T0283332

HOW SONDHEIM
CAN CHANGE
YOUR LIFE

HOW SONDHEIM CAN CHANGE YOUR LIFE

RICHARD SCHOCH

ATRIA BOOKS

New York   London   Toronto   Sydney   New Delhi

ATRIA
BOOKS

An Imprint of Simon & Schuster, LLC
1230 Avenue of the Americas
New York, NY 10020

First Atria Books hardcover edition November 2024

ATRIA BOOKS and colophon are trademarks of Simon & Schuster, LLC

Simon & Schuster: Celebrating 100 Years of Publishing in 2024

For information about special discounts for bulk purchases,
please contact Simon & Schuster Special Sales at 1-866-506-1949
or business@simonandschuster.com.

The Simon & Schuster Speakers Bureau can bring authors to your live event.
For more information or to book an event, contact the Simon & Schuster
Speakers Bureau at 1-866-248-3049 or visit our website at
www.simonspeakers.com.

Interior design by Joy O'Meara

Manufactured in the United States of America

1 3 5 7 9 10 8 6 4 2

Library of Congress Cataloging-in-Publication Data has been applied for.

ISBN 978-1-6680-3059-2
ISBN 978-1-6680-3061-5 (ebook)

for Paul McCarren, SJ

CONTENTS

OVERTURE

It was about seven o'clock on a Saturday night when I learned—in a text message with a link to his *New York Times* obituary—that Stephen Sondheim, aged ninety-one, the man who lifted the Broadway musical to new heights of artistry, had died the day before, November 26, 2021, at his home in Roxbury, Connecticut.

He had not been noticeably ill. Eleven days earlier, as I told the students in my musical theatre class, he had attended the first performance of the acclaimed gender-swap Broadway revival of *Company*. Greeted with cheers and a standing ovation, Sondheim rewarded the stunned audience at the Bernard B. Jacobs Theatre with a flash of that famous lopsided grin. He moved haltingly, but unaided, gripping the seatbacks for support as he inched his way to his own seat in the fifth row. The day before his death, Thanksgiving Day, Sondheim and his husband, Jeff Romley, dined with friends in Roxbury. He was frail, they recalled, but as quick-witted as ever and bursting with backstage gossip. Yet he collapsed soon after returning home with Romley and never regained consciousness.

That Saturday night I was at my home, watching *tick, tick . . . Boom!*—the musical biopic about Jonathan Larson, composer and lyricist of *Rent*. In director Lin-Manuel Miranda's film, adapted from the stage version, Sondheim becomes a true-to-life character: part idol, part crusty critic, and part mentor who had learned from his own mentor, Oscar Hammerstein, the power of a nurturing word. Bradley Whitford played Sondheim with studied precision, contorting himself, as he put it, into "a crooked smile on an unmade bed."

Yet the scene in the film that really got to me was when Sondheim, just as he did in real life, leaves a message on Larson's answering machine after attending a fraught workshop of the young composer's musical *Superbia*. "It's first-rate work and it has a future," Sondheim said; "and so do you." He wrote that line himself for the screenplay; he recorded it, too, for the film. The prophetic voice on the telephone was, thrillingly, Sondheim's own.

At that moment, at that *very* moment, the ping of my cell phone announced the text message telling me that he was dead.

Instead of clicking on the link to Sondheim's obituary, I returned to his voice on the answering machine. And I kept replaying that scene, obsessively—just as I imagined Larson himself did, back in 1985, listening to Sondheim's uplifting words over and over, wearing the cassette tape thin. For me, it was an act of pure denial: Sondheim can't be dead if I can still hear him on the telephone. The telephone, of course, wasn't mine, and it wasn't even real. Yet it consoled me, in my sudden sadness, to believe that his message on the answering machine was meant for me. Sondheim was speaking to me—and *about* me.

———

Haven't we all felt just this way about a favorite artist? As much as we admire the painter's skill, the novelist's style, or the singer's perfect pitch, what we really respond to in a work of art is how it speaks to us. Our private bond with it. Not, or not just, the connoisseur's appraisal of its formal qualities, but something more intimate: how the painting or the book or the song makes us feel, what it opens our eyes to, the way it—not always comfortably—enlarges our life.

The artist, to *be* an artist, must "give us more to see." Dot asks George for exactly that in "Move On," their soaring final duet from Sondheim's *Sunday in the Park with George*. Her deceptively simple words—so short in length, so extended in meaning—are her call for something new. She doesn't just mean new works of art, although that's how it starts. Dot wants to pass through George's art—move on—to arrive at a greater understanding, a sharper perception, a fuller way to make sense of her world.

In his Manhattan town house, Sondheim kept an impressive collection of Japanese wooden puzzle boxes. He had a lifelong fascination with puzzles of all kinds, from cryptic crosswords to scavenger hunts to escape rooms. Unlike a jigsaw puzzle, where the goal is to assemble interlocking pieces to form a complete picture, the point of a puzzle box is to figure out how to dismantle it. This, to me, seems the perfect metaphor for what Sondheim's works accomplish. He doesn't put the pieces of life back together again; he takes them apart. What Sondheim offers us is not life with all its riddles happily solved, but life deconstructed and laid bare, in all its confusion and disarray.

Musical theatre is often branded, and mocked, as a form of trivial escapism, and, doubtless, some instances of the genre are. But not Sondheim. *Never* Sondheim. Because through his works we do not so much escape life as confront it. His words and his music feel not like a denial of reality but rather its unsparing exposure. Virginia Woolf once described George Eliot as a novelist for "grown-up people," and the same is true of Stephen Sondheim.

His musicals are for grown-ups. My students regard his songs as a rite of passage, their own induction into adulthood.

The formal tributes to Sondheim began within days of his passing. It was a moment for eulogies and reverences, for praising a legendary career and being grateful that we were around to witness some of it. Still, I remember feeling a little unsatisfied. Unsatisfied, because all the eloquent panegyrics didn't reach what was, for me, the heart of the matter: how the theatre of Stephen Sondheim rhymed with my own life. Not just one show or at one time, but all his shows and all the time. Isaac Butler, writing in *Slate*, came closest to what I was feeling: that Sondheim's works "follow us through each stage of our own lives."

I kept wondering, what is the "more" that Sondheim gives us to see? What do his music and lyrics bring into focus? How are his works like a message to us, and about us? Such questions crystallized in my mind in the wake of Sondheim's death. Yet in all the words of praise that I was reading, those questions weren't being answered; they were barely being asked.

That's when, and why, I decided to write this book.

———

I begin with deep respect for Sondheim's artistry. At age eighteen, I saw Angela Lansbury as Mrs. Lovett in the first national tour of *Sweeney Todd*. I stayed up late in my dorm room at Georgetown reliving the show and then bombed my economics final exam the next morning. (I don't regret it.) That was just the beginning. Since then, I've seen Judi Dench as Desirée Armfeldt, Maria Friedman as Fosca, Adrian Lester as Bobby, and Victor Garber as Franklin Shepard, Inc. In *Elaine Stritch at Liberty*, I saw the original Joanne in *Company* perform her iconic number "The Ladies Who Lunch." In London's West End, I heard Barbara Cook sing mostly Sondheim, along with some of the songs that he wished he had written. And I'm grateful to have seen the first production of Sondheim's last work, *Here We Are*.

I've spent the past four decades, nearly all my adult life, working in the performing arts. I started out as a theatre director in Washington, DC, and New York City, putting onto the stage new plays and new musicals, plus a few classic old ones. Later, I worked at the New York Public Library for the Performing Arts, raising money for its extraordinary archives in theatre, music, dance, and recorded sound. Getting to know those collections, which are housed in the library's Lincoln Center branch, helped me to realize that I enjoyed studying theatre as much as I enjoyed making it. For nearly thirty years now, I've been a university professor, a role that allows me to be both a scholar of theatre and a teacher of theatre practice. My experience has taught me that these roles are mutually enriching, each one inevitably enhancing the other.

What's made it possible for me to write a book on Stephen Sondheim are the years I have spent teaching his works to aspiring singer-actors, guiding them through the particular journey of each particular song. My students, not entirely in jest, call my class "Sondheim boot camp," because we start with the toughest of musical theatre workouts: "Rose's Turn," from *Gypsy*. If you can handle *that* song, you can handle any song. It's a useful number for students to tackle early on, because its story—finally, Rose gets to be the star—resonates with their own desire to stand in the spotlight and be applauded. There's something in Madame Rose that's also in *them*, and the song reveals it. I hope that in this book I can make similar, but much broader, connections between Sondheim's music and lyrics and what they can mean for us individually.

And so, this book is not so much about Stephen Sondheim as about what we can *learn* from him. The more I think about Sondheim's works, the more I realize that their greatness—beyond the clever lyrics, beyond the complex music—lies in telling stories that insinuate themselves into a spectator's own life story, until in some way the stories click. His works understand us as much as we understand them. Sondheim, if we let him, can change our life.

"Being Alive," the final number in *Company*, is Bobby's late-in-the-game plea for intimacy and love. It's up for debate whether Bobby is truly ready for someone to hold him too close, but the song itself declares what the theatre of Stephen Sondheim is all about: being alive. Being alive not in the sense of controlling our life, but of bearing witness to it; being fully present to its terrors as much as to its joys, to its conflicts as much as to its concords, and to its mysteries as much as to its banalities.

Sondheim's theatrical worlds open our eyes to our own world. He lures us into the lives of imagined others—lives that are always knotted, often tormented, and never tranquil for long—only to return us to the here and now. Yet, and here's the twist, we return to the world *changed*, because as Little Red Riding Hood puts it in *Into the Woods*, we "know things now / many valuable things" that we "hadn't known before." The ambitions, dreams, disasters, and fixations of Sondheim's characters can teach us how to get through our own lives—so that, like Petra's vow to herself in *A Little Night Music*, we'll not have been dead when we die.

Sondheim always rejected the notion that his shows were veiled autobiographies. There may well be parallels between him and solitary figures like Bobby in *Company* and George in *Sunday in the Park with George*, but that hardly equates to self-portraiture. It's precisely because Sondheim's works are not explicitly confessional that they can be continually relevant to us; that they can be *about* us. Sweeney Todd's revenge lust, Fosca's humiliating passions, Louise's triumph when reborn as Gypsy Rose Lee, and Ben's regret over the dreams he didn't dare. Those aren't just Sondheim's stories; they're ours too. I have, in my own way, lived out each one. And I suspect that you have done the same.

As Oscar Hammerstein put it, "The Song Is You." Sondheim often said he envied Hammerstein and Jerome Kern for writing that song, and I think I know why: because it dissolves the barrier between art and its audience. For all its brilliance, Sondheim's work is not trying merely to divert us; it's trying, in fact, to *involve* us.

That's the nub of my argument: his song is you.

This book is not a Sondheim biography, although it traces his career more or less chronologically. Nor is it a "behind the curtains" stage history, although it tells many stories about performers and productions. Still less does it aim to be a formal critical study, although it offers close readings of most Sondheim musicals.

Most, but not all. Because I have not sought to write a comprehensive study, I have been free to approach Sondheim's works selectively. I have focused on those that in my opinion best reveal what Stephen Sondheim can teach us about life. The omission that might surprise, or disappoint, you the most is *West Side Story* (1957). It was Sondheim's first Broadway show, was twice turned into a film, and is still performed around the world. But to the end of his long life, Sondheim disdained his own lyrics, judging them overly grand for the show's youthful characters and lacking the spark of spontaneity. Nor do I look at *A Funny Thing Happened on the Way to the Forum* (1962), although it was the first musical for which Sondheim wrote both music and lyrics and had the longest initial Broadway run (964 performances) of all his shows. Nevertheless, the songs in *Forum*, as Sondheim himself admitted, served mostly as delightful respites from its zany plot. Neither of these well-known musicals offers the mature "life lessons" found in his later works.

I've also left out Sondheim's least-produced stage shows—*Saturday Night* (1955), *Do I Hear a Waltz?* (1965), *The Frogs* (1974), and *Road Show* (2008)—on the grounds that readers are least likely to know them. (I do glance, though, at his 1966 television musical *Evening Primrose*.) Even so, you will find in the pages ahead a sustained look at most of Stephen Sondheim's theatrical legacy: thirteen shows in total, from *Gypsy* (1959) to the posthumously produced *Here We Are* (2023).

Sondheim freely acknowledged that everything he achieved came about through collaboration with other theatre artists. The stories I tell include them—directors like Hal Prince and James Lapine, librettists like Lapine and John Weidman, and performers from Ethel Merman to Len Cariou to Lindsay Mendez—but the figure who unites these disparate stories is Stephen Sondheim. He is the thread that runs through it all.

Each musical gets its own chapter, and the chapters run in chronological order. Mostly, I take a rounded view of each show, looking at its range of characters and songs. Sometimes, though, I focus on a single topic—the Baker's Wife in *Into the Woods*, say, or "Someone in a Tree" from *Pacific Overtures*—if such intense scrutiny helps me to argue my point. Yet whatever approach I'm drawing upon, I'm doing it to make this one claim: Sondheim's works can change your life. A prolonged encounter with them will reveal predicaments—and the paths out of them—that we recognize as our own. The better we understand Sondheim, the better we will understand ourselves.

A musical becomes a hit when its songs "land" with the audience. No longer merely watching, the audience, now stirred to respond, reaches out and grabs the songs, absorbs them, becomes one with them, and then enacts them in their own way: toe-tapping, finger-drumming, quiet sobbing, wriggling in their seats, clapping in time, or holding their collective breath on the high note. A fifteen-year-old Stephen Sondheim wept into Dorothy Hammerstein's fur coat at the end of the first act of *Carousel*. It was permanently stained with his tears.

In such moments of transference, when the song *leaps* from performer to spectator, Sondheim's musicals are no longer just about Madame Rose burdening her daughters with her own frustrated dreams, Sweeney Todd vowing revenge upon the entire world, or the painter George spurning the woman who loves him because he must finish the hat. It's now also about you and me. Building upon, but then wholly surpassing, the accomplishments of his predecessors, Sondheim created musicals that don't just entertain or fascinate us, but also include us. That are, ultimately, about us. Like a message from him on our answering machine.

INTRODUCTION

The Song Is You

Grateful, no doubt, for having Oscar Hammerstein as his mentor, Sondheim always called teaching a "sacred profession." Sondheim was himself carefully taught for the first time in the summer of 1945, when Hammerstein spent an afternoon at his farmhouse in Bucks County, Pennsylvania, pointing out to fifteen-year-old "Stevie" (a friend of his son Jamie) the many flaws in a musical that the boy had written. Sondheim later boasted that he learned more about musical theatre in those four hours than most librettists or composers do in a lifetime.

Teaching became Sondheim's profession, too, and not just in the master classes he offered over the years. Everything he wrote was a lesson in life—and it's all there for us to take to heart.

Yet to become himself a teacher—our teacher—Sondheim had to learn one important lesson: the people who truly own a musical theatre song are neither those who write it nor those who perform it. They're just, to echo Madame Rose in *Gypsy*, "spreading it around." The ones really in charge are those who receive it. Every musical theatre song, as Sondheim had to learn, is ultimately about its own audience. Have, by all means, something of consequence to share with your audience—but be careful how you do it. If you're careless, you might not get your point across.

1

Before we look in depth at Sondheim's works, let's "pause for a mo'" (as Buddy sings in *Follies*) to look at how Sondheim learned that the audience comes first. Hammerstein tried to teach him just that lesson: by critiquing the novice's work, by the example of his own songs written with composers from Jerome Kern to Richard Rodgers, and even (the tale is a theatrical legend) by persuading Sondheim to change the ending of "Rose's Turn" so that the audience could applaud Ethel Merman's unforgettable Madame Rose. But still, Sondheim had to learn the lesson for himself. He learned it the hard way, and early on, with the disastrous original production of *Anyone Can Whistle*.

Sondheim once found himself seated on an airplane next to the English dramatist Peter Shaffer, best remembered now for writing *Amadeus* and *Equus*. Later, they became good friends, with Shaffer advising on the Cockney slang in *Sweeney Todd*. But at the time, around 1965, they didn't know each other well. Yet, in a remarkable coincidence, Shaffer numbered among the few people who had seen the original production of Sondheim's *Anyone Can Whistle*, which closed at the Majestic Theatre in New York on April 11, 1964, after only nine performances.

Now a cult classic—I've seen it performed in a tiny basement theatre near London's Piccadilly Circus—the show was then Sondheim's first flop. A stinging belly flop, too, after the stunning high dives of *West Side Story*, *Gypsy*, and *A Funny Thing Happened on the Way to the Forum*. An "exasperating musical comedy," bristled Walter Kerr in the *Herald Tribune*. "Anyone can whistle, but nobody can sing." (Angela Lansbury, by the way, was one of the leads.) The *New*

York Times, dispensing a little mercy, noted the show's "attempt to be meaningful" in its critique of bourgeois conformity, McCarthyite red-baiting, and nuclear weapons. Still, its drama critic Howard Taubman chided Sondheim and director-librettist Arthur Laurents for not leavening their blunt, partisan commentary with a single spoonful of "entertainment." It does sound like heavy going for a musical that opened four months after *Hello, Dolly!*

Sondheim never courted failure, but neither was he ashamed of it. "I don't mind putting my name on a flop," he insisted years later, "as long as we've done something that hasn't been tried before." What hadn't been tried before was transplanting the dark mood of European absurdist theatre—plays like Eugène Ionesco's *The Bald Soprano*, Jean Genet's *The Balcony*, and Samuel Beckett's *Waiting for Godot*—into American musical comedy, an art form so unstoppably optimistic that even saddle-sore Oklahoma cowboys begin their day with an ode to a beautiful morning.

The graft did not take. Convinced, though, that they had created a work of some importance, Sondheim and Laurents pulled out all the stops to keep the show running. They even paid $3,000 for an advertisement in the *New York Times*, hoping that word of mouth would cancel out the bad reviews. It was the *Mad Men* era, but not even Don Draper at Sterling Cooper could have salvaged *Anyone Can Whistle*.

So eye-blinkingly short was its run that the cast album, produced only at the insistence of Columbia Records executive Goddard Lieberson, who believed that Sondheim's score deserved a legacy recording, was made *after* the show had closed. How the abruptly unemployed actors got through that funereal day in the CBS 30th Street Studio remains a wonder.

All the more surprising, then, that Peter Shaffer, sitting next to Sondheim in the airplane, told him that *Anyone Can Whistle* was "among the most brilliant and original theatre pieces" that he had ever seen. The show's composer-lyricist was now, with or without a midflight vodka stinger, flying high. "As well as," Shaffer continued, "one of the most irritating."

Crash landing. More intrigued than downhearted—Sondheim had, after all, survived the scorching reviews—he listened as his newest critic pinpointed the end of the show's first act as the reason why the press and the public had been so hostile. It committed, Shaffer explained, the mortal sin of insulting the audience. Arthur Laurents, a man for whom flinging abuse at others was the highlight of each day, rejected that judgment, even though Sondheim himself came to see the wisdom of it.

Musical theatre audiences are a forgiving bunch, but one thing they won't forgive is "being made asses of." So pronounced Angela Lansbury, who played the lead role of Cora Hoover Hooper in that ill-fated production. Yet, as she regretted, that's just what happened with *Anyone Can Whistle*: it mocked the people who had paid to see it. Sondheim and Laurents crafted a lengthy musical scene—the one that Shaffer felt was both brilliant and irritating—that ended with the cast laughing at and then sarcastically applauding the audience. A striking *coup de théâtre*, yes; but it totally backfired. Instead of captivating the audience, it only irked them.

The number was titled "Simple," though it was anything but. In fact, it remained Sondheim's longest and most complex musical sequence for two decades, until "Putting It Together" from *Sunday in the Park with George*. "Simple" flipped from singing to speaking, and then flipped back, but all the while the orchestra never stopped playing.

They devised it while sitting side by side on a piano bench. In a jazzlike back-and-forth, Sondheim developed a melody at the keyboard, Laurents ad-libbed some rhythmic dialogue to be acted over it, and then he handed the song back to Sondheim, who came up with the accompanying lyrics on the spot. This particular scene had to be created in tandem, because the whole point was to blur any distinction between the score and the script. The result was a fifteen-minute tour de force that alternated between solo, chorus, spoken lyrics, dialogue, and rhythmic movement. A typical 1960s show tune lasted barely three minutes. In the published libretto, "Simple" takes up a whopping twenty-nine pages.

Let's back up for a moment. *Anyone Can Whistle* takes place in a bankrupt American town whose mayoress, the loathed Cora Hoover Hooper, stages a phony miracle: curative waters gushing from a rock in the town square. Her fraudulent plan is to attract "pilgrims" who will spend enough money in the town to save it from financial ruin. Nearby is a mental asylum, known as the Cookie Jar because its residents are called "Cookies" (kooky) by the locals. As it happens, the residents are not insane but only social nonconformists. Fay Apple, the asylum's chief nurse (a role created by Lee Remick), releases them to take the miraculous waters. Filling the town square, the pilgrims and the Cookies intermingle so much that no one can tell one group from the other. Cora, alarmed by this mass confusion, recruits the asylum's new psychiatrist, J. Bowden Hapgood—who, it later transpires, is not a doctor at all but a mental patient—to divide the crowd into the sane and the insane. Yes, the plot is convoluted and wholly improbable, but so is *Hamlet*.

It goes on. Hapgood, swearing a pretend fidelity to "logic," conducts six nonsensical interrogations, all set to music, in which he divides the crowd into the equally nonsensical "Group 1" and "Group A." Each group is certain that only *its* members are sane. But it's impossible, as Hapgood's questioning reveals, to distinguish between the normal and the deviant, because any apparent difference between them is meaningless. As meaningless as the difference between, say, "1" and "A." This is "Simple," the ironically titled number that closes the first act of *Anyone Can Whistle*.

It's also the number that insulted the audience. It ends with the stage lights dimming to an eerie glow at the footlights, as Group 1 and Group A rush to the front of the stage, chanting, faster and faster, "Who is what?" and "Which is who?" Those are illogical questions, each formed with mixed-up words. Everyone falls silent as the stage goes suddenly black, except for a tight spotlight on Hapgood. He looks straight out at the audience, smiles at them, and whispers, "You are all mad."

Instantly, the stage explodes with sound and color. As galloping "circus music" plays, a strip of lights, like a theatre's balcony rail, descends from the fly loft over the stage and covers the audience in a wash of pink, blue, and yellow light. At the same time, the lights on the theatre's actual balcony rail switch back on to illuminate the stage. During the blackout, the scene had changed. When the lights come up, the audience sees the entire cast sitting on the stage in a row of theatre orchestra seats—as if *they* were the audience—and fanning themselves with their programs. The actors, staring back at the real audience, begin laughing and applauding. Their jeers and their claps get louder and louder, until the act curtain falls.

The curtain falls, but on whom? Or, as Sondheim put it, "Who is what?" Hapgood has only pretended to separate the rational people from all the irrational ones because there's no actual difference between them: *everyone* is mad. The actors taunt the audience by mimicking them to their own faces, insisting that they, too, are acting out an illusion. Yet so virtuosic is their collective performance that they deserve a round of hearty applause.

———

Truth lurks in this taunting. In our daily lives, we *do* perform the identity roles that over the years we have learned to master. If we've been lucky enough to choose our roles, they're usually flattering: "Happy and successful! Liked and loved and beautiful and perfect!" as Cora promises her depressed citizenry. Yet the roles can feel like burdens if others have imposed them upon us, as usually happens to outcast groups like the Cookies.

Either way, these roles become how we make our impression upon others. Those same others are, likewise, enacting their own roles to make an impression upon *us*. Although the persona we show to the world may be an obligatory charade, it's a charade all the same. As Shakespeare knew, "all the world's a stage."

How talented we are. We inhabit our accustomed roles so thoroughly, and so automatically, that it takes the jolt of a stranger laughing in our face to make us admit that our life has indeed been a kind of performance. Not necessarily a dishonest one, but necessary, for sure, to get through the day. Our reality is structured, because it *must* be so structured, like a theatre. This, to me, seems the lesson we are meant to learn when the actors and the audience in *Anyone Can Whistle* swap their roles.

That moment when Hapgood, standing in his spotlight, confirmed the audience in its mass delusion was not so different from the ending of Genet's *The Balcony*, when Irma, madam of the "House of Illusions" brothel, tells her own audience, "You must now go home, where everything—you can be quite sure—will be falser than here." Genet's play had its New York premiere just four years earlier, at the renowned Circle in the Square. And the urban liberal elite to whom *Anyone Can Whistle* so obviously catered may well have been familiar with Erving Goffman's landmark sociological study *The Presentation of Self in Everyday Life*, published in 1956, which first made the argument that day-to-day social behavior is essentially theatrical, with each of us being simultaneously an actor and a spectator.

Sondheim's insight, although not unique to him, was certainly significant—and *Anyone Can Whistle* was the first American musical to express it. That's why, as Shaffer told Sondheim, when they were speeding at 36,000 feet above the planet, the show was so brilliant. But so irritating, too—because it belittled its own audience. The performance had crossed the line, as Sondheim himself later conceded, from "smart" to "smart-ass."

And so the lesson that *Anyone Can Whistle* worked so furiously to impart—be aware of the roles that you enact in your life—never really broke through in any of its nine performances. Overly enamored with the boldness of his artistic vision, Sondheim forgot the elemental lesson that Oscar Hammerstein had taught him: put the audience first. Or, to use the famed lyricist's own words, "The Song Is You."

Sondheim never forgot it again.

1

GYPSY

How to Be Who You Are

Looking back on *Gypsy*—the 1959 musical inspired by the life of celebrity stripper Gypsy Rose Lee, but whose irrepressible lead character is her mother, Rose—Sondheim judged it one of the "best" (also, one of the "last") musicals in the Rodgers and Hammerstein tradition. He meant that its songs were dramatically purposeful: they revealed the show's characters and they drove the story forward.

I wonder about that. There's richness of character, for sure, in *Gypsy*'s songs. Only Madame Rose could sing "Rose's Turn," her own macabre inversion of the eleven-o'clock showstopper. (Musical theatre fans often call her "Momma Rose," but nobody in the show itself does.) Only Louise, the neglected tomboy not yet reborn as the burlesque star Gypsy Rose Lee, could sing the plaintive "Little Lamb." And who but those clapped-out strippers Mazeppa, Electra, and Tessie Tura could entertain us so shamelessly with their trademark gimmicks?

And yet there isn't much obvious action in those and other songs. Rose doesn't get eighty-eight bucks from her father for the act's new costumes. Louise, on her birthday, never figures out her true age. Nor does she become a star overnight just because Momma promises it. Rose doesn't get married, let alone stay married, even

11

though her daughters June and Louise beg her to walk down the aisle. And boyfriend-turned-manager Herbie, locked in Rose's gripping arms, isn't going anywhere. The world at the end of all those songs is pretty much the world at their beginning. Lyrical time has passed—music aplenty has been heard—but dramatic time has stood still.

I couldn't, at first, make sense of it. Sondheim was the lyricist, after all, so these songs must be accomplishing *something*. Then I wondered if maybe I was looking for the drama in the wrong places. It took me a little while to detect Sondheim's pattern, but it's consistently there. And it's brilliantly condensed in Rose's lyric "you'll never get away from me," one of the many in *Gypsy* that sound endearing right up until they sound sinister. *That's* the action in the songs: not getting away; not moving on; and not having what you want, whether it's bright lights, a quiet family life, or just a life of your own. Mostly, you're stuck with life as it is. Now that's an action that some people can definitely relate to.

Everybody in *Gypsy* wants to *get away*, even Tulsa and the other chorus boys named for the cities from off whose streets Madame Rose had more or less kidnapped them. But nobody wants to get away more than June and Louise. It's not a place, though, but a person—Momma—that they need to escape from. June is more honest about it than Louise, but the truth is that they both feel trapped by their own mother.

Who wouldn't feel trapped? It's a crushing burden that Rose forces on her children, pushing them onto the vaudeville stage because she "was born too soon and started too late." Madame Rose could have been, *should* have been, the greatest star, if only those lucky stars above had aligned for her just once. So says Madame

Rose. But the stars never did align for her, and that loss has marked her sorry life ever since.

To survive it, she tasks her daughters—first June, then Louise—with succeeding where she failed. Succeeding no matter the cost. It's now the child who, in a reversal of family values, must sacrifice for the benefit of the parent. There's no getting away from that distorted fact of life. Sure, Rose relishes playing the martyr: the mother who gave up everything, or so she tells everyone, for the sake of her two precious girls. But that's just an act, and not a particularly good one. Wherever Madame Rose goes, and whatever Madame Rose does, you can bet your bottom dollar that it's all for the greater glory of Madame Rose.

Well, you gotta get a gimmick.

———————

The famed Swiss psychologist Carl Jung believed that the greatest burden placed on a child is the unlived life of the parent. Not material lack, not school or peer group pressure, and not even family instability. He said that the heaviest burden for a child to bear is the psychological distress felt by a parent, because all that distress gets pushed onto them.

The trouble starts with whatever has been left unrealized in the parent's own life: a risk never dared, a talent never nourished, a height never scaled. Instead of taking a deserved pride in whatever they have achieved, they sabotage themselves. They accuse themselves of missing the mark in their own lives. "I could have been," that's their petulant motto.

Who among us has never uttered a similar word of regret or self-reproach? Perhaps fear of failure holds us back, or lack of encouragement, or being shamed for being different from everybody else. I've felt each of those rebukes, and sometimes still do. Or maybe we never got that one lucky break. Everything's coming up roses, just not for us. Naturally, we would resent those who did get all the breaks. Why *them*? More importantly, why not *me*? Yet we would also resent ourselves, for never having become the bigger person we set out to be. We would feel, instead, only the smallness of our lives. How it diminishes us. How every day it reminds us of all that we have not yet done, and likely never will do.

It's intolerable that our unfinished business lives on, lives on to mock and to berate us for leaving it unfinished. We have no choice but to demand, although the demand itself is mostly unconscious, that somebody else get up and finish the job for us. That's how some children get saddled, so unfairly, so damagingly, with the responsibility to fulfill a parent's unmet needs.

Madame Rose is positively bursting with unmet needs. Bursting like one of those brightly colored balloons at Uncle Jocko's Kiddie Show, where we first meet her as the stage mother straight from hell. She barges her way to the front, shouts everyone down, and says what she wants to hear. Her tiny dog, Chowsie, peeping out of her handbag, makes Rose look only more formidable. Get off her runway. And get Baby June booked on the Orpheum Circuit pronto.

Why the rush? Because Madame Rose scorns the humdrum life of "playing bingo and paying rent." That's swell for *some people*—Rose's most sneering epithet—but not for a dreamer and a hustler like her. She's got to "get up and get out." Yet in the next scene she's back at her childhood home in Seattle, pleading with her grumpy father for the umpteenth time to fork over a lousy eighty-eight bucks. He turns her down, so she steals his gold retirement plaque, shoving it furtively into her handbag. Rose sings her first song, "Some People," with a fierce passion—but it's the passion that comes from being locked outside your own life. From not yet being "all the things that I gotta be yet."

Her song begins on a plunging low note. That's tough, Sondheim conceded, for a singer. But the note is pitch-perfect because the whole song is excavating a depth of character, hauling up to the surface what's been at the bottom of Rose's obsession with stardom. Years ago, when Rose was still a little girl, her mother walked out on her. Never did come back. It's now decades later, and her own father can't stop bringing up that trauma, almost throwing it in Rose's face. Lack of a mother's love, and the lack of everything good that such love would have made possible, is the sad, central theme of Rose's life. Here is the primal wound that she has been trying ever since to heal.

Being a domineering parent is how Rose compensates for the harm she suffered as a child. Neglected by her own mother, she must control, and not set free, her own children. She must be the parent who *never* leaves them alone. While it's too late for her failed dreams, maybe there's still time for them to come true for her girls. "I'll be damned," she swears, "if I'm gonna let them sit away their lives like I did."

———

If only every parent spoke with such ringing clarity about making their child responsible for their own unmet needs. Life would go much easier for them both. Far more typically, though, what's driving this sort of behavior—not from all parents, of course, but unfortunately from some—remains largely unconscious: never reflected upon, and so never dealt with.

Every Little League dad, to give a classic instance, believes that he's doing the right thing when he pushes onto the baseball field an unwilling child (say, a ten-year-old me) who would rather be reading a book. It's to toughen them up, they insist; build a sturdy character; and make them winners. Rose is hardly the only mother convinced that she's doing her girls an unappreciated favor by dragging them and their toe shoes from one dance audition to the next. After all, isn't it everybody's dream to be desired and applauded?

Most parents are, thank goodness, loving, nurturing, and well-intentioned. But even the most caring of parents must deal with the fallout of how their own parents once treated them. There is no avoiding the familial hand that life has dealt us; there is only how we choose to play it. I do not blame anybody's pushy parents, including my own. But I do want to think about why they push so hard—and why, sometimes, they enlist their own children in the pushing.

In extreme cases—and in *Gypsy*, it's extreme—the parent's obsession with their own unfinished business is revisited upon the child as a curse. As a fate so heavy that it cannot be lifted. An implicit bargain is now struck: "I will love you, my child, but only if you do what I want. Don't you dare let me down." The child will internalize the demand (to be loved, I must . . .) because their very survival depends upon it. When you're in a tight corner, that's a rational and self-protective response.

Unfortunately, it's damaging in the long run. As psychologists Robert A. Johnson and Jerry M. Ruhl explain in *Living Your Unlived Life*, a child will feel a parent's inner conflict as if it were the child's own, and so devote all their efforts to resolving it. How sneaky this dynamic is, for it depends upon the child identifying with, and so never questioning, a parent's wishes. Yet the child can never resolve the conflict because it's not theirs to begin with. Worse still, they are utterly unaware of that liberating fact. They do not know that the burdens they feel belong to someone else. A deeply traumatized child, as Johnson and Ruhl elaborate, is barely conscious of the scant regard they have for themselves. Gradually, they lose a sense of selfhood.

I admit that the ordeal I've just outlined is an unusually grim topic for a book on Broadway musicals. And yet, I think it's a pretty fair account of Louise in *Gypsy*. Especially the Louise who celebrates her birthday in an Akron flophouse. For breakfast, there's a smashed-up cake, part of it already eaten by Gigolo the monkey, and some leftover chow mein. On that paltry cake stand ten paltry candles, the same as last year, even though Louise clearly merits more. Yonkers, one of the chorus boys, tries to remember for how many years now Louise has been celebrating her "tenth" birthday when Rose cuts him dead: "As long as we have this act, nobody is over twelve and you all know it!"

Those cheap candles will melt, but Louise remains frozen in time. Forever a child. Forever a child doing her mother's bidding. And doing it with a quiet, servile smile. Louise's birthday gift from Momma—a lamb—is no gift at all. It's just the latest gimmick for June's barnyard act. Louise's party gets cut short by the arrival of Mr. Mervyn Goldstone, who bears the astonishing news that Dainty June has been booked on the Orpheum Circuit. Festivity turns on a dime, and the birthday party, measly though it is, abruptly ends. Rose all but snatches the food right out of Louise's mouth. Those egg rolls are for Mr. Goldstone.

Amid the ensuing ruckus, Louise slips away—unnoticed, unwanted, unnecessary—grateful for a moment of solitude. She sits, as the lights come up, on a mattress, alone expect for the birthday menagerie that she has gathered around her: the lamb, a stuffed bear, a stuffed cat, a wooden hen, and a drawing of a goldfish. Then she sings, so softly, the only true love song in *Gypsy*.

What a strange love song "Little Lamb" is. Louise sings not to another person, but to animals—and not real animals, but fake ones. These inanimate objects are, in turn, less and less plausible versions of what they purport to be. A stuffed bear is fine; we all had one as children. But that sketch of a goldfish? It's tacky and ridiculous.

For Louise, though, it's serious. She confers upon each substitute figure a reality that is as compelling for her as it is illusory for us. Being dragged into service as a newsboy in a lousy vaudeville act—an imposture forced upon her year after year, even though she's constantly being scolded for how little talent she has—is taking its toll. So great a toll that Louise now finds it hard to tell the fake from the real.

One of my students recently performed "Little Lamb" in my class on Sondheim. She brought with her all the toy animals named in the song. She placed them carefully around her, looked fondly at each one, and then sang straight to them. We in the audience were just eavesdropping. That's when I understood that the toy animals are utterly real for Louise because they *are* Louise. They are the outward show of her inner state. Unable to admit her own sadness—and who wouldn't be sad, stuffed into the back end of a cow costume because that's where the ugly and the untalented ones belong—Louise needs an external object or two to carry her sadness for her.

Sondheim's lyrics make this clear in their juvenile purity. Little bear sits reassuringly on her right, "right there." Little cat looks so forlorn; it must be the cat's birthday too. Louise asks the goldfish if her wishes will come true. And she shares with little lamb the great unknown of her life, "I wonder how old I am?" This most innocent of songs reveals the most scandalous of truths: that Louise herself is the lamb, the sacrificial lamb, whose life is offered up in selfless service to Momma.

Poor Louise. So totally does her life belong to Rose that she cannot sustain a reality any sturdier than a tea party with toy animals. The self-knowledge that she seeks ("I wonder how old I am . . .") is always disappearing into whatever lunatic fiction Rose concocts and then preaches to the world as gospel truth. The biggest lie that Rose tells, the lie that almost nobody in *Gypsy* believes, and that the audience has *never* believed, is that the big time is only minutes away. Louise is stunned to learn how dreadful the act really is. Stunned, because she had always seen the world through Rose's distorted eyes.

Before it got to New York, *Gypsy* was clocking in at nearly three hours. To trim the running time, director Jerome Robbins cut "Little Lamb" from one performance. Jule Styne, the composer, was so outraged that he threatened to pull all the other songs in the show unless it was put back in. It was put back in.

I can understand why Robbins chose "Little Lamb" for the chop. It's a quiet number, and so maybe it feels like a letdown after Mr. Goldstone and his egg roll hullabaloo. But I'm glad the song stayed in. Because for the audience, it's deeply moving. It hurts our hearts to see Louise be such a loving mother to those stuffed animals, giving to them—and through them, to herself—all the tenderness and care that her own mother withholds from her. And, maybe, mixed up in all our hurt is a remembrance of being once in that same lonely place, coping as best we could.

———————

Siblings often cope in different ways. For Louise, there's safety in cheerful compliance: whatever Momma wants, Momma gets. But for her sister—the cosseted Dainty June, star of the act—rebellion feels right. A cutie-pie onstage, the real June exudes a fierce bitterness: "It's a terrible act and I hate it!" Waiting to learn if Rose will ruin June's chance of becoming a legitimate actor under the patronage of Mr. T. T. Grantziger—she *does* ruin it, as you always knew she would—the sisters sing of how much better their lives would be "If Momma Was Married." Louise, not pining for stardom, wants only to live with Momma, Herbie, and "six turtles" in a house "as private as private can be." June, the feisty one, dreams of getting Momma, plus all those baby-doll hair ribbons, out of her hair. The melody is a playful waltz, but June is sternly resolved: it's time to cut those ribbons and run.

We never see June again. She marches straight out of the story, along with Tulsa, her husband of three weeks, headed for Kansas City, where they've lined up a booking for their new double act. So absolute is June's rebellion that she doesn't hang around to tell Momma the news. She puts it all, rather, into a scribbled note, which she hands to Louise, who hands it to Rose, who reads it, and then throws it away, on the railroad platform in Omaha where they've been wondering why June's running so late.

She's not running late—she's running away. Yet her defiance of Rose accomplishes nothing. June hasn't grabbed the spotlight for herself so much as she's surrendered it. She is *gone*, and it's not yet the end of the first act. The play still belongs, as it always has belonged, as it always will belong, to Rose. She is, for a second, floored to read June's kiss-off note. But only for a second. People have been walking out on Rose for years, so what's one more? The irony is that June, in the moment of her seeming triumph, remains a bit player in the long-running melodrama whose one singular star is Madame Rose.

This can't be a surprise. So often, a rebellious child's vow—"I won't be like *you*!"—doesn't help them to rebel. In fact, their hostility keeps them tethered to a parent as tightly as ever, just in a more spirited way. Same with a compliant child—looking at you, Louise—except that it's a bit quieter. Now that June has fled the scene, Louise gets shoved to center stage. And the mother who until this moment has all but disowned her elder daughter now promises her the whole world on a plate.

It doesn't much matter if a child identifies *with* or *against* a domineering parent, because either way the domination holds. Either way, the child's sense of selfhood—of identity, of individuality—still derives wholly from the parent. Louise and June, even when they are alone (but are they ever *really* alone?), sing about Momma, the character so firmly in control of events that she steals focus even when she's offstage.

Meekness gets you nowhere; but then, neither does insolence. To break free from this pernicious cycle, we've got to live our own life honestly and to stop living someone else's life dishonestly. We've got to be conscious about the choices that we make. For it's the consciousness—and not the impulse to wound, or appease, an already wounded person—that will set us freely on our way. We must step *off* the Orpheum Circuit, for that path never goes forward but only round and round, a forever loop, returning us without fail to all the same familiar places.

———

For Louise, the path that leads away from Rose—and toward herself—starts in the most dubious of sites: a sleazy burlesque house in Wichita, Kansas, where the only reason "Rose-Louise and her Hollywood Blondes" have been booked is to stop the cops from raiding the joint. Here, in a world that does not dance to Rose's regimental tune, a world in which Rose's nerve counts for naught because everybody else has *more* nerve, Louise can—at long last—come into her own.

On the final night of their booking, the top-billed stripper gets busted for soliciting and the stage manager needs somebody to go on in her place, and quick. Rose, offering up the sacrificial lamb one more time, volunteers Louise for the dirty job. This mother's hunger for stardom, for stardom even in a dump like this, is so insatiable that she will pimp out her own daughter to snatch a crumb of it and then applaud herself for the feat.

Louise, in her borrowed silver heels, is at first wobbly with fear—and who wouldn't be? But her fears fall away as easily as the shoulder straps on the gown she has been stitching for Tessie Tura but now shimmies into herself. And now, for the first time, she *sees* herself. The person who looks back at her in that dingy dressing room mirror is not the old, unloved Louise—the forever ten-year-old, the newsboy, the farm boy, the tin soldier, and the rear end of a goddamn cow—but Louise rebirthed in womanly triumph as Gypsy Rose Lee.

Gypsy is no new creature, though, but rather the unveiling—long desired, yet long obstructed—of the self she has always been. The self that has waited so patiently to emerge from underneath all the heavy layers of disfigurement and disguise. But the wait has been worth it. We know this from Gypsy's first words: "Momma . . . I'm pretty . . . I'm a pretty girl, Momma!" I like to imagine that Gypsy speaks these words so quietly that they can be meant only for her. When you can see what is beautiful about yourself, you do not need anyone else to tell you so—or to tell you otherwise.

It's a sublimity to be savored—yes, even a tatty strip joint in Kansas can be sublime—that Louise sheds her dependence upon Rose by shedding her clothes in public. If the real Gypsy Rose Lee had not provided us with such an enticing metaphor for self-actualization, then where would we be? But we're right here, a few rows behind the out-of-tune upright piano, our eyes fixed on this new divinity as she peels off a long white glove here, dips on the drumbeat there, and unzips just one zipper (the tease!) as the spotlight goes out on her.

Sondheim's reprised lyrics are working all their smutty charms. What had been innocence itself ("And if you're real good, I'll make you feel good") becomes now the erotic promise of the temptress at whose slinking approach we fall silent. Until, that is, we explode into wolf whistles and shouts for encore.

A star, as they say, is born. Three midwives—Mazeppa, Electra, and Tessie Tura—attend the birth. For it is they who, in their salty and wisecracking way, deliver Louise into the brave new world of burlesque. They even christen her Gypsy Rose, and the stage manager adds "Lee." So fondly do they care for this newborn that we may justly call them her surrogate mothers. In the warm limelight glow of such unexpected, but undoubted, maternal love, their daughter Gypsy thrives and blooms.

"To be a stripper, all you need to have is no talent." So declares Tessie Tura in one of her backstage tutorials for Gypsy. The real Gypsy, in her memoirs, stated the same: "I didn't have to sing or dance or do anything. I could be a star without any talent at all." I don't think that Gypsy—in life, in the musical—is giving herself nearly enough credit. For it seems to me that she possesses the truest talent of all: the talent of being yourself. And being yourself means *not* being someone else. It may look like Gypsy has merely a gimmick—a flashy falsehood—but all along she has been telling the absolute truth: "I *am* Gypsy Rose Lee! I love her!"

By the decree of the gods, Louise, whose heaven-sent name is Gypsy, must spend her days—I mean, rather, her nights—stripping her way down to the purity of selfhood, all the way down, removing with delight every last burden that has been imposed upon her.

—————

Eleanor Roosevelt, who knew all about living in the shadow of a larger-than-life figure, sent a telegram of well wishes to the real Gypsy Rose Lee at the Shubert Theatre in Philadelphia during the show's tryout. What bliss to have been at Western Union on the evening of May 8, 1959, as her message came in over the wires: "MAY YOUR BARE ASS ALWAYS BE SHINING." This telegram still exists, and you may see it for yourself at the New York Public Library. Some have claimed that Mrs. Roosevelt was too dignified a lady to send so vulgar a message. Who knows? It pleases me to think that she did, and so I do.

What I hear in her words is not vulgarity but wisdom. The

profoundest wish we can have for someone (ourselves included) is that they *be* that someone, naked in soul and spirit in the way that a stripper is naked in the flesh. To me, there is a bare candor in that telegram, one that recalls a state of grace—maybe now lost, but it once was there—before any of us learned the dark arts of beguilement and masquerade.

Perhaps, like Louise, we have felt cornered in our own life, blocked from following our own course, and curbed by another's demands. But there *is* a way out: Louise found it, and so can we. We find it when we stop trying to complete someone else's life and start trying to complete our own. Louise doesn't so much solve the problem of Rose being so overbearing (Momma, no matter what, will always be Momma) as she outgrows it. The problem doesn't disappear, but it does cease to matter. For Louise, her mother's presence in her life—that fixed presence, alterable only by death, and maybe not even then—no longer worries her, because as she tells us, "for the first time it *is* my life!" Louise is, by the end of the show, living out what had for so long been unlived in *her.*

The surest sign that Louise—now Gypsy—has transcended the very problem that had kept her trapped for years is that, in the end, she does *not* walk out on Rose. She does not coldly abandon her mother. In fact, she keeps her warm, though when you're the headliner at Minsky's, you do it in style with a mink stole. In that moment—in that final scene, which Sondheim knew was so crucial to the audience—the cycle of trauma breaks for good. The suffering has stopped; and, in its place, compassion takes hold. Louise, because she has set herself free, is now free to look lovingly upon Rose—even though everybody else in the show has walked out on her—and stand right by her side.

It has an extraordinary effect. Rose, the rejected daughter, gets a mother's love from the daughter that she herself had rejected. Getting it, she takes it. For once in her life, instead of barking commands at others, Rose looks calmly into herself: "I guess I did do it for me . . . Just wanted to be noticed."

Nowhere in *Gypsy*, not even in its final cathartic scene, will you find a hint of sentimentality, for that is merely a pleasant fiction. In this show about theatrical illusion there is only truth to be found. Ugly truths, at first—no getting around that—but, eventually, they turn consoling. The truth that we are not doomed to be prisoners in our own lives. That with the right encouragement from the right person, we can see the goodness in ourselves, and so find ourselves. That hurtful patterns can be disrupted and then replaced by the benevolence of a nurturing heart, beginning with our own. That everything *can* come up roses for you and for me. If only, like Gypsy, we dare to let our bare ass shine.

2

COMPANY

How to Get Close

After the ninth try, they send her home. Nobody is happy, least of all the singer herself. "Wrong!" she screams in self-reproach, listening to the playback, before commanding her recorded voice to "Oh, shut up!" Maybe it's the late hour, past five on a Monday morning, and they've been locked inside the Columbia Records studio since early Sunday afternoon. Maybe it's the case of chilled white wine that Elaine Stritch, much like her character Joanne, in *Company*, couldn't ignore. Or maybe it's fear of displeasing Sondheim. After all, he wrote "The Ladies Who Lunch"—the song she has now sung, wrongly, nine times in a row—just for her. Too much is *not* enough for producer Thomas Z. Shepard, who tells Stritch to leave the studio. Let's try again tomorrow, he quietly, and tiredly, adds. Or maybe the day after.

Dismissed, she grabs her pack of cigarettes off a nearby chair, and, with her eyes downcast in shame, heads straight for the door. To get there, she must walk right through the orchestra. Not a single player, not one, looks up at her. Not the slightest nod as she passes by. It's not disdain, though, or awkwardness, that stops the musicians from noticing Elaine Stritch as she departs. Unlike her, they're still at work, about to record her song's backing track. (It's too expensive to have them on hand for the extra recording session.) Stritch leaves

29

the studio a veritable outcast: a lonely, abject figure whose loneliness is only accentuated by the buzz that surrounds, yet disregards, her.

She returns, a day or so later, a changed woman. Crisply coiffed, mascara just right, and looking assured in a white blouse: finally, the star we've always loved and feared even more. Naturally— inevitably—*necessarily*—she nails the song. Hammers it straight in. This is the version destined for the original cast album, the signature song of a unique talent. Yesterday she was left for dead. But today Stritch is the recording studio's pulsing heart, the very source of its life and spark and gleam.

D. A. Pennebaker's camera caught every unsparing bit of this drama for his documentary *Original Cast Album: Company* (1970). It's a good thing, too, because the scene of Elaine Stritch collapsing in solitude and then bursting back into vigorous life is a concise symbol for *Company* itself. What she goes through, so does Bobby, the thirty-five-year-old bachelor, and best friend of five married couples, whose hard-won defeat of loneliness gives this plotless musical its semblance of a story. The character has, in recent years, become Bobbie, a single woman of the same age who can hear all too clearly the ticking of her biological clock. It's a tall order for any musical, even one whose lyrics and melodies are the work of Stephen Sondheim, to anatomize the loneliness of modern urban life—and then to show us how to overcome it. But in *Company*, Sondheim did just that.

You can, for sure, be lonely anywhere. Still, there's no feeling quite so miserable as being lonely in a city—the one place where, it might be supposed, no one need ever run short of company. To live in a city is, after all, to feel the pressure of agglomerated humanity, the relentless heaving of each upon the other.

Yet mere density of others is no stay against feeling empty in

yourself: depleted on the inside, even as the outside goes throng-
ing on. To feel lonely while others swarm all about you practically
defines this insufferable state, and with the keenest acuity. Because
loneliness, as critic Olivia Laing has explained, means not "soli-
tude, but rather an absence or paucity of connection, closeness,
kinship." Loneliness, then, is less the withdrawal of others than
the withdrawal of the intimacy that others could offer, and that we
could offer them. In a city, it is hard to get close to other people,
hard to share a spark with them, and hard simply to idle a few hours
away together. It's the fertile soil in which loneliness will take root
and then sprout. This was very much my experience when I lived
in New York City in my late twenties: feeling all alone in a crowd.

Marta, one of Bobby's three girlfriends, knows this feeling. She
moved to the city to put herself at the center of the world, only to
discover, as many have before her, and so many more will, that
it's a "city of strangers." Yes, New York is teeming—every day, *an-
other* hundred people get "off of the train / And the plane and the
bus"—but nobody ever meets anybody. They look for each other
in vain. They speak through messages that don't always get a reply.
Their plans are hardly ("shall we let it go?") worth the planning.

If, defying the odds, they do find each other, the signs of the
times—defaced posters, "rusty fountains"—will only discourage
them. When words fail to signify because so much graffiti obscures
them, and when the flow of life-giving water is impeded by so
much corrosion, then what chance does anybody have of staying
for long with anybody else? They keep their hearts as guarded as
the parks through which they warily, and hurriedly, pass. In New
York, the answer to an overture of any kind from anyone is always
the same: a busy signal.

Yet, if you listen closely to a busy signal—one beat on, one beat off—you might mistake it for a heartbeat. Both are pounding rhythmic vamps: so persistent, so *insistent*. No wonder the busy signal is the driving sound of *Company*'s title song, which also opens the show. Six quarter notes in a row, all on the same pitch. Those repeated thumps enliven and yet alienate us at the same time, like hearing about a party we haven't been invited to.

I find it easy to sympathize with Marta, who's all dressed up (or down, for she never roams north of Fourteenth Street) but has nowhere to go. Though she belts "Another Hundred People" with gusto, and though she finds fault with Bobby, down to the metaphorical and no doubt literal tightness of his asshole, her real audience may be only herself. Marta's true subject—that of which she sings—is the conflict between the New York she came in search of and the New York she actually found. This city may be, as she boasts, the center of everything; yet it is also, and for that exact same reason, the center of *nothing*—a great mass, but diffused, splattered, and shattered into broken bits. It's a place where the promise of intimacy is dangled just out of reach.

Marta has brought herself to a powerful insight: that loneliness is not a personal defect, not a weakness of character, and certainly not anything to hide or to feel embarrassed about. Loneliness, she's learned, is a feature of life as it comes to us, like the battered barks on the sidewalk trees.

Company crams the hard work of intimacy—the messy entanglements, the risk of commitment, and both the desire for and the fear of coupling—into a container labeled "marriage." That was, in 1970, a safe and sensible thing to do. Still, matrimony itself has never been the show's central theme. Sondheim and librettist George Furth had no interest in the sociology of marriage. Two gay men in the Stonewall era, why would they? Having, back then, no experience of marriage, Sondheim quizzed his close friend Mary Rodgers on what being married was like before he started working on the lyrics.

It seems to me that *Company* is mainly about overcoming the fear of intimacy. Heterosexual marriage (at the time, the only kind) serves as a convenient shorthand for that universal theme, an easy frame of reference for the audience. But it's nothing more than that. From this perspective, the long-standing question of whether Bobby is a closeted homosexual—Sondheim said he wasn't, but it's not hard to think otherwise—doesn't feel quite so pressing. The people in *Company* are definitely obsessed with who is and isn't married, but their true obsession lies in what marriage itself signifies: the risk of knowing another and of being known by them.

If, as the couples keep insisting, marriage heals the wound of loneliness, then why do the husbands feel so ambivalent about it? Bobby watches Harry and Sarah, the karate couple, pretend not to notice each other's little lapses. He's sworn off booze, yet pours himself a nightcap. She swears by her diet, yet devours a brownie. Bobby then asks Harry if he's ever sorry that he got married.

There's a beat before Harry sings his reply, but he's not pondering Bobby's question, let alone mulling over his answer. He knows the answer already, and takes his time to give it: he's sorry *and* he's grateful. In this balanced refrain, which gives "Sorry-Grateful" its title, he is joined by David (married to Jenny) and then by Larry (married to Joanne), all three husbands agreeing that marriage is mostly a mixed bag, with satisfaction and regret found in equal measure. You do feel safe, except when you feel trapped—or you might feel both at the same time.

These shared refrains—which could be real, or just imaginings in Bobby's mind, though it hardly matters—add up nearly to an axiom that matrimony is a condition in life better accepted than interrogated. To whatever question you may wish to ask about someone else's marriage, no simple answer can be given. Bobby's mistake is to suppose that feeling ambivalent about your marriage is an error that needs correcting, a shortcoming to be surmounted, if the relationship is going to flourish. Yet what the husbands tell him, and tell us, is that a marriage succeeds not when its contradictions are resolved—they won't ever be resolved—but when they are *withstood*.

If we hear only the lyrics in "Sorry-Grateful," as Bobby seems to do, then we will likely come away from it with a dismaying view of married life, a state marked chiefly by unmet desires and the undimmed allure of "what might have been." That's true for both spouses, each one sometimes longing to escape but also worried that the other is plotting to escape first and so leave them all alone.

Yet if we listen to the music, we might arrive at a new perspective. Because while the lyrics spell out the spousal predicament of being sorry-grateful—both emotions, each wrapped up in the other—the music offers a response to that predicament. A response filled with patience, acceptance, and tolerance. The song preceding it, "The Little Things You Do Together," is quick in tempo and tight in rhythm, barreling toward its sardonic finish. "Sorry-Grateful" strikes a poignant contrast: long in musical line and relaxed in its phrasing. The melody isn't just repetitive, it's *contained*—held safely

34

inside its own frame of sound, its key passages fluctuating within a comfortably narrow vocal range. Instead of ending, the song melts smoothly away: three voices reduce to two, two yield to one, and we're back where we started, with Harry singing alone.

So mellow is "Sorry-Grateful" that it threatens to become an easy-listening parody of itself. But Sondheim is too subtle a composer for that. Instead of Muzak banality, he gives us—three times over—the heart's full resolve to stay true and stay the course. The husbands know perfectly well that their feelings, and those of their wives, are divided, but—and here's the astonishing part—they aren't in turmoil about it. They're not fighting themselves, as Bobby does whenever *he* sings. Unlike him, they're not trying to change the tune. Instead, they sing it—and sustain it, just like their married lives—all the way through.

In one of Sondheim's most exquisite touches, lyrics that divide the character's feelings—"You're always sorry, / You're always grateful"—are bridged in the melody, with each new phrase ("You're") beginning on the last beat of the prior one. Here the music does not resolve the stated tension but rather holds it, lives with it, and moves through it. In short, the music does what we should do.

This, to me, is the sound of good counsel. Our task is not to banish all ambivalence from our emotional life—that's impossible for anyone—but to withstand it, to tolerate it, and, somehow, to bear all the contradictions that won't ever go away. The work that sustains a marriage, or any other kind of intimate relationship, is not denying (or worse, rejecting) our equivocal feelings, but accepting them. And in accepting them, to not be overwhelmed by them. To not be defeated by our own contradictions.

Bobby has not yet learned this lesson, and by the end of the show, he may still not have learned it. But the husbands *have* learned it, and they did so well before the show began. What about us? What's our learning curve? The more I listen to "Sorry-Grateful," the more I feel that this gentle ballad, and not the troubled star turns "Being Alive" and "The Ladies Who Lunch," is the true masterpiece in Sondheim's score for *Company*.

Bobby, the poor baby, has just one way of reacting to his own emotional ambivalence: he gets defensive. He denies all his doubts. Insists that no bachelor is more willing than he—"I have no block, no resistance"—to getting hitched. His friends stay skeptical: "I don't feel you're really ready," Jenny tells him. That's because Bobby betrays himself at every turn, protesting, but a beat too quickly, that's he ready to settle down; or vowing, but a tad too eagerly, that *huge* changes are in the offing.

Mostly, though, he's deluding himself. Still, it's hard *not* to get carried away when you sing a song as fervent as "Marry Me a Little." Dropped from the original production, the number was restored, at director Scott Ellis's suggestion, in the Roundabout Theatre Company's 1995 revival. Boyd Gaines, playing Bobby, sang it at the end of the first act, where the song has remained ever since. That's a good place for it, because "Marry Me a Little" works as a proper soliloquy: Bobby reveals the truth about himself to himself. He wants to get married. It's time. He's *ready*, a word that he repeats compulsively, and, at one point, holds for twenty-three and a half beats. That's a fierce readiness.

Except it's not. What makes this song a classically Sondheim soliloquy is that the truth insisted upon by the character turns out to be a lie. For us, the lie is easily detected, because hypocrisy is so apparent in the song's title: no one, after all, can be a "little" married. Intimacy at a guarded distance doesn't count as intimacy. Vows you're not expected to keep are scarcely worth the vowing. And a fidelity that can be haggled over is nothing of the sort.

I'm wary of coming across as a cranky moralist—but remember, the terms are Bobby's own, not mine. He's the one pledging himself to the venerable institution of matrimony, even though his pledge amounts to nothing. He's hinting madly that no one, himself especially, will ever be held to account. No demands. No sacrifice. No honesty. "You promise whatever you like, / I'll never collect."

We're halfway through the evening, and Bobby remains as stuck as ever. He's lost, but he can't see it. Confused, but doesn't know it. Unable, still, to grasp that being in a relationship means allowing another person to make an impact upon you—to *alter* you. Otherwise, what's the point? Bobby's clever lyrics and sweet melody do not solve his problem so much as they restate it: it's easier to hide behind style than to look at the truth.

But we, in the audience, see right through Bobby's style. We've witnessed so much of it that by now we're more than a bit suspicious. And so, the song's effect on *us* is different, fully opposite, from its effect on him. The louder that Bobby sings, and the higher his notes jump, and the longer he holds them, the less we believe him.

Maybe we've already stopped believing him. After all, this guy doesn't trust his own or anybody else's words. His surprise proposal to Amy after she gets cold feet about marrying Paul (wisely, she turns Bobby down) is too rash to be credited. His morning-after plea in "Barcelona" for air stewardess April to put her "wings down" and "stay a minute" is wholly disingenuous, pure performance art.

So well performed, though, that she takes him at his word. To the couples, he speaks in greeting-card platitudes—"Thank you for including me in your thoughts, your lives, your families." From one scene to the next, Bobby uses language not to reach out, but to withdraw; to render impossible the very closeness that he professes to seek. April, Marta, and Kathy got it right: he "titillates a person and then leaves her flat."

Yet the person Bobby *won't* leave flat is the one who doesn't exist. He tells us this at length, getting an entire song ("Someone Is Waiting") to devote himself to an imaginary woman. Not entirely fanciful, this "someone" is an amalgam of all that he admires in his female friends: Susan's warmth, Jenny's softness, and Amy's blue eyes. Even so, a "Susan sort of Sarah," or a "Jennyish Joanne," describes no actual person. No plausible partner for him in life. Bobby wonders if he has already met his "someone"—but how would he know? You cannot spot in the street a lover who lives only in your head.

Sondheim once remarked that "Someone Is Waiting" is the one song in *Company* that nobody ever performs in concert. He exaggerated, no doubt, for effect. But it's true that this song is not particularly popular outside the show itself. Granted, its full effect depends on its dramatic context; but that's true of many Sondheim songs. Nor is it especially difficult to sing: a slow waltz, with no melodic leaps. If anything, its notes are tightly sequenced—half-step up, half-step down, and repeat—compressed and bounded like Bobby himself.

The real reason, I suspect, why this song has failed to become a cabaret standard is that it can be painful for the audience to hear. Not musically painful, of course—indeed, the opposite—but dramatically so: the character is lying about himself. Either that, or he's a fool. For the truth of the song is that *no one* is waiting for Bobby. The music may soothe—so languid, so seductive—but trouble is brewing in the lyrics. Bobby seems to be declaring a becalmed readiness for love, but actually he's terrified—and looking, frantically, for the nearest exit.

———

Bobby adores the coupled women in his life, but maybe that's because there's so much about them that he overlooks. There's Sarah, whose repressed hostility springs to life in a karate kick. Or Amy, who falls to pieces on her wedding morning. And who would make a goddess of vodka stinger Joanne? Bobby won't admit the full truth about these women—his blinkers are tightly in place—because he needs them to be *other* than who they really are. He adapts them, and then combines them, into an exalted fantasy figure whom he can gallantly worship from a distance. In short, he idealizes them.

They, in return, idealize him. They cast Bobby in the role of surrogate spouse, the man who will reliably escort them to the opera, or take their kids to the zoo, when their own husbands won't. Other times, he's a boy who needs mothering, which usually means compulsive feeding. He can also, when necessary, act as a therapy pet. His quiet, passive companionship—"Angel, I've got something to tell you"—will steady even the most agitated soul. The husbands do much the same, but in a cruder way. They project onto their bachelor buddy their own frustrated wish for erotic freedom— "Chinese techniques," "exotic mystiques"—the very freedom that their own marriage vow has curtailed.

Over and over, Bobby's married friends exclaim how glad

they'll be to see him, but it's not actually *his* company that cheers them. The Bobby they want in their lives is the one whom they have created in their minds—because *that* Bobby can satisfy all their emotional needs. In the title song, they serenade him frantically: "we looooooooooooove you." That's straight from the libretto, and it takes a full fifteen seconds for the couples to declare their shared love for Bobby. The actors were given so much time to sing one word (more precisely, to hold one vowel) because they had to get out of their elevated compartments in Boris Aronson's chrome-and-Plexiglas set and down onto the stage floor. Yet this freakishly elongated note works in a paradoxical way, becoming less credible the longer it is held. It calls too much attention to itself, especially when Elaine Stritch, always the loudest voice in a cast album, goes flat. The more we listen to it the hollower it sounds, a mere performance of love. And this is how the show starts.

To be, as Bobby is, *unseen* by his dearest friends—the ones whose company he keeps—must be the epitome of loneliness. It's hard enough to suffer the peculiar alienation of the urban mass, being thrown into the crowd and yet still feeling alone. How much more awful, then, to be denied the balm of friendship. To be locked outside its sanctuary, never accepted (or, perhaps, forgiven) for being who we are. That feels, to me, like the definition of despair, being invisible not to the nameless many but to the person nearest in heart. I've had to bear that particular agony before, and it nearly broke me.

Yet here's kiddo Bobby kidding his way through life, always happy to twist or to bend himself into whatever version of himself that for the time being his friends need him to be. "Whatever you're calling about"—he's just so darn agreeable—"my answer is yes." Plasticity is his style. Or, maybe, it's mirroring. David likens him to the Seagram Building, the 1950s Manhattan skyscraper whose glassy surface reflects the onlooker's image back to them. That's Bobby summed up: when you look at him, you see only yourself.

Bobby, meanwhile, has nobody to look at. This truth is glaringly exposed at the top of the second act, in the rousing hat-and-cane routine "Side by Side by Side." Michael Bennett, the original choreographer, felt that the number's vaudeville extroversion was a mask (no matter what, keep dancing) to hide Bobby's loneliness amid all the couples who need him so desperately to stave off their own loneliness. Bennett devised the sequence of marital tap-dance routines—each husband does a time step, then each wife repeats it—that ends with Bobby dancing alone. He extends his hand—your turn, now—but there's no one to complete the move. No requital, just the empty space next to him. (Desirée in *A Little Night Music* has a parallel moment of forlornness: she makes her entrance, but no one is there.)

For a dangling—terrifying—instant, everything on the stage stops. Astonished, we hold our breath. What next for Bobby? Will he rally? Will he collapse? The music crashes in quickly and saves him, pulling him back into the collective whirl. But for us, the silence and the stillness and the sadness linger on. Linger on because we sense that a mistake has unwittingly revealed the truth.

The truth is not that Bobby is secretly lonely—this we know already—but that his "good and crazy" friends have conspired to keep him that way. They *want* Bobby to stay locked inside the prison house of loneliness, even though they profess in honeyed words that no one wants him to be happy more than they do. But deep down, so deep they may not even know it, they want Bobby to make *them* happy, or at least to try—"sharing a tear, lending a shoulder." In

"Being Alive," they exhort him to change: "Don't stop now! Keep going!" But these urgings are flatly negated by their wish for Bobby on his thirty-fifth birthday: "Stay exactly as you are." Cruel words, in a way, for what the couples seek is to hold their friend back; to arrest him, and so keep him stuck unhappily in place.

Sometimes, alas, our friends do want us to be lonely. And to stay lonely, so that they can call upon available us to ease *their* loneliness. They need us to be at home on the sofa every night playing solitaire. Or reverse the dynamic, and it's we who find it so oddly uplifting to have a friend whom we can pity. Company, you might say, loves misery.

That's a travesty of how friendships ought to work. Friends are meant to be conduits, not positive barriers, to connection. They are supposed to escort us into the wider world, not plunge us deeper into our solitude. Above all, they are meant to reflect our essential goodness back to us. In a genuinely loving relationship, and friendship may well be reciprocal love in its purest form, we like who we are when we're with that other person. We feel seen. We feel, in our strongest friendships, enhanced and enlarged; the best we'll ever be. A friend who reduces us with their shaming, even in the guise ("Poor baby") of tender care, is no friend at all.

———————

One woman *does* reflect Bobby's goodness back to him. It's not sweet Jenny, though, and not loving Susan, and not even the ever-indulgent Amy. It's mean girl Joanne who turns out to be Bobby's best friend.

While all the others merely pity Bobby for his misery, Joanne provokes him out of it. Shakes him up. Slaps him awake. Throws a dry metaphorical martini in his face. Her tactic is a drunken grilling in a nightclub near closing time. Instead of pushing Bobby onto the disco floor and into the arms of a woman his own age, she proposes a hookup ("When're we gonna make it?") and tells him to show up at her place tomorrow afternoon, when her husband, Larry, will be at the gym.

It's a canny setup. They both know it's not going to happen. But Bobby is so rattled by Joanne's brazen offer of casual sex (where did *that* come from?) that for once he can't come up with a glib retort. Thrown off script, as it were—and how Bobby loves the safety of a script—he crashes into the truth. Perhaps for the first time in the show, Bobby speaks honestly about himself. (All credit to George Furth for *Company*'s sharp libretto.) When Joanne promises to take care of him, he replies, almost as if someone else were saying it, "But who will I take care of?"

The door long sealed has now been pried open. The someone who speaks these strange new words is none other than the *real* Bobby, the person he has exhausted himself in concealing from everyone, and most of all from himself. Courtesy of Joanne, ice queen of the insult, Bobby has melted just enough on the inside to admit his yearning to love someone else. Not to be loved, but to love.

Joanne is right to say that she's done Bobby a "big favor"—the biggest—because she has given his life back to him. More than just challenging Bobby to stop pretending, she has created a space in which he can risk being vulnerable with another person—and then find that he is accepted in his vulnerability. If you want to matter to someone, they have to matter to you. It's Bobby's openness to needing someone else that makes this the most truthful scene in *Company*. In its own startling way, it's also the most loving scene. For what is love if not knowing the height and depth of another person's being, and allowing them to know the full dimensions of you?

The question that hangs over the last moments of *Company*—and especially Bobby's solo "Being Alive"—is whether he can continue to be *himself*. Not the psychoanalyst on the cheap for his married friends. Not the maladjusted zombie that drives his three girlfriends crazy. And certainly not the Bobby baby, Bobby bubi, Bobby darling, or any other infantilizing diminutive that his friends bestow upon *Robert* (as Sondheim always called him) to deny this thirty-five-year-old man any semblance of adult integrity.

Most often, "Being Alive" is performed as Bobby's breakthrough. Finally, and at the last minute, he stops playing emotional games and gets serious about settling down. Urged on by the voices (in his mind?) of his married friends, Bobby starts, though, by scorning the spousal bond: "What do you get?" He worries that if someone holds him too close they are bound to hurt him too deep. He fears drowning in the dark tangle of someone else's life. But in the final refrain, he reverses course: "Somebody crowd me with love." What he once feared, he now embraces. What he long spurned, he now pursues. It's a petition—a prayer—a *demand*. In its closing lines, the song pivots one last time. Instead of seeking it, Bobby now offers love: "Somebody let me come through, / I'll always be there." He ends the song, and the show, as the kiddo who isn't a kid anymore.

So state the lyrics. The music, however, demurs. The images in "Being Alive" convey openness—lowering your guard, letting someone in, needing too much—but their *sound* is closed and tight. Even when the melody climbs in crescendo, it reaches the top reluctantly, hauling itself up the scale, note by hard-won note. The final ascent to the high G, unusual in a Sondheim song, can be painful to the ear. When Bobby moves from an embittered to a hallowed point of view, the music—by design—refuses to follow him. The too-predictable key change adds the expected intensity; still, it's the same old tune.

Each year, I caution my students not to make "Being Alive" sound too polished. And each year, they ignore me. There is value, I tell them, in giving the song a wrenching sound, because it's true, and unapologetically true, to the hard work of intimacy. After all, what Bobby is calling for is not anything pleasant. Not at all. When he cries out for someone to sit in his chair—to be as close to him as he is to himself—it's not to ease his burdens, but to make them bearable. It's not to shelter from the world's harshness, but to endure it together. Love isn't there to make our lives less frightening and more agreeable. It's there, if we can find it, and then hold on to it, to give us more life: "To help us survive / Being alive."

———————

The wisdom of Bobby's words is undoubted. What's doubtful is whether he actually believes them. "Being Alive" could certainly be a liberating moment of triumph—that, indeed, is the standard view of the song. But it could likewise be another instance of Bobby trapped in pathetic self-delusion: he thinks that he's learned his lesson, but he hasn't. More cynically still, Bobby might only be *performing* his readiness for love (remember, "Barcelona" showed us how gifted an actor he is), delivering his aria of falsehood so convincingly that his married friends stop badgering him about getting married.

Who can say? Bobby's hardly been a reliable source of his own biography. So why, at the last minute, should we trust him on this crucial matter? "Being Alive" was not Sondheim's first, or even second, choice for the show's final song. He thought it was a dramatic "cop-out," a change of heart so abrupt that no audience would find it credible. Cop-out or not, it's there to be sung. And everyone who sings "Being Alive" must decide for themselves whether it's the most heartfelt, the most deluded, or the most fraudulent moment in *Company*.

But I'm not sure that *we* must decide. By this, I don't mean that we shouldn't be involved in the song. We absolutely should be—that's why we're there. Our involvement, though, might not require us to discern Bobby's motives. Nor does it depend upon our feeling any heightened compassion for him. Michael Bennett recalled that Dean Jones, the original Bobby, was effective in the role, although he played it for only a few weeks, precisely because he never bid for the audience's sympathy. He stood, rather, at a cool remove. His Bobby didn't have time to deal with our feelings because he was too busy dealing with his own.

In this voyeuristic way, Bobby becomes the archetypal lonely New Yorker, a figure glimpsed through his apartment window but never really known. He's less a person than a parable. Like a parable, he teaches through his story. Indeed, he exists solely so that we may learn from his story. What we learn is to be alive in the time of our life. Here's how: Need someone too much. Know someone too well. Crowd them with love. Force them to care. And always, even though you're frightened, come through.

Perhaps, then, the worthiest response we can bring to *Company* is neither to admire it nor to solve its riddles, but rather to let it work on us. Let it have its way with us. It may well be that the story unfolds in a flash in Bobby's mind, but in our minds, it can unfold at leisure. So instead of hoping that Bobby will make himself whole, let us hope it for ourselves. Instead of wanting loneliness to be banished from his life, let us resolve to banish it from ours. Above all, let us do what Bobby never does: make a wish, and not just at birthday parties, on our own behalf.

3

FOLLIES

How to Survive Your Past

My advice to high school drama teachers: Get your students to perform *Follies* instead of *Into the Woods*. I grant you that neither penciled wrinkles nor gray-streaked hair will let a sixteen-year-old pass for sixty. Or even fifty. Or, for that matter, a spry forty. But passing is hardly the point. The point is what a youngster stands to gain from impersonating an elder. If young people can imaginatively experience now a version of the future that awaits them—turning the illusion of theatre to their actual advantage—they will have a far better chance of not messing that future up. The world will be a much happier place in twenty-five years if more teenagers today are encouraged to sing, "I'm just a Broadway baby."

Go ahead, laugh. *Follies* was, in its time, the most expensive Broadway musical in history, costing nearly $800,000. It closed in July 1972, after 522 performances—a decent run, but you'd expect longer for a show that captured seven Tony Awards, including Best Score—and lost nearly its entire investment. One reason it fared so badly was that older theatregoers, those closest in age to the show's characters, loathed it. Why? Because a story about middle-aged people stuck in the past—that's *Follies* in a nutshell—disappointed an audience mainly in search of escapist pleasure. The show's nostalgic title led them to expect an old-time entertainment, and they didn't get it. Well, not exactly.

Younger people, though, adored the show. For them, *Follies* was less a wistful return to a bygone era—few of them cared about a prewar musical revue—than a cautionary glimpse of their future. The stage was filled with semblances of their own anguished parents, as librettist James Goldman observed, and it transfixed them. Transfixed them in the ghoulish way that spectacles of catastrophe always do. A twenty-year-old Frank Rich, reviewing the Boston tryout of *Follies* for his Harvard student newspaper, likened its "upsetting" pastiche songs to "our parents' old 78 records." Aghast at the emotional wreckage of an older generation—and primed to use the past to redeem the future—the young ones resolved, "That's not going to happen to me!"

———

Still, it happens. Most people, as Sondheim himself remarked, "have one foot in the past and one foot in present." Nowhere do past and present collide so forcefully as at a reunion. Any kind will do. School, family, work, even meeting an old flame for a drink. No matter the setting, the same dynamic holds: we are returned, in a flash, to our past. A backward trip in time can be irresistible, for none of us is immune to the fantasy of saving ourselves by getting a *second chance*. We can settle old scores, call a truce, untie some knots, or tie up some loose ends. So many ways to revise the world.

But alongside the thrilling prospect of making the past perfect, there's fear that the past won't oblige. We worry that revisiting the past will expose, and expose in front of our gleefully judging peers, how much we remain in thrall to our yesterdays. So deeply enthralled that by now it feels natural. Every reunion threatens to reveal that our life, although it may seem exciting, has slowed to a stop.

Follies makes good on those threats. It's New York City, in 1971. The once-glittering but now-derelict Weismann Theatre will be demolished in a few hours—the wrecking ball hangs ominously at the ready—to make way for another Midtown parking lot. It won't take long, though, because the conspiracy of time, neglect, and gravity's downward pull is doing that job just fine. Dimitri Weismann, the impresario who for thirty years produced his *Follies* in this very theatre, has invited the surviving "Weismann Girls" to a cocktail party held on its bare, ruined stage. A last chance "to glamorize the old days, stumble through a song or two," he offers—and "lie about ourselves a little." The aging former showgirls are played by similarly aging actresses—the youngest are in their fifties, the oldest in their eighties—a physical equivalence that gives an undeniable truth to the whole performance.

The women do glamorize the old days. Heidi Schiller, oldest of the Weismann Girls, boasts that a Viennese composer once rushed straight to her drawing room to place before her ("Liebchen, it's for you") his latest waltz. Heidi can't recall whether it was Oscar Straus or Franz Lehár, but no matter. The choicest memory is how grandly the song was bestowed upon her. And they do stumble through a few of their signature songs. Stella Deems leads a chorus of old-timers in "Who's That Woman?," all of them braving a tap routine untapped these thirty years. Their hoofing skills may be in perilous decline, but they're still here.

Mostly, though, they lie about themselves—a lot. The chief liars in *Follies* are its four leads: Sally and Phyllis, the youngest of the former Weismann Girls, and their husbands, Buddy and Ben. Once inseparable, the couples haven't seen each other in thirty years.

Until tonight. First up is Sally Durant—"*Di*-rect from Phoenix, / Live and in person," as she jokily broadcasts her own arrival—now a bored housewife who wonders why she settled for the traveling oil rig salesman Buddy Plummer. Back in 1941, though, in the distant days when everything seemed possible, Sally and her best pal Phyllis Rogers shared a fifth-floor walk-up on East Forty-Fourth Street. Phyllis, a beauty from the sticks, had a wardrobe that extended to two dresses, one of them borrowed. In the years since, she's prospered greatly, having married the wealthy politician and diplomat Benjamin Stone. But he wasn't rich and famous when they met. He was just "Ben," little more than a smitten kid, who hung around the stage door with his friend Buddy. The boys waited, not so patiently, for the girls upstairs to wriggle out of their tights, clamber down the backstage metal stairs, and head out with them for some late-late-night dancing at Tony's.

These four have some serious history together, and it all gets played out at the reunion. Sally arrives early, nervous about whether to confront Ben, the man she's never stopped loving, despite the fact that thirty years ago he ditched her for the more presentable Phyllis. Sally settled instead for Buddy, even though she can't stand him. Buddy, knowing that his own wife finds him repulsive, seeks comfort in the open arms of Margie, his on-the-road mistress. Yet he can't bring himself to love the woman who does love him because he's still stuck on the woman back home who thinks he's a jerk. For this, Buddy hates himself.

Back to the reunion. It takes Ben a little while, but he realizes that Sally—he struggles to place her, but then remembers that she ate Baby Ruth candy bars for breakfast—is still in love with him. He had no idea. But he has every idea that his wife, Phyllis, despises him. Hostility runs mutual in their sham marriage: outwardly enviable in affluence and status, but dead and loveless on the inside. So many wasted years. Yet, as Phyllis tartly observes, there's no point now in leaving him (and their Chagall paintings), because she left long ago. Ben, set free by his wife's scorn, begins to think that Sally—the girl he remembers, though, not the woman at the reunion—might have been the great love of his life. Which leaves a humiliated Buddy to watch as his wife flings herself at the feet of the man who used to be his closest chum.

These four are ensnared by their own history, caught in its net, unable to get free of it. They now lead separate, and such different, lives—one glamorous, the other tedious—but they have not relinquished a shared past. Or rather, it hasn't relinquished them. Because the past is right here, on the empty stage of the Weismann Theatre, surging up in front them, like the return of the repressed.

Such is the feeling that a reunion is bound to provoke. The discomfiting feeling that no matter how much we claim to the contrary, we have not changed one little bit. No sooner do we arrive at a reunion than we slide right back into our old, accustomed roles. (That happened to me at my ten-year high school reunion. Which is why I've never gone to another one.) We can find ourselves replaying all those not-so-little dramas whose final act, or so we thought, had concluded long ago.

Keep in mind, this is just the play's premise. Though *Follies* lacks a linear plot—party guests wander in and out, sometimes singing, other times squabbling—it's positively brimming with action. This being a Stephen Sondheim version of the follies, the action is mostly internal: what the characters are hiding, what they know but refuse to say, what they feel but wish they didn't. Sondheim called it "subtext," a well-known term in actor training that he borrowed from the great Russian theatre director Konstantin Stanislavski.

In *Follies*, Sondheim lifts the subtext right up into the text. Characters who for decades have been deceiving everyone, and deceiving themselves most of all, are slowly brought to full account. None of the leads—Sally, Buddy, Phyllis, Ben—will survive the torments of the reunion evening unless they admit the "folly" of their lives. And *folly* in its double sense, as Hal Prince, the original director, told the company: foolishness and madness. Before the bulldozers arrive at dawn to demolish the Weismann Theatre—a site haunted by shapely ghosts in stilettos and black-and-white headpieces, the relics of a history that refuses to die—they have one last chance to heal the wounds of the past. Either that, or they will lose their minds.

———

Losing their minds does seem to be their preferred option. Whenever a disturbing impulse, or a painful memory, confronts these characters, they push it deeper down. So far down that it slips beneath their consciousness. Ignoring the truth makes them feel, for a while at least, that they've overcome their anxieties. Sally convinces herself that she does love Ben because she certainly doesn't love Buddy. Ben feels it's too dangerous to remember the man he'll never be. Phyllis keeps her snappy alter ego locked up for fear of splitting herself in two. And Buddy's got the blues because the things that he gets aren't the things that he wants.

The four of them have become their own distorted reality, and this distortion becomes central to their persona. Unwilling to part with it, they must defend it to the end. To them, facing the truth feels like a leap into the dark abyss. And so, they won't face it. Ben, with his customary terseness, makes the matter clear: "I'm in no mood for honest talks."

Instead, they settle for deceit. Sally, when she first spots Ben, the very object of her obsession, acts surprisingly coy: "No, don't look at me." Who's she kidding? Getting Ben to look at her—and to remember her—and to fall back in love with her—is why Sally threw down those gardening shears in Phoenix and caught a flight to New York City.

The lies keep coming. Picking up on Ben's hint that their old romance won't be rekindled—for her, an almost instant defeat—Sally airily pretends that no such prospect was on her mind. After all, Buddy is the best thing that's ever happened to her. Really? She wasn't sure that he would follow her to New York. Her song, "In Buddy's Eyes," opens with a confession of regret—"And yes, I miss a lot / Living like a shut-in"—that is quickly retracted. Sally prefers to indulge the fantasy that "in Buddy's eyes" she is forever young and beautiful.

Sally has convinced herself that her never-at-home, adulterous husband is also the one man who makes "life worth living." Preposterous, of course. Yet Sally's denial of the manifest truth that her life is empty is what gives her song its irresistible drive. No wonder Sondheim likened it to "self-hypnosis," a state of altered perception.

But we, in the audience, can perceive things rightly. Sally's song is certainly sublime in mood. I would be in raptures if someone looked at me the way that Buddy (so she says) looks at her. But there's something in the music putting us on high alert. Maybe it's the sudden key change when Sally sings of Buddy. Or maybe it's how the dry woodwind accompaniment—the work of orchestrator Jonathan Tunick—challenges the ecstatic lyric. "This number drives me bats!" Barbara Cook complained in rehearsals for the 1985 Lincoln Center concert version of *Follies*. "It's the intervals," she said. It *is* the intervals—they don't land comfortably where they should. The melody of this song disputes all the beautiful lies told in the lyrics. You don't need to be a musicologist to hear, and to feel, how it warns us, as Roscoe sang in the first number, "Caution, / On your guard with / Beautiful girls."

We ought to be on our guard with Ben too. In "The Road You Didn't Take," he sings his firm refusal to dwell upon the past. "I don't remember," he insists, by turns defensive and glib. Don't stew over choices you never made. Don't brood over dreams you never dared. Don't fret over doors you never opened. That's just, Ben says, how it goes: "one's life consists of either/or." Nor, he adds, would these other options have changed much of anything had they been chosen. Life would be different, of course, but not better. Just different.

Yet Ben's confidence, his *over*confidence, erodes from within. His pronouncements are called into lyrical question—"Does it?," "Was it?," "Would they?"—in the same breath in which they are so blithely delivered. Musically, the song's "stabbing dissonance," as Sondheim described it, tells us that Ben is wary of delving into the past not because it's futile, but because it's tormenting.

Torment over the past is indeed what this song heaves upon him. Two flashback scenes play out between its verses, the first with younger Ben and Buddy (the "boys downstairs," waiting for their girls upstairs) and the second with younger Ben and his girl Phyllis. *This* is the past he insists that he doesn't remember. Yet here he is, painfully remembering it all.

Sally and Ben use their songs to hide from the truth. She hides from the present, and he from the past. Either way, they're not looking at what they most need to look at. What I hear in their songs is an echo of how we are all prone to push aside the truth about ourselves. We might, like Ben, refuse to take stock of the past (although secretly we do, replaying it obsessively in our minds) because it hurts to admit that we got things wrong. Or we might, like Sally, whistle gaily past the graveyard, ignoring the awfulness that everyone else can see.

Whenever I'm in the mood to torture myself, I know exactly how to do it. I return to all the roads I didn't take, and then I take them. Foolish, I know. But I do it anyway—and I'm not the only one. Where to start? That time (all right, times) I put career over love. What if I hadn't? For years, no commitment for me was fixed; my life was revisable in every moment. What if I had been more settled? Less wandering? And why did I spend my twenties in the closet? Coming out is the healthiest thing I've ever done. I could go on, but you see what I mean. Somewhere, out there, is another me. This other Richard is leading a parallel life—the life that *this* Richard might have led, but now never will. It's too late. Nothing for it. Trouble is, I do remember him. And I can't help but think— not always, not even often, but sometimes—that his life is better.

———

Right from the start, *Follies* switches between two kinds of theatre songs. The ensemble characters get "pastiche" songs—that is, songs deliberately reminiscent of the theatrical past. When Hattie belts "Broadway Baby," or when Solange purrs "Ah, Paris!"—or Heidi warbles her Viennese waltz, "One Last Kiss"—they are re-creating at the reunion their long-ago numbers in the Weismann Follies. These songs are, in the world of the play, reprises of decades-old stage routines: mini-performances unto themselves. And so, Sondheim wrote the pastiche songs for *Follies* not in his own style but in that of his musical forebears. He wanted them to sound, and they *do* sound, as if they had been composed by George Gershwin, Jerome Kern, or Cole Porter.

By contrast, the four leads sing traditional "book" songs that are character-based and woven into the plot. Broadly realistic, these songs arise logically from the dialogue and, indeed, are inseparable from it. We've looked at the ones sung by Ben and Sally, but there are two more: Buddy's "The Right Girl" and Phyllis's "Could I Leave You?" They are all conventionally dramatic in that they all carry the action forward. For these songs, Sondheim composed, so to speak, in the voices of the several characters. The melodies sound fresh and modern (for the 1970s, at least) and definitely not like tokens of the past.

Different types of songs are meant to work in different ways. Typically, pastiche numbers are performed to return the audience to a bygone era. They offer the comfort of nostalgia. Yet as re-imagined by Sondheim in *Follies*, these delightful "routines" from the past don't stay put in the past. Instead, they offer a weighty commentary on the present. How ironic that the pastiche songs in *Follies* end up behaving like conventional book songs. Though it all feels topsy-turvy, these seemingly frivolous songs become part of the plot.

That's why "Who's That Woman?" has stopped the show ever since Mary McCarty, the future Mama Morton in *Chicago*, first performed it with her five chorines. The gist of this jazzy tune is that a woman looks in a mirror and sees a sad, pathetic figure—a lady who's let her life go by—only to realize ("Lord, lord, lord!") that she's been looking at herself. A fun, gimmicky number for the Weismann Girls in the 1940s.

But when performed, badly, thirty years later—dance steps stumbled over, notes neither hit nor held—the song tells a different story. Remember, the actresses are themselves in late middle age, or even older, just like the characters they portray. Gone is the rapture of youth, and in its stead appears the full evidence of time's ravaging. The tremor. The creak. The wobble. The croak. (The ghostly appearance of their once-lissome selves only heightens the shocking contrast.) These reunited troupers merit our cheers not for their virtuosity—that's long gone—but for their total vulnerability. Where we might be fearful—getting on a bit, not what we used to be, worried we look absurd—they show only bravery. They risk it all, and for them, the crowd roars.

Here is instruction, and a clue. The instruction is to live out the song's own metaphor: to look in the mirror, to *reflect* on that disturbing reflection, and to accept with a good grace what the years have made of us. "It's very poignant," said Phyllis Newman, when rehearsing the number for the Lincoln Center concert, "especially when you're over twelve." She laughed nervously at her little joke, knowing it was not a joke. The song's repeated, insistent question—"*Who's* that woman?"—becomes the existential question we must all answer in our lives. We risk, as we age, clinging to a lost youth, and so being unaware that we may have turned into a parody of our former selves. We might be ludicrous, like a worn-out hoofer convinced that time has not weakened her double-time step.

The clue lies in the nature of the song, and what Sondheim did with it. He made an old-fashioned song do new things. He took an escapist tune and turned it into a discourse on life. How deftly Sondheim used the illusion of theatre to install a palpable reality. And so, it will be by the means of theatre—by the power of stage artifice to summon forth the truth—that Sally, Buddy, Phyllis, and Ben will save themselves. No more book songs that let them get away with telling lies. It's time, well past time, for each of them to step into a surreal spotlight.

————————

When Sondheim smashes a theatrical frame, he really smashes it. Halfway through the second act, just when we've started to think that nothing will get resolved for the lead characters, we find them arguing with their younger selves, blaming them (not forgiving them) for their ruined lives today. "You had it all," Ben rebukes Young Ben, "and you threw it away." "You lost me everything," Sally accuses Young Sally. "I could kill you." The book of life is not yet written for the young—but its pages do fill up, year by quickly turning year. I can well understand all this middle-aged outrage.

It must feel cathartic to shift all that guilt onto somebody else, and then vow God's coldest fury upon them. The irony, so invisible to them, yet so manifest to us, is that they are blaming themselves. *They* are the miscreants whom they harangue. *They* are the culprits they refuse to forgive. Unable to be kind to themselves, they are, likewise, unable to grow through their mistakes. It is bad enough to endure a harsh past, but it is worse by far to have learned nothing from the harshness.

A fanfare of trumpets, coming out of nowhere, silences the hysteria. The empty stage, flooded now with sudden color and light, transforms itself into the follies extravaganza of "Loveland," that mythical world where "everybody lives to love." It's less a smooth segue, though, than a hostile takeover. A leap not just into a new story, but into a new dimension of being.

We're watching a new musical now, but it's being performed by the characters and cast of the old one. Somehow, the four leads have been stolen away from the Weismann Girls reunion and forced onstage in a bizarre version of the Follies. In the twenty uninterrupted minutes of theatre music that now follow, each of them gets a star turn: for Buddy, a rapid-fire comic patter song; for Sally, a torch song; for Phyllis, a burlesque routine; and for Ben, a top-hat-and-tails number that would make Fred Astaire proud. They've gotten, at last, their own pastiche songs. Songs of yesterday that will, in their own magical fashion, unveil the truth of today. Through the Follies, these wandering souls will find their way back home.

Buddy, dressed in a clown's baggy trousers and sporting a too-small derby hat, darts through the show curtain and hails the audience: "Hello, folks, we're into the Follies!" He's got a problem, you see, and he needs to share it. He's feeling "very betwixt and between." What's the trouble? He tells us, at lung-depleting length, in "The God-Why-Don't-You-Love-Me Blues." Buddy's crazy for the gal (Sally, his wife) who ignores him, but runs a mile from the one (Margie, his mistress) who adores him. What gives? Scooting around in the toy car hitched absurdly to his suspenders—chasing and chasing, but never reaching—he finally figures it all out. Buddy's problem, and the reason why he's "very perturbed," is neither that Margie loves him too much nor that Sally loves him not at all. It's that he doesn't love himself. The lowness of this slapstick clown's self-regard—in his own eyes, he's still second banana—stops him from accepting love and keeps him stuck looking for it from the wrong person.

That wrong person is Sally, who, as fate would have it, suffers from a contrary ailment. She thinks highly of herself—don't let that faux modesty fool you—so highly, in fact, that she's fallen victim to her own fantasies. This much is evident from how she appears in her torch song, "Losing My Mind." The stage curtains part, but only enough to frame her in a tight spotlight. How glamorous this fiftysomething Phoenix housewife now looks in a hugging silver-beaded gown. Undeniably, it's the portrait of a star, but a star lost in pointless reverie. Like those 1930s Hollywood musicals that turned their backs on the breadlines, simply declined to see them, this song refuses to admit what it secretly knows.

But then, that's Sally's own truth. I've known this song for decades, and heard it sung in concert frequently by Barbara Cook, one of Sondheim's favorite singers. But it didn't dawn on me for quite a while that it's not a love song. It is, rather, an ode to obsession. Sally is not so much pining for Ben as luxuriating in—making a positive luxury of—her own unrequited longing for him. Hence, the upbeat word "bright" strikes a worryingly low note. Sally allows this never-to-be-fulfilled longing to shape her every second and to mold her every move. Or, rather, her inability—"Not going left, / Not going right"—to move at all. Yet Sally is no hapless victim, for she chooses, over and over, to "spend sleepless nights" obsessing over the man with whom she has not shared a single morning. She plots her misery with pride, just like she plotted her entrance at the reunion. Poor Sally, she will be ruined before she will let herself be changed.

Phyllis knows that *she* needs to change, and fast. Perhaps that's why she struts so quickly across the stage, with a leggy confidence that Gypsy Rose Lee herself would envy. She launches, not a beat skipped, into "The Story of Lucy and Jessie." We know, of course— her winks and wiggles announce it—that the song's "two unhappy dames" are the two contradictory sides of herself. Her own, but much prettier, Dr. Jekyll and Mr. Hyde. When Phyllis sings of drab youthful Lucy longing to trade places with mature dressy Jessie—or wrung-out Jessie wishing she were juicy Lucy—she's admitting the split in her own psyche. There's young Phyllis, naive but full of life, and the Phyllis of today, urbane but dead on the inside. (The number that Sondheim first wrote for this spot, "Uptown/Downtown," makes the dual point in its title alone.)

To win over Ben, all those years ago, and so gain the status and the affluence he promised, Phyllis had first to deny herself and then to remake herself. Turn herself into the curated consort he demanded. "I'll study and I'll read," she vowed. "You'll be so proud of me." At the time, the choice must have seemed smart to Phyllis, but it's harming her now—and leading her to harm Ben. As she sings her life story, with the chorus boys willing her on, this former follies dancer knows what her next step must be. The only way for Phyllis to piece back together a fragmented selfhood is to claim as her own those very fragments. What she has divided, she must now unite. What she has shunned, she must now embrace. "If Lucy and Jessie could only combine," Phyllis hints, then somebody "would finally feel just fine."

Here comes Ben, crooning that he does feel fine. The other three have faced the truth about the awful mess they've made of things. Not all are ready to change—only Phyllis stands on the cusp—but they have named the problem in their lives, showing an honesty that was absent in all their bantering and bickering at the reunion. The holdout is Ben, who starts "Live, Laugh, Love" in slick denial. And why not? He's debonair "Mister Whiz," so the ensemble flatters him, the dandy who laughs and smiles through it all—not caring about, in fact barely noticing, the crumbling walls all around him. He's getting away with it too. Nobody dares to contradict his bullish credo: "Me, I like to live, / Me, I like to laugh, / Me, I like to love."

Enter fate, to claim its revenge. Ben goes blank, forgets everything, and looks down at the conductor (remember, it's a follies performance) to throw him the next line. John McMartin, the original Ben, was so convincing that half the audience at the Winter Garden Theatre feared he really had forgotten the lyrics. The orchestra quickly reverts to a vamp, giving him a chance, before panic takes hold, to find his way back into the music. He can't. Stumbling through the next verse, Ben mangles his tagline so that it comes out "I DON'T LOVE ME!"—which are, of course, the first honest words he has spoken all evening.

It was bound to happen, for pride will have its fall. Crashing out of his song, Ben screams in his wretchedness—"Look at me. I'm nothing. Can't you see it?"—as the orchestra and the singers drown his screams out. It has cost him everything, but Ben has finally stopped believing his own bullshit.

One honesty begets another. Now, for the first time, Ben asks for help. It's hard to hear him, what with the cacophony of everyone singing disordered fragments of their songs. A "Broadway Baby" here, a "Rain on the Roof" there. But, somehow, Phyllis does hear him. She rushes to his side, though her action is hardly cloying. Both ready, at last, to speak truthfully, they stage their own private reunion. No more "martyred looks." Enough with "cryptic sighs." This night has taken them to hell and back—something out of Dante—but the harrowing has been worth it. "Bet your ass," to invoke Phyllis's idiom of choice. For compassion has now replaced cruelty. As we watch Phyllis and Ben step out into a new morning's brightness, we can extend to them the hope for healing that we hold in our hearts for ourselves.

———

I had forgotten somewhat, until I wrote this chapter, just how startled, and then how moved, I am by the ending of *Follies*. Because in that ending, we behold nothing other than the ruin of the show itself, a kind of reverse creation tale. It starts when Ben drops out of his song. Then the whole "Loveland" sequence comes to its riotous, chaotic halt. For a moment, we are back at the Weismann Theatre reunion. And then, finally, the characters quit the world of the play. It's a tribute to James Goldman's libretto that the audience follows this unwinding action so easily. At day's break, the party guests wander out of the theatre—and back into life—surrendering that beloved site of memory, and also of illusion, its perennial twin, to the ghosts who have stood silent vigil all this while.

A thrilling moment, the undoing of theatre by the means of theatre. How apt are Roscoe's words from hours earlier, when he warned (but were we listening?) that at the theatre "your reason is undone." Yet as the trials of Phyllis and Ben have shown us, it is only by being undone—shocked out of our delusions, mocked for our fantasies, evicted from the safety of self-image—that we stand any chance of finding our true selves. (Pay heed, high school drama students.) That is, the kind of person who admits, and so can forgive, each misstep and each mistake. Who doesn't lose their mind in nostalgic obsession. Who leads a congruent, and not a fragmented, life. And who knows that you cannot get through the show all by yourself. Not even if you are unlucky enough to be the famous Benjamin Stone.

4

A LITTLE NIGHT MUSIC

How to Handle Your Regrets

They enter in front of the act curtain and sing. They're not really singing, though, just warming up: trills, scales, "la-la-la." Yet already, they're glancing at us—toying with us—aware that we want the real music to begin. Our patience is rewarded when they give us a preview of three songs—"Remember," "Soon," and "The Glamorous Life"—that we will hear in full before the first act ends.

An unusual way to start—a *vocal* overture—and yet it feels so familiar. Three women wear long black gloves and sweep across the floor in sparkling mauve gowns. How they keep the plumage in their hair from tipping over is a marvel. Meanwhile, two men strut in vintage white tie and tailcoats. On the spinet, a candelabra gleams. Their music is composed in a lilting waltz rhythm—*one*-two-three, *one*-two-three. You might assume, if you didn't already know otherwise, that the curtain has just gone up on yet another Sacher torte revival of *The Merry Widow*.

But something feels amiss. The more this quintet sings, even now, before the play proper has begun, the more we sense an imbalance. Perhaps it's the odd number—five—of the singers themselves. Mathematical oddity gives rise to a dramatic one: a group of five cannot be split into couples, cannot be neatly paired off, which is how an operetta ends. With five, someone will always be left out, and left over—like the remainder in a long-division *problem*. However much they sing of lovers and their liaisons—and they sing of nothing but—one of them will be cut out of the coupled equation. Five will not go evenly into two.

The trouble only compounds when we listen to their words. The music spins in a romantic waltz, but the lyrics force us to a halt. We get only snippets of three full songs, but it's enough to know that the substance of each is not the union of lovers, but their division—whether because of memories mismatched ("Remember?"), desires thwarted ("Soon"), or never being together in the same place ("The Glamorous Life"). In the supporting vocal harmony, a single vowel sound is shifted: "la" slides into "lie." That dishonest word becomes the repeated refrain, so that the song, this *first* song, calls out its own lies in the very moment of their elegant utterance.

The lie is that the lovers will end up together. They won't—of this we are forewarned—and the consequence of their missing out will be a lifetime of regret. Not romance, but *regret*: that's the story we're about to see.

So don't be tricked by the witty libretto, or the charming music, or the waltzes that swirl in from nowhere. In this world where nothing seems to happen—much politely evasive talk, but nary a word of candor—every day brings a little death. A fresh regret to cut you off at the knees while you're playing croquet on a manicured lawn. Remember, it's adapted from Ingmar Bergman's 1955 film *Smiles of a Summer Night*. No wonder Hal Prince, the original director, described this musical as "whipped cream with knives."

One last thing before the act curtain rises. The five singers have names—Mrs. Nordstrom, Mrs. Segstrom, Mrs. Anderssen, Mr. Erlanson, and Mr. Lindquist, so the program tells us—but they are not part of the emerging story. True, their singing offers a running, and largely scornful, commentary on the main characters, but they are not themselves integral to the plot. They observe more than they enact.

Much like the audience. We, too, are engaged, but from a distance. We, too, form impressions, not uniformly favorable, of what we observe. And when we laugh, or applaud, we do it mostly together, and together in perfect time. Whenever I hear the quintet in *A Little Night Music* warming up, I hear a rehearsal for life. Real life, not just its theatrical image. Singers aren't the only ones who need to draw a deep breath, summon their strength, attack the note, and keep time with others.

The sharp knives of regret are out, and they're pointed at us.

―――――――

It is not the wisest gambit to begin rehearsals for a Broadway musical with five of its fifteen intended songs still unwritten. But that's how, on December 10, 1972, things started for *A Little Night Music*. Of the ten songs that Sondheim had finished, two were cut almost immediately. Hal Prince judged them too heavy for what he considered a delicate comedy of manners. Over the next four weeks, as the company rehearsed in New York, Sondheim kept supplying new songs until only one gap in the score remained.

The plot revolves around two characters: the middle-aged Swedish lawyer Fredrik Egerman and his old flame Desirée Armfeldt, a slightly fading stage actress. Fredrik has been married for about a year to Anne (an eighteen-year-old virgin who won't sleep with him) when he reunites with Desirée, who's been performing at a local theatre. Their romance is fast rekindled, but Fredrik spurns her more serious offer to settle down after so many years of gadding about. Sondheim proposed writing a song for Fredrik late in the second act when he tells Desirée that their affair is over and he's going back to his young wife.

This was the final piece of music that Sondheim needed to write—and quickly, too, because the company was just days away from leaving New York and moving to the Colonial Theatre in Boston for the out-of-town tryout. But at least he knew the angle to take for this one last song.

Or so he thought. For five weeks, Hal Prince had directed the scene in question with Fredrik, and not Desirée, as its focal character. Fredrik is, after all, the one who takes control. *He* rejects Desirée. *He* walks out. *He* returns to his wife. (Spoiler: she's already run off with his twenty-year-old son, Henrik.) And he gets an eloquent speech by librettist Hugh Wheeler—"To flirt with rescue when one has no intention of being saved . . . Do try to forgive me"—to apologize for being such a heel. All this time, Desirée only reacts. She listens to Fredrik, and then she watches him leave. No grand gestures. No big speech.

But after the first run-through with Len Cariou and Glynis Johns, the original actors, Prince realized that the scene's energy comes from Desirée. She takes the risk of confessing to Fredrik, her old lover, her new hope that they might together "find some sort of coherent existence after so many years of muddle." (I hear in Desirée's words an echo of *Follies*, Sondheim's previous show, another musical about midlife regret.) Fredrik turns her down, but that's not what the scene is about. It's about—and here the actors agreed—Desirée finding the courage to speak honestly. In a play crowded with characters who live to deceive, or to posture, or to engage in all manner of masquerade, here is someone—an actress, no less—who dares to speak the truth. She is the one who has changed. The scene, they all decided, really belongs to her. Which means that the song still to be written also belongs to her. Somebody ought to tell Sondheim.

Prince got on the telephone and told him to come right away to the rehearsal studio. Arriving by taxi minutes later, Sondheim settled in to watch the scene performed as written, but now tilted toward Desirée. He needed only those few minutes—followed by a drink with the director in a nearby bar—to work out what Desirée's new song had to accomplish. Glynis Johns long admired Hal Prince's knack for knowing precisely "what Steve needed to see to tip him off."

––––––––––

Back at his town house in Manhattan's Turtle Bay neighborhood, Sondheim set to work. First, he wrote down all the thoughts he supposed were running through Desirée's mind at the top of the scene: "I want to right it all before it's too late. . . . But how can you rescue somebody who doesn't want to be rescued?" Then he turned her thoughts into an imagined monologue, what she needed to say to Fredrik: "It was a good thing we didn't get married back then—I was too busy or other things. . . . There's a time to stop opening doors." That metaphor made it into the final version. Sondheim's last task for the evening, although it was by then early morning, was to convert all this preliminary material into the finished lyrics for what would become his most popular song—his one and only palpable hit.

The following day, he showed Hal Prince and Hugh Wheeler

the lyrics to "Send in the Clowns." They liked what they read. Sondheim then spent the second night writing out the vocal line and the piano accompaniment, beginning with those now-famous arpeggiated chords running under the triple-beat melody. (All these notes and first drafts are in a folder labeled "Desirée Act II," part of Sondheim's personal papers in the Library of Congress.)

In rehearsal the next morning, he played—and sang—the full song in front of the two actors. "I was a little pissed off," Len Cariou later admitted, for he was hoping that the new song would still be given to Fredrik. But the song was given to Desirée—and to the particular Desirée that Glynis Johns had created. Just as Sondheim had done first in *Gypsy*, and later in *Company*, he tailored his song to fit the singer. In this case, neither Ethel Merman's trumpet blast nor Elaine Stritch's growl, but the small, silvery voice of Glynis Johns. He crafted a ballad that she could handle without a worry: a modest octave and a bit in range, short phrases firmly closed off with consonants ("Isn't it rich?"), and plenty of rests in between for taking a needed breath. In shaping the melody to suit the performer—though wobbly on long notes, Johns could phrase an intricate lyric like nobody's business—Sondheim found the steadiness of rhythm and the maturity of tone that make us believe Desirée when she declares herself ready to start over with Fredrik.

Johns, a trouper from the old school, learned "Send in the Clowns" in two days flat. She performed it for the first time, glancing not once at the typed lyrics in her hand, at the company's last rehearsal in New York. When they arrived in Boston for the tryout, Jonathan Tunick stayed up all night in his hotel room to orchestrate the song. As Tunick recounts in his introduction to the published libretto of *A Little Night Music*, he opted for the delicacy of strings, a harp, and that low clarinet whose lonely solo is the very sound of middle-aged regret.

———

In the Columbia Records studio, Glynis Johns, who had been in such a room only once before—for the 1964 Disney movie *Mary Poppins*, in which she played Winifred Banks—recorded "Send in the Clowns" in a single take. The same cannot be said for the more than four hundred (and counting) other singers who have recorded it since, everyone from Judy Collins to Shirley Bassey and from Lou Rawls to Frank Sinatra. It's Barbra Streisand, though, who made the most popular cover version to date. Her Grammy-winning *Broadway Album* (1985), whose eighth track is "Send in the Clowns," has sold over four million copies.

Despite—or because of—its lasting popularity, "Send in the Clowns" remains a misunderstood song. Sondheim, ever pessimistic, felt it better suited to a Greenwich Village piano bar than the boudoir of an aging Scandinavian actress. An unerring prophecy, for that is precisely the sort of venue where this song lives on. It's "too pretty," he grumbled to Hal Prince, "too easy to remember."

Over the past fifty years, ballad singers from Manhattan to Manila have lodged no such complaints. Too often, though— and especially when singers stretch the melody out to flatter their voices—"Send in the Clowns" gets warped into a sentimental love song. Which, most definitely, it is not. "It's not even a torch song," Sondheim explained in a television interview for the 1995 revival at the National Theatre in London. "It's quite an angry one. It's a song of enormous regret and irony."

Anger, regret, and irony: that's dark and serious stuff. Which is exactly how Judi Dench performed it when she starred as Desirée in that London production, for which she won a Laurence Olivier Award. As Dench told theatre critic Sheridan Morley, she treated Sondheim's song as a speech for a dramatic actor: "[Desirée's] looking back at her life and realizing that she hasn't made a coherent whole of it. She's made a bit of a mess of it. She's mis-timed it . . . You're one thing, I'm the other." A love song, perhaps—if you insist. But a love song that cannot find its right time or its natural place. A love song in which love is offered only to be spurned. She's "here at last on the ground," but he's lost "in mid-air."

The song's central image—the clowns—hits home hard. A veteran performer, Desirée speaks in theatrical patois: losing her timing, making her entrance, knowing her lines. Extending the theatrical metaphor, she depicts Fredrik and herself as a tired double act whose performance (which is to say, the botched handling of their lives) is so awful that they flee the stage to end the misery for everyone, themselves included. When an act bombed in an old-time vaudeville show, the stage manager really did bring on the clowns to give the audience a little comic relief after the fiasco they had just witnessed. When Desirée invokes that same image she is admitting that she's made a mess of her life.

But there's an ironic edge to it. Desirée calls for the proverbial clowns only to realize that they've been there all the time—because *she* is the clown. She is the buffoon in her own life. No matter how much applause she gets from the audience for playing Ibsen's Hedda Gabler in Halsingborg, or in Rottvik ("and don't ask where is it, please"), Desirée cuts a figure of pure absurdity off the stage. What we witness in this song is Desirée facing the truth that the joke is on her. That is why "Send in the Clowns" ought never to be performed as a gentle air, and why, for that matter, I have been delving so deeply into its backstory. That Desirée can withstand playing the fool in her own life—it hurts, but she stays with the hurt—ought to give us a fright of recognition, but then also a hope strong enough to overcome that fright.

That's what Sondheim told the two students who sang "Send in the Clowns" in his master class at London's famed Guildhall School of Music and Drama in 1984. The event was recorded and then broadcast on London Weekend Television's South Bank Show to coincide with an interview of Sondheim. In a way, the performers had two strikes against them. (Three, if you count the throat-parching pressure of singing Sondheim in front of Sondheim as the cameras and the hundreds in the audience looked on.) Firstly, they were too young, by decades, to play Desirée. Young adults may well know emotional distress, but they are less likely than their elders to be burdened with regret. There simply hasn't been enough time for them to make a multitude of bad choices. (Their time will come.) Secondly—and I cannot decide whether this is more or less significant than their age—a strong, trained voice risks distorting a melody composed for a performer with not much of a voice at all. The temptation to allow the act of singing to override what is being sung—because the singing itself is so exquisite—proves all but irresistible. And yet it *must* be resisted. Every year, I watch my own well-meaning students struggle to let their voice serve the song, and not the other way around.

An expert teacher, Sondheim gently guided the two students back to the song's dramatic core. Namely, Desirée's regret that her every encounter with Fredrik has been badly timed; her thinly concealed anger at him for being an old fool; the ironic reveal that she is the greater fool for supposing he had changed; and the hesitant pivot from despair to hope. Sondheim advised keeping it light when Desirée indulges her glamorous self-image—"my usual flair"—and then darkening the tone when self-reproach wounds her most deeply: "No one is there."

It's a hard balance to strike. That such talented singers did not always fulfill the dramatic demands of the song tells us more, of course, about the song than about them. It tells us that the only way to inhabit this song—and by inhabiting it, to offer the audience a metaphor for life—is to accept humiliation. Here the plainness of the melody speaks so perfectly the plain truth of a life that has lost its way, and knows it. The steady rhythm—now advancing, now holding back, but always in that pensive triple beat—evokes the steady gaze Desirée now fixes upon herself. It is her honesty that touches us most poignantly. Her readiness, not just to forsake all stratagems to win Fredrik back, but to claim as her own all the pain of her life—the anger, the sorrow, and the epiphany that comes too late.

When Desirée caught sight of Fredrik at the theatre—a surprise, fourteen years after their last tryst—she was playing the Countess Célimène in the eighteenth-century comedy of manners *Woman of the World*. That's a fictitious work, but it's based on plays of the period. The Countess, a signature role, was created in Desirée's own image: a woman besieged by suitors who bored her. Yet, how much both women delight in making willing slaves of their serial lovers. The secret, as the Countess reveals to her ladies-in-waiting, is to affirm, uphold, and harden a man's "dignity."

But what about *her* dignity? Perhaps it is because Desirée has devoted so many years to protecting a lover's dignity—no small feat, especially when the lovers are as ridiculous as the current one, the toy soldier Count Carl-Magnus Malcolm—that she leaves her own dignity undefended. She has seen the absurdity of bolstering the ego; she has, in fact, been the ego's accomplice and crafty enabler. But, as she tells Fredrik in their pivotal scene, it's now time to renounce the illusions of the ego. He's not ready, but she takes the risk anyway. She lowers her guard—and gets badly hurt.

Which means that to perform "Send in the Clowns," you must relinquish your poise, sacrifice your cultivated persona, and let go of your need to make a fine impression. It is, in the oddest way, a song in which talent may well hinder you. It's definitely the right song for Desirée Armfeldt, for she has no talent whatsoever in the art of living. I have intentionally blurred the line that separates the performer from the character, the actor from the enacted, because to me that seems the crux of Sondheim's song: to sing it and to live it are one and the same.

And so, I will blur yet a further line, the one keeping the audience at a secure distance. If we feel that Desirée's sorrow for the wreckage of her life has nothing to do with us—and, indeed, if we applaud her sorrow for precisely that deflective reason—then we are missing the point of her song. The point that we, too, might be acting the fool in our own lives, being at right this moment the witless choreographers of our own stumbling.

That's a humiliating truth. Once admitted, it might well turn us angry—just like Desirée—angry at supposedly guilty others. For nothing yields more comfort than blaming someone else for the mishandling of our own affairs. Still, such lashing out is but a protective first reflex. If we can step back from our anger, as Desirée does by the end of her song, then we can allow ourselves to feel something else: regret. Regret that our own choices have led to our discontent.

———

Perhaps it's unfair of me to accuse Desirée of being deficient in the art of living. Because by the end of her scene with Fredrik, she does admit the unfortunate truth about herself. She grieves over her past. And from within her grief, she finds the strength to ask for a second chance. The chance, not to stew over her remorse, but to set things right. Desirée's plea to start over with Fredrik is a wise and mature response to a persistent regret. It is the life-giving response we might all hope to have in such a moment. Anyone bowed by the weight of regret would surely wish to be free of it.

Still, no assurances can be given. Fredrik admits that he's a fool for trying to renew his youth by taking a virginal ingénue as his bride. He also admits that he's content to keep on playing the fool, even though he realizes that it's time to wise up. He does wise up, and that same night, but only after suffering a few more indignities. For now, though, the door that Desirée had the courage to open is closed right in her face.

Yet in that dispiriting moment, the moment that segues so perfectly into "Send in the Clowns," she has never been more alive. No longer pretending, no longer performing, and having cast her accustomed disguises aside, Desirée emerges—how forlorn she looks—as the broken figure she really is. No doubt she chose that red gown to inflame Fredrik's lust. But now it signifies only the raw, bleeding wounds of the heart she can no longer hide. Like her gown's ripped hem, her life is in tatters. Even so, I cannot imagine that Desirée would wish it otherwise. For she is now no longer in thrall to her regrets, and no longer held hostage in her own life, like an actress on tour at the constant mercy of her lady's maid and the railway timetable.

What, then, should we do if we find ourselves consumed by regrets? It's no good ignoring them, for that only makes things worse. Fredrik walks out on Desirée, and straight into trouble: a pistol shot grazes his ear in the absurd game of Russian roulette that he plays with Carl-Magnus. The pair of them, idiots pretending at bravery. Far better to meet our idiocy—it's there waiting for us—with a gentle forgiveness. Let us admit that our timing has never been worse. Let us reclaim all the sides of ourselves that we have angled so tactically out of sight—like an actor showing himself only in flattering profile—but which are, nonetheless, still part of us.

Because then we can do something about our remorse. Where amends can be made, make them. Where circles can be closed, close them. Where hurts can be healed, at least try to heal them. It won't always work, and some of our overtures will be rebuffed. Still, there is honesty, and integrity, in our efforts. And perhaps a bit of learning, too, so that next time our timing will be better. When the smiles of a summer night grant you the grace of second chance, don't be a fool and miss it. Be like Desirée and take it.

———————

Happy are they with nothing to regret. The serving maid Petra earns her place in *A Little Night Music* in the way that minor, but somehow unforgettable, characters often do: by being the person she is. The unsparing self-scrutiny that the lead characters mostly avoid comes so naturally to her. We first meet Petra as the Egermans' flirtatious maid, tempting pious Henrik, Fredrik's son, into afternoons of carnal delight. Alas, he cannot rise to the sinful occasion. She mocks his impotence by patting the spot where his bulge should be. Then comes a weekend in the country, an exciting respite from all the silly people she spends her days serving.

Inside, gathered around Madame Armfeldt's candlelit table—the hostess, you see, is Desirée's mother—the guests are playing their old tricks. They double-deal in artifice and speak only in barbed innuendo. Gamely, they toast to life. And yet their scene of repressed passion feels more like a living death.

Meanwhile, Petra is out in the garden with Frid, a fellow servant, gorging first on bread and wine and then on him. Petra lives her allotted life to the heartiest, while all the fancy, but shallow, others are only pretending to. While they're stuck deep in quagmires of their own making, she's "just passing through." Petra is not simply a weekend visitor at the Armfeldt estate, but a visitor in the wider world. She travels through it unencumbered, ready to savor all its offerings.

Appetite for life—in its rawness, in its zestfulness, and, yes, in its discontents—is the theme of "The Miller's Son," the showstopper that Petra sings near the end of the second act. With her hair and her skirt still damp from the garden tryst with Frid, who dozes contentedly at her side, Petra turns to the audience and recounts the story of her life. Also, the imagined lives that she knows will never be hers. First, she pictures herself married to the miller's son. That's her charted destiny, the best match a housemaid could make. Then she speculates a bit, fancying herself first as a businessman's wife (unlikely, but not impossible) and then as being married to the Prince of Wales (now that's just absurd).

The twist is that while the husbands ascend in wealth and stature, married life gets no better. In 1900, about the time when *A Little Night Music* takes places, the Prince of Wales was the soon-to-be-crowned King Edward VII, a man piggish in shape and equally piggish in his varied appetites. Hardly a bridegroom of choice. No matter the husband, so the song says, marriage will always be a variation—his grouchiness, her saggy breasts, somebody's pressing thigh—on the theme of disappointment.

Yet Petra knows better than anyone how to handle life's disappointments. Stop trying to forestall them—you can't—and start getting busy in the meanwhile. Seize glad occasion while you may ("And there's many a tryst / And there's many a bed") to sample and savor what you can. No matter who we are, and no matter the circumstances we find ourselves in, there will always be a "meanwhile": a parallel moment to slow down, take stock of what lies within reach, and then leap at it. Meanwhile is the time with no time for regret. For "there are mouths to be kissed / Before mouths to be fed."

George Furth, who had written the book for *Company* (and would do so a decade later for *Merrily We Roll Along*), had a friend whose six-year-old daughter was born on Christmas Day. When asked which occasion she preferred to mark, the girl guilelessly replied, "I just want to celebrate everything that passes by." Struck by the wisdom of that youthful credo, Sondheim gave the line almost verbatim to Petra, who declares near the end of her song that "a person should celebrate everything / Passing by."

As should we. Don't judge what the parade of life will put before you. Don't wear yourself out angling for a better view. Don't, above all, take any of it—or yourself—too seriously. Instead, laugh at yourself. Laugh at yourself so loudly that others will hear. That's

Fredrik's problem. That's Henrik's problem. That's pretty much everybody's problem in *A Little Night Music*: they are characters in a farce who act like they're playing high tragedy. Yet who can stay serious for long when their petticoats are flung high? Or their trousers dropped low? Better to follow Petra's lead—and celebrate all that comes your way in the time of our life. You don't want to be already dead when you die.

———————

One character does die in *A Little Night Music*: Madame Leonora Armfeldt. Hours earlier, she lifted her glass to the twinned realities of life and death. Perhaps, in that moment, she felt a tremor of foreboding. But what a life she led. A life once crowded with "liaisons," when in exchange for her sexual favors, the nobility of old Europe rewarded her with "some position / Plus a tiny Titian." (Titian never painted small, but it's a fittingly arch rhyme.) She welcomed all such tangible bounties, drawn more to business affairs than to love affairs. And yet now, in old age, with her mind drifting, Madame Armfeldt recalls the Croatian count, a lover from long ago, who made her a gift of a plain wooden ring. Plain, but a centuries-old heirloom. Scoffing at its coarseness, she tossed aside both the ring and the man who offered it. "Who knows?" she now wonders. "He might have been the love of my life."

All evening long, Madame Armfeldt has disdained the romance—"disgraceful," "shoddy," "indiscriminate," she laments—that swirls all around her. But now, remembering the count's gift (no one forgets their first lover), she weakens just enough to feel what she has so far refused to feel: the pang of regret. She dies soon after, when the long summer night smiles its last smile, upon "the old who know too much." What is the "too much" that Madame Armfeldt knows? I suspect she knows that a life spent in "discretion of the heart," which is her poetic euphemism for being hard-hearted, might leave you brooding on your deathbed, fretting over that lost moment when a little indiscretion was required.

Mortality's intrusion is never far from the scene in *A Little Night Music*, especially in its uneasy final waltz—more Ravel than Strauss, more a seizure than a sweetness—which is also a kind of danse macabre, a spin around the floor in death's tight grip. For the characters, their old life has died—spouses left, vows betrayed, families forsaken—and their new life is scarcely born. Still, this is romantic operetta—ladies dwarfed by their feathered hats, gentlemen stuffed into swallowtail coats, and each *mésalliance* put right by the final curtain—so on death we must not dwell too much. It's life that we need to think about. Then, when we make our entrance again, and let us hope for that second chance, we will time it better. So that next time, someone *will* be there.

5

PACIFIC OVERTURES

How to Be a Part of the Whole

The date is April 26, 2020. The occasion is a tribute to Stephen Sondheim as he turns ninety. Musical theatre greats—Raúl Esparza, Bernadette Peters, Lin-Manuel Miranda, and the list goes on—gather online from their dispersed lockdown locales to perform in the concert extravaganza *Take Me to the World: A Sondheim 90th Birthday Celebration*. Livestreamed on YouTube—fifty years to the day after *Company* opened on Broadway—it has since been watched nearly three million times.

The concert takes its name from one of Sondheim's loveliest songs. He wrote it for *Evening Primrose*, a 1960s television musical about a group of eccentrics who live secretly inside a department store, never leaving it and coming out only at night when the store is closed. Its theme of retreat from, and longing for, the world takes on a poignant new meaning. We, too, are cut off from the world—because of the pandemic lockdown—yet are united in our desire to be taken back to it.

It was quite something, then, to watch Patti LuPone sing "Anyone Can Whistle," another song of lament, standing not in her accustomed spotlight but alone in her Connecticut house, in front of a plain wooden bookcase. She who is renowned for berating anyone who dares to switch on a cell phone while she's onstage now looks fragile and pensive, as if she's about to cry. She's not alone. Tearful confessions pop up on the live chat screen: "Oh wow I'm already crying" . . . "Anyone else sobbing?"

Sobbing overtakes me during "Someone in a Tree," a song from *Pacific Overtures*, one of Sondheim's lesser-known works. It's sung by four actors—Ann Harada, Thom Sesma, Austin Ku, and Kelvin Moon Loh—from the Classic Stage Company's 2017 Off-Broadway revival, directed by John Doyle. We're ninety minutes into the concert, more than halfway through, and this is the first ensemble number. It's tricky to make four Zoom squares—behind them, different people in different places, all using recorded music—look and feel like live theatre. But it works. When the actors "turn" to each other during the song, I can hardly stand it. I know it's an optical illusion—they're still trapped, like all of us, in their virtual cells—but what is theatre if not a house of illusions? And this one convinces. The virtual fragments recompose themselves into a unity. This song feels, as one ecstatic viewer types in the chat screen, "Deliciously NOT REMOTE."

Later, I reflected on why this performance in particular moved me to tears. (I'm in good company, though: Sondheim burst into tears when he first played the song for librettist John Weidman.) I was grateful for a chance to ease my loneliness for a few hours, if only through a virtual gathering. But that was true of the whole concert. It was joyous to watch performers be so relaxed, even affectionate, with each other—not allowing a little thing like lockdown to rupture the bond between them. But that, too, was part of the event.

Something deeper was happening. It wasn't clear to me at the time—I was too close to the moment—but I can see it now. "Someone in a Tree" captivated the online audience not because it revealed its own story—a treaty signing in Japan in the 1850s—but because it so perfectly revealed ours. The song is about living at a turning point, and yet not fully seeing the turning. It's about being part of history, and yet finding it only in fragments. The parallels were uncanny. The COVID pandemic was an epochal shift (hence, we refer to "the before times"), but one that we experienced mostly in isolation. History, and with a capital *H*, was happening—that much we knew. But it was happening somewhere else, not here. Here, we were but fragments of the day.

That I failed to grasp this fact of life at the time when I was living that same life is an irony worthy of Sondheim himself. It is also the theme of "Someone in a Tree."

———

A tree grows in Kanagawa, the Japanese port where Commodore Matthew Calbraith Perry of the United States of America was permitted to land in June 1853 during his gunboat diplomacy expedition on behalf of President Millard K. Fillmore. *Pacific Overtures*—Perry's own words, taken from his politely threatening letter to the Japanese emperor—tells how the island's centuries-long isolation from the West came to an end. It tells that story entirely from the Japanese point of view.

The formal historical record gives *Pacific Overtures* its narrative high point: Commodore Perry coerced Japan into signing a trade treaty with the United States. In retrospect, the treaty signing was an epoch-making moment, a point of no return in the floating island kingdom's encounter with the mercantile West. It was the moment when Japan started down the path of becoming a global economic superpower.

But in 1853, all that lay in the unknowable future. Right now, the four American warships menacing the coast—"four black dragons," the Japanese call them—herald not an opportune beginning, but a tragic ending. Commodore Perry, in six days' time, will disembark his side-paddle steam frigate, the USS *Susquehanna*, and come ashore. He will request that Japan enter into a treaty with the United States. Should his request fail, the shell guns and the cannons that he has ordered pointed at the shoreline will doubtless secure him the outcome he desires. The ending to this story feels like it's already been written. Written, that is, by the Americans.

The Japanese, however, look at things from a different angle. To the ruling shogun and his councilors, the mere idea that a foreigner should set foot on Japanese soil, and do it by threat of violence, is utterly abhorrent. Sacred protocol forbids it. Yet nothing will stop Perry and his crew from reaching land. What to do? If the Japanese cannot alter the outcome, and they definitely cannot, then they will forget that it ever happened. They will write a rival history, one that suits *them*. This suitable history will state that "the Americans were never here."

And so, a hopeful ruse forms in the mind of one Kayama, the minor, but rapidly promoted, Samurai functionary tasked with erasing the Americans from Japanese history. Let Perry's frigates sail, he advises the shogun's councilors, into the lesser port of Kanagawa. There, let the expanse of sand be covered by tatami mats. Let a wooden treaty house be built to receive Perry and the letter he bears from President Fillmore. Let all graces be observed. Let the Americans depart in peace.

Then, let us wait. Wait for the Americans to board their gunboats, to pull up anchor, and to chart their homeward course. Once it's safe, burn every last mat—rice straw catches flame so easily—and raze that treaty house to the ground. "The Americans will have come and gone," the crafty Kayama explains to Lord Abe, the shogun's chief advisor, without ever having stepped on actual Japanese soil. Better still, all evidence of this unwelcome intrusion will be destroyed. Japan will suffer no dishonor, and its decree against foreigners will remain inviolate.

Everyone can go back now to the ageless island serenity from which they were momentarily dislodged. Commodore Matthew Perry? Never heard of him. President Millard K. Fillmore? Doesn't ring a bell. July 14, 1853? Just another day.

Except that it wasn't. Those brightly colored kites descending from the theatre's fly gallery tell us that it's a singular day, a day marked out, an *occasion*. So much is happening before our eyes. Here is the treaty house being built onstage; built, of course, only to be demolished. A samurai warrior wedges himself under its wooden floor, ready to attack should the devious Americans draw their guns. A fully mature tree, ready for someone to climb it, slides in next to the treaty house. Lord Abe and the Second Councilor enter the house, disappearing from the audience's view, and wait inside for the Americans to arrive.

No sooner are the tatami mats unfolded down the length of the *hanamichi*—the traditional kabuki theatre runway—than the American entourage enters to the braggart sound of its own marching band. Yankee sailors keep guard outside the treaty house as Commodore Perry and his officers go inside it to conduct a little forced diplomacy, the conduct of which remains deliberately hidden from view. If you can't see it, it didn't happen.

In a sense, the play stops here. Everything comes to a halt just when the story reaches its climax. The scene we've been waiting for, the scene of Commodore Perry and Lord Abe squaring up to each other, never does get seen. Everything is frantic for a while—and then, nothing. Just nothing.

Well, nothing but a song. What about? It can't be about the treaty signing, at least not directly, because nobody can give a full or fair account of it. But as the librettist John Weidman knew, a song can proceed by indirection, sneak up on its theme, follow an "oblique" route. And so he outlined a scene in which two (in a way, three) people try, but fail, to remember that unusual day. This emergent scene, which would later become entirely musical, was about things *not* happening. People who don't see. Who don't hear. Who can't recall. Sondheim doubted at first that he could write music and lyrics about nothing. Yet the more he pondered it, the more he realized that a song about "nothingness," as he later explained, might well become a song about "everythingness."

Everything starts with the Reciter, the kabuki-like narrator who shifts our attention from the treaty signing (which we can't see, anyway) to how that elusive event was later described. How it found its way into the annals of history. Or, rather, never found its way there—because the shogun's councilors never spoke a word about it. The Americans spoke plenty about it, and then wrote even more. But the Reciter puts no trust in biased histories compiled by uninvited foreigners. What a pity, he reflects, that "no authentic Japanese account" has survived.

Enter, to the sound of a brisk clarinet, an old Japanese man who politely, but emphatically, corrects the Reciter's mistake. He, himself, "was there"—at the treaty house—and saw everything. Being then a boy, just ten years old, he scampered high up a nearby tree—*this* tree, the one onstage—the best of all possible lookouts. We're inclined to believe this man. Old age dignifies him, as do his delicate spectacles and his bowler hat. Wait, the hat is a Western import—and his attaché case, another foreign object, is likewise a bit suspect. But they do lend him a serious air. Let's give this eyewitness a chance.

———————

So begins "Someone in a Tree," the song that promises to tell us what happened in the treaty house. Our hopes shoot high, as high as that overlooking tree, that everything long hidden from us will be revealed at last.

What's revealed, though, are doubts and difficulties. The old man can't remember exactly where the tree was. Yet it hardly matters, because he's now too feeble to climb up it, though he tries a full eight times. What began as laudable has become laughable. "I was younger then," he apologizes.

Indeed, he was—and here comes his youthful avatar, bouncing onto the stage and up into the tree. But the ensuing colloquy between young and old adds little to our knowledge. What they can see through the eaves—mats on the treaty house floor, men in parley—doesn't amount to much. Worse, they dispute the details. No, the old man retorts, the negotiators were not old. No, the boy insists, only *one* American officer sported gold braid on his coat. They agree on this: the tree, it then being mid-July, was green and leafy.

Even in his double incarnation, our witness has not witnessed very much. He sees into the treaty house—a bit—but he hears nothing. His perspective is one-sided. Totality eludes him. We need fuller evidence.

Right on cue, a samurai warrior—the one hiding in armed readiness beneath the treaty house floorboards—joins the song. This seems promising, for he adds a new perspective: though he cannot see what's happening, he can *hear* it. He listens for two knocks—the agreed signal, as Kayama explained, for him to unsheathe his sword, burst up through the floorboards, and attack the Americans. His ears are tuned to the frequency of that one alerting sound. Meanwhile, other noises—creaks, thumps, clinks, growls—seep through, all muffled and indistinct. Snippets of arguments can be heard, but it's only "droning."

We're no better off than when we started. There are two witnesses to the treaty signing, but neither of them knows much. One, moreover, keeps changing his story. We hope that these divergent points of view will compensate for each other, filling in the blanks, but that doesn't happen. Throughout, the Reciter questions the witnesses ("You were where?") and urges them to elaborate ("Tell us what you hear"), but all to no avail. Even he, longing to possess an "authentic Japanese account," admits defeat. But still, he has an opinion. "Whatever happened," the day went exactly as the Japanese had planned: the Americans came and the Americans left. They left, of course, but only to return—along with a reinforcement of trade-hungry Europeans. Even this summary of events is misleading.

And so the song ends the only way it can: with a chorus in jubilant praise of its own failure. "Someone in a Tree" tells us nothing about the past, and takes a marathon three hundred and two bars to tell it.

Yet the more I think about it, the more I'm convinced that this song *must* extend itself to the point that its length compels our fascination, like a high note held to the limit of a singer's endurance. How long, we wonder, can it go on? Going on—and on—is the song's true achievement. Not explaining the past. Not documenting the past. Not even agreeing on the past. But, rather, letting the past *be* the past: a river of time, flowing without cease, into which we now and then wade in our futile, but predictable, effort to alter its course.

Sondheim's true subject, it turns out, is less a given historical event than the workings of history itself: how we give meaning to the past. History is, of course, always specific, and Commodore Perry's mission to Japan is a worthy case study, a dramatic and globally consequential event. We can scrutinize this event from different angles—in "Someone in a Tree," literally from different angles—and try to make sense of it. The *making sense* of it, though, is the actual task, the real story. But to reach that real story, we must first pass through the apparent one.

In March 1976, Frank Rich, then a young *New York Post* film critic, arrived at Sondheim's town house on East Forty-Ninth Street to interview him and John Weidman about, as he put it, "how a [musical theatre] song is conceived, how it's written, and how it is refined until it's ready to be performed." The result was "Anatomy of a Song," a short documentary produced for the CBS Sunday-morning arts program *Camera Three*. The chosen song was "Someone in a Tree," one of Sondheim's self-professed favorites. Anatomizing it, he said this: "The song's about history the way the show is about history and what that means."

Back to the song's unusual length—and sound. Working out a musical analogy for the sweep of history—its equivalent in pitch, tempo, rhythm, and harmony—Sondheim was inspired by what he called the "relentlessness" of Japanese music. How it rolls on and on—and ever on—always stretching forward but never reaching its end. He tried to capture this repetitive sound in "Someone in a Tree." As it turned out, Sondheim's music felt more Indonesian in tone than Japanese; or, indeed, more like the iterative music that Philip Glass had been developing in the 1960s. But strict cultural authenticity was not for him the point. The point was to create for the listener a desired *effect*—and Sondheim did.

As the Old Man enters, we hear the four-beat vamp on a single chord that sustains itself throughout the entire number, repeating hundreds of times with only small variations. Those variations are perceptible to the ear—the music edges up a note here, drops down a note there—but never jarring to it. The Old Man explains— the Boy climbs the tree—the Warrior crawls out from under the floorboards—the Reciter poses questions—and, eventually, their voices unite in chorus. Yet all this time, the underlying harmonics do not change. Not even in its sixty-six-bar crescendo does the song develop. It offers only *more* of itself. The rhythm holds. The beat goes on. Goes on as inevitably as each tomorrow becomes a today and each today drifts back into a yesterday. Sondheim latched on to the sound of history itself, making music that, in its serene unfurling, felt to him like "the endless stretching out of time."

In the music, we hear time's passage; on the stage, we see it. In Hal Prince's original version, the number ends with the Old Man in the center, flanked on the left (from the audience's view) by the Boy perched high in the tree and on the right by the Warrior aisémentcrouched low on the floor. Together they form a strong diagonal traversing the width of the stage. It looks like time's own arrow in flight.

The character in *Pacific Overtures* who most wants to make sense of history is the Reciter, the lone figure who bridges long ago and right now. He speaks with the past, but always from the present. He wants to know how the past bears upon the present. How, indeed, the past *creates* the present—which means, of course, that the past is never entirely past.

No naive investigator is he. The Reciter is canny, for he knows that all histories are slanted in sly, self-serving ways by the people who write them. He also knows that there's no point in appealing to so-called objective evidence—because that evidence, too, will be biased in a particular someone's favor. That's why he's so intent on finding a *Japanese* account of the treaty signing. He wants to bend the historical record away from the Americans— hard to do, for that record is deeply rooted in America's ideology of "manifest destiny"—and back toward the Japanese. Because as his compatriots see it, Commodore Perry's expedition did not end with Japan's disgrace.

It's a long story, and more intricate than it might seem. The incursion of Westerners in the second half of the nineteenth century fueled a simmering Japanese anger that led to its economic rivalry with those same nations, culminating in the 1970s—the decade of *Pacific Overtures*—when Japan beat America at its own export-import game. That Japan's economy has slowed down markedly in recent times makes exactly the same point, just in a different way: history keeps changing. The Reciter is well aware that there can never be a total or definitive account of the events of July 14, 1853. That's

crouched low on the floor. Together they form a strong diagonal traversing the width of the stage. It looks like time's own arrow in flight.

The character in *Pacific Overtures* who most wants to make sense of history is the Reciter, the lone figure who bridges long ago and right now. He speaks with the past, but always from the present. He wants to know how the past bears upon the present. How, indeed, the past *creates* the present—which means, of course, that the past is never entirely past.

No naive investigator is he. The Reciter is canny, for he knows that all histories are slanted in sly, self-serving ways by the people who write them. He also knows that there's no point in appealing to so-called objective evidence—because that evidence, too, will be biased in a particular someone's favor. That's why he's so intent on finding a *Japanese* account of the treaty signing. He wants to bend the historical record away from the Americans— hard to do, for that record is deeply rooted in America's ideology of "manifest destiny"—and back toward the Japanese. Because as his compatriots see it, Commodore Perry's expedition did not end with Japan's disgrace.

It's a long story, and more intricate than it might seem. The incursion of Westerners in the second half of the nineteenth century fueled a simmering Japanese anger that led to its economic rivalry with those same nations, culminating in the 1970s—the decade of *Pacific Overtures*—when Japan beat America at its own export-import game. That Japan's economy has slowed down markedly in recent times makes exactly the same point, just in a different way: history keeps changing. The Reciter is well aware that there can never be a total or definitive account of the events of July 14, 1853. That's fine. All he wants is to ensure that the American version of those events isn't the only one.

In its final, flash-forward scene—and especially in the convulsive modern rhythms of its final song, "Next"—*Pacific Overtures* tells this alternative history. How the real legacy of American imperialism was, at least for a time, the economic ascendancy of Japan, the ancient floating kingdom that floated right to the top of postwar global capitalism: Mitsubishi, Toyota, Seiko, and Sony. Today we might envy Japan's cultural power—"Cool Japan"—with its global brands of manga, Pokémon, and (my own favorite) Hello Kitty. Sondheim's lyrics were written in the mid-1970s, but their point still holds: "Who's the stronger, who's the faster? / Let the pupil show the master."

———————

Such reversal of fortune was hardly what Commodore Matthew Perry had in mind when he sailed out of Norfolk, Virginia, in November 1852, headed ultimately for Japan. But it was most definitely what Hal Prince had in mind when he urged John Weidman, who had studied East Asian history at Harvard, to dramatize Perry's mission from the Japanese standpoint solely, thus making outsiders of Americans and Europeans in a Broadway musical. The coup de grâce was to stage *Pacific Overtures* in 1976, the year of America's proud bicentennial.

How radical the change was. Rodgers and Hammerstein, only twenty-five years earlier, had written *The King and I* from Anna's point of view, not the king's, and thought nothing of it. *South Pacific*, their earlier musical, promotes racial and ethnic tolerance ("You've Got to Be Carefully Taught") but always through American eyes.

Within the show, Pacific Islanders—that is, the Indigenous people—are still always the "other."

Granted, *Pacific Overtures* was put together by a team of white Americans. In casting, though, it has always been diverse. Granted, too, it trades in some tired Orientalist stereotypes: warrior men and submissive women. Still, I think, a larger point is valid: here was an effort, and a provocative one, to call history itself into question. To make it known that what you can see of the past depends upon the place, the necessarily *limited* place, from which you are seeing it. Similar themes recur in *Assassins*, whose libretto was also written by Weidman, Sondheim's most politically minded collaborator. Everybody's got a right to their own version of history.

When Perry's four frigates arrived in Japan in July 1853, local artists rowed out in small boats to draw him and the four black dragons of his fleet. Thus began the flourishing cottage industry of depicting Commodore Perry in Japanese woodblock prints. Many of them can been seen today in museums from Honolulu to Washington, DC, to Salem, Massachusetts. By far, though, the greatest collection of such artifacts is housed in the Ryosenji Treasure Museum in Shimoda, the first Japanese port opened to America, in 1854.

Perry, in most of the Japanese prints, looks nothing like the staid, double-chinned plumpness—the "Old Bruin," as his sailors dubbed him—found in Mathew Brady's posed daguerreotypes. What the Japanese artists conveyed was not how Perry appeared to his fellow Westerners, but how he appeared to *them*. To them he was a barbarian invader on the rampage. And so he is depicted with his eyes alert, stare intent, sword brandished high, and with enough matted facial hair to rival a werewolf. Both likenesses are true, but not universally so; they are true in a particular context. To the Americans, Perry cut a dour figure, a Boston grandee. To the Japanese, though, he was a brutal invader, a figure of menace and fright. How could one single portrait encompass two such different, but equally valid, realities?

Costume designer Florence Klotz, who won a Tony Award for *Pacific Overtures*, must have studied these woodblock prints, because the Commodore Perry who comes ashore at Kanagawa is the Commodore Perry who alarmed the Japanese. In the show, he's a white-maned Kabuki lion in fierce, exaggerated makeup and dressed garishly as Uncle Sam. A complete portrait of alien terror. The victory march that plays as Perry struts in his wordless, yet intense, scene that concludes the first act underscores the point fully: whatever you see, you are seeing it through your own eyes. Just as everyone else is seeing it through theirs. There is no other way.

———

Risks abound when a Broadway musical takes as its theme the process of history: namely, how the past is documented and interpreted. Almost by definition, such an undertaking will come across as too abstract, too academic, a dull textbook in theatrical form. Sondheim worried that *Pacific Overtures* would feel like homework to its audience. He was right to worry. After all, most of us don't spend our days pondering the fundamentally contingent nature of historical truth. We have much better things to do.

Sondheim, then, had to *dramatize* the making of history, turning a cerebral insight into a palpable reality—something personal, even intimate, and relevant to life as we now live it. For we are, all of us, whether we realize it or not, inserted already into history. From birth to death, and maybe thereafter, we are historical figures. We occupy history. How does that feel? Sondheim's answer: it feels like being a fragment.

"Fragment" is the key word in "Someone in a Tree." In working out the song, Sondheim began with Weidman's idea about an old man who struggles to recall the past. What, Sondheim asked himself, was at stake in this moment? It must be significant, because we've not seen the Old Man before, and we won't see him again. Picking up one of the soft lead pencils that he always used when writing songs, he scribbled these words onto a yellow legal pad: "it's the details that count." Then a series of paradoxical images came to his mind, images of the part being greater somehow than the whole: "pebble not the stream," "word not the sentence," "stroke not the painting." Sondheim had found, in this reverse logic, his perfect metaphor—the fragment—and he made it the song's central refrain: "I'm a fragment of the day."

In Japanese haiku, a single delicate image, just a wisp of words, can betoken the whole world. Its sparseness of form, with seventeen syllables arranged precisely over three lines, leaves a space for thoughtful readers to occupy. With a similar poetic exactness, Sondheim's lyrics—"It's the pebble, not the stream. / It's the ripple, not the sea / That is happening."—collapse the vastness of history into tangible immediacy: things seen and known and handled and felt in the course of a day. The world comes to us, as it must come to us, in the bits and pieces of life as we live it. Yet these fragments, in their aloneness, reach also beyond it, inclining toward the unity from which they have been sundered. The poets call it synecdoche: the part, though it never stops being a part, stands in for the whole. We might call it someone in a tree.

This, it seems to me, is why a song about failure sounds so jubilant. Not naively jubilant, but wisely so. The Old Man, the Boy, and the Warrior aren't fooling themselves. They know they are but a *part* of the larger event: "I'm a fragment of the day . . . I'm the part that's underneath." Yet they respond to these inescapable limits not with the anger of an ego threatened at being so diminished, but with a gentle humility. Humility born of a consoling awareness that even the humble fragment—the sliver, the scrap, the bit snapped off—carries within it the trace of the whole. No one in this trio is ever really alone. Singing a litany of setbacks that set nothing at all back, they cannot help but smile.

The *Camera Three* documentary filmed in Sondheim's town house ends with a powerfully intimate rendition of "Someone in a Tree." The original performers—James Dybas as the Old Man, Gedde Watanabe as the Boy, Mark Hsu Syers as the Warrior, and the inimitable Mako as the Reciter—gather around a grand piano to be accompanied by the composer himself. Charmingly, Sondheim needs his own sheet music. They look, from today's perspective, like the contents of a time capsule from the 1970s—history, again—with their long hair, velvet blazers, and chunky, nubby turtlenecks. Yet time's distance erodes once the music starts. It takes the singers a while to settle in—they're nervous, no doubt, with the camera rolling and Sondheim playing—but come the exultant chorus they are all nods and bounces and grins. Except for the coolly restrained Mako, who nods only. In the unbroken silence that follows this long song—something akin to the silence granted by a haiku—the camera pans right and rests on Sondheim, still at the keyboard and still staring at his music. Beat. Glancing up, he looks right into the camera—and smiles. His shy smile, the one we know so well. The one hinting at the depth of feeling to which we have all just surrendered.

————————

This is when the tears flow—I write from grateful experience—because this is when the music heals. Heals not by hiding how fragmented we feel, but by exposing the value of that very feeling, daunting though it is. The almost Zen minimalism of "Someone in a Tree"—its endless vamping, its precise, elemental metaphors, its resistance to finality—makes us aware that we are all but fragments of the day. How could it be otherwise? All we can do, all we ever can do, is to stay mindfully in the moment, alert to the lack that shapes our perception of the whole. And yet we gain something from that same lack. We gain the self-possession of the beam that holds the building up, knowing all the while that its test of strength must be shared. We gain the calmness of the ripple that knows no matter how far it extends, the surrounding sea extends yet farther. And were it not for that wider sea there would be no rippling, none at all. That's a wisdom for all the seasons of a lifetime.

6

SWEENEY TODD

How (Not) to Deal with Injustice

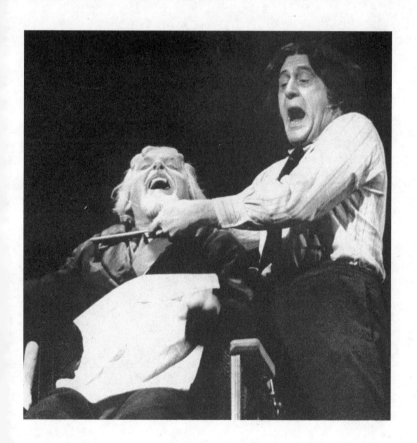

It took five years for the 1979 Broadway musical *Sweeney Todd* to be performed as an opera. Hal Prince, who mounted the original production, directed it in 1984 for both the Houston Grand Opera and New York City Opera. Whether it's due to Sondheim's mostly through-composed score, or to how easily this Victorian revenge tale lends itself to epic staging, *Sweeney Todd* has become a fixture in the repertoire of opera companies the world over—from the New Zealand opera in Auckland to the Icelandic Opera in Reykjavik to the Zürich Opera in Switzerland.

If you're going to perform a show about revenge—which is, after all, Sweeney's driving compulsion—Zürich is a fitting place to do it. For it was in this city that a team of cognitive neuroscientists conducted one of the world's most thorough experiments in the psychology of vengeance.

Researchers at the University of Zürich devised a game in which two players (both men) were given equal amounts of money. Let's say ten Swiss francs each. Player A was told that if he gave his portion to Player B it would be quadrupled. He'd have nothing left, while the other player would be enriched: forty bonus francs added to the original ten. In nearly all cases, Player A handed over his money, trusting that Player B would share the multiplied bounty.

That would, of course, only be fair—what justice demands—because the outcome depended on Player A taking a risk. The other player, although he gained, risked nothing. Most times, Player B did split the rewards, leaving both of them better off.

Sometimes, though, Player B kept the spoils for himself. This is what the scientists were hoping for because the experiment was designed to incite acts of revenge. Revenge—why we do it, when we do it, and how we feel about it—was their object of study. And so they gave Player A, when he felt cheated, the power to punish Player B by taking away some of the hoarded money. This was *not* restorative justice: the deducted money wasn't returned to Player A. It was, rather, revenge in its purest and swiftest state—as swift as the avenging slash of Sweeney Todd's razor.

Nobody gets through life without wanting to hurt the people who have hurt them. A cheating lover, a faithless friend, an irksome neighbor, a nasty boss, or that son of a bitch who cuts us off at the intersection. "Road rage" and "air rage" are phrases in common usage now, while "revenge porn" is a criminal offense enabled by social media. We don't (thank goodness) always follow through with our revenge fantasies, but the impulse is there. I can barely get to and from my local coffee shop each morning without entertaining murderous thoughts about the sidewalk dawdlers blocking my way. How I would love to push each of the offenders into the oncoming traffic—and continue merrily on my way. You know what I mean. Fortunately, for *them*, I lack Sweeney Todd's resolve.

We indulge our revenge impulse because it's so pleasurable. In that Swiss experiment, real-time brain scans showed that the mere *thought* of inflicting punishment on the guilty would activate (that is, increase oxygen flow to) the dorsal striatum, the front part of the brain that deals with reward processing. The scans lit up, showing a rush of neural activity. Revenge—pondering it, plotting it, picturing it—makes us feel good. It's the same high we get from looking at our spouse's photograph or anticipating this month's paycheck. Or, for that matter, rubbing cocaine into our gums. In the brain's chemistry, there's no difference at all: pleasure is pleasure.

I wonder if any of those Swiss neuroscientists saw the Zürich Opera's production of *Sweeney Todd*. If so, they would have witnessed a grandly macabre enactment of what their clinical study had confirmed: sweet revenge is one of life's tastiest treats. Some like it cold, and others piping hot. No matter how this delicacy is served, we do like it.

———

The 1979 musical is based on Christopher Bond's play *Sweeney Todd, the Demon Barber of Fleet Street*, which thrilled Sondheim when he had seen it in London six years earlier at the Theatre Royal Stratford East. Bond's script looked back to George Dibdin Pitt's gory melodrama from 1847 but turned the fictional Sweeney Todd into a more complex character. No longer a stock villain, Sweeney emerged as a wronged man who destroyed himself by seeking revenge at any cost upon his tormentors. It was this revenge motif that Sondheim wanted to explore in what he called "a musical thriller."

Sondheim and librettist Hugh Wheeler altered Bond's story only a little. The Fleet Street barber Benjamin Barker was convicted by the corrupt Judge Turpin on a fake charge and sentenced to life in prison in the penal colony of Australia. Fifteen years later, when the play begins, he escapes and returns to London under an assumed name—Sweeney Todd—to avenge himself upon the judge.

Sweeney's hunger for revenge becomes only more intense when Nellie Lovett, his former landlady, reveals two horrible truths: his wife, Lucy, poisoned herself with arsenic after Judge Turpin raped her; and ever since, his daughter, Johanna, has been kept a virtual prisoner in the judge's house, where he plots to make her his bride.

Gone forever is honest, but naive, Benjamin Barker. In his place stands Sweeney Todd, with his pale visage and his odd eye and with something more than mischief on his mind. It is Sweeney who, with a feral justice on his side, declares that the "hour has come" for the guilty to be punished.

A raging intent, but how will it be fulfilled? The enterprising Mrs. Lovett supplies the answer, for she has kept safe Sweeney's own silver razors. Restored, at last, to the arm they render complete, these blades will sing once more as they slice open the "throats / Of hypocrites." Sweeney will lure the unsuspecting Judge Turpin into the death trap of his soon-to-be renowned "tonsorial parlor" on Fleet Street, where the judge will get the closest shave of his life. Providence itself could not have devised a scenario more fitting.

———————

For all his grim resolve, Sweeney Todd smiles at the prospect of putting his old razors to new and vengeful use. It happens in "My Friends," his first extended song—his first aria, really. Sweeney sings it not to Mrs. Lovett (she coos at his elbow, though, a hesitant lovebird), but to his razors. *They* are his much missed and most necessary friends. Sweeney caresses his weapons of death, holds them lovingly up to the light, sings to them tenderly, and promises them "splendors / You never have dreamed all your days." He means, of course, the splendor of being drenched in Judge Turpin's blood. But when blood is so deserving to be spilled, its dribbling down the blade will look more like "precious / Rubies," a string of gemstones set in a silver base.

Here, then, is our first taste of sweet revenge, with even the music notated *sempre dolce*. Hatched in an instant, Sweeney's vengeful plot will now unfold as easily as his chased silver razors. On the threshold of revenge, Sweeney stands in full hypnotic rapture, transfixed by the glinting of the blades in a light so strong that it can shine through the grime and the dust that obscure the windows in Mrs. Lovett's pie shop.

Yet this is not the whole song. Throughout it, Sondheim warns us not to get drawn into that hypnosis, not to be seduced by a revenge fantasy. Sweeney's lyrics are unrhymed, which grants them the intimate forthrightness of a Shakespeare soliloquy. (Was Sondheim thinking of Macbeth's ode to a hallucinated dagger?) Here is a tormented soul who longs for an end to all his torments. We believe Sweeney when he sings "My Friends." Maybe we also pity him. Yet still, we stand apart. For we have heard what Sweeney cannot hear: that his song is unstable.

Its melody surges in majesty, but the tide beneath is drifting. Three steady beats fill each measure, yet the strummed chords underneath are held for seven beats. A count of three or six in the accompaniment would, as Sondheim later explained, make perfect rhythmic sense—*with* the downbeat. But a seven count is irregular. Those chords heard underneath Sweeney's singing are, in the fullest sense of the term, *offbeat*. His song's meter and tempo never vary—from start to finish, it's a slow waltz—but the musical accents never land where they should. They exceed the metrical mark, seeping into a part of the music where they should not be found. We feel, even if we can't precisely account for it, this song's oddity. Not so much the oddity of Sweeney himself as that of the path he is embarking upon. This is Sondheim's way of alerting us to the likelihood that Sweeney's revenge quest might not go as neatly as planned. Watch out for excess bleeding.

We're now slightly on our guard, but Sweeney throws himself in his work. Restless, he frets that Judge Turpin has not yet visited his shop. Mrs. Lovett, in her lullaby to a grown man, counsels patience ("Wait," her song's title) but to no avail. Though Sondheim never much liked this song, it does reveal that Mrs. Lovett hasn't a clue about what Sweeney really wants. He wants to claim his vengeful prize. And soon enough, it appears. Beadle Bamford, the judge's factotum, has persuaded his lordship that a close shave and a sprinkle of cologne will render him more appealing to young Johanna. Straight he goes to Fleet Street, in search of the barber Sweeney Todd. At last, the waiting game is over. Sweeney's anxious, jittery fingers have only to clutch the blade and sink it into the old man's throat.

Yet here, on the verge of retribution, Sweeney stays his murderous arm. At the very instant when his deepest desire can be satisfied, and be satisfied at the quickest stroke, he pauses. Why? Because the pleasure of revenge (recall the Swiss brain scan experiment) lies mostly in its expectancy. "Patience, enjoy it," he whispers to the killing blade, and to himself.

Not needing to rush, Sweeney indulges in the nearly erotic thrill of stropping his manly razor, sharpening its edge with a rhythmic rubbing along the length of a leather strip. I say nothing of the white froth he smears on the judge's upturned face. Prolonging this moment—edging, really—he joins Judge Turpin in a lilting waltz in praise of women. A gorgeous song, certainly, but it's also teased-out queer foreplay, a mutual heightening of arousal to each man's breaking point. The judge, partial to whipping himself into a guilty ecstasy, knows better than most that to bring your pleasure to a peak you must resist it for as long as you can. Why else would Sweeney not go in for the kill, when the judge sits at last so submissively in the barber's chair, with his head tilted back and his scruffy throat exposed?

To linger, as Sweeney does linger, on the threshold of retribution—not the doing of the deed, but the exquisite *nearly* doing of it—is to ignore the demands of justice. If justice alone were Sweeney's true aim, then he would not tarry. But tarry he does—and for so long that he cannot finish the job. When Sweeney is, finally, about to slash the judge's throat, the sailor Anthony barges in and blurts out his plot to steal Johanna from the judge's house that very night. Judge Turpin flees in furious alarm, not knowing that he came within a hair's breadth of his demise.

Sweeney now rages in impotence and lashes out first at Anthony for ruining his plans, and then at Mrs. Lovett for urging him to wait. But, really, he must bear the blame. He has spoiled the moment all by himself. Spoiled it by putting his own ego needs above any moral claim for revenge. Sweeney, it turns out, doesn't want to settle the score—he doesn't want to see justice done—because once the score is settled, the game is over. And when the game is over, so, too, is the pleasure of playing it. What Sweeney wants, instead, is to turn the game of rough justice into one that *never* ends, and with himself as the only lead player.

How fitting that a Fleet Street barber should be transfigured into an angel of vengeance, for his life's mission is to cut away the badness, shear it clean off, leaving only a smooth goodness to shine in the mirror held up at the end. Granted, an awful turn of events—the loss of his wife, his daughter, and, indeed, his own self—justifies Sweeney in his revenge quest. Yet he survives this inciting catastrophe only to bring upon himself a far worse one. Sondheim was right that Sweeney was the play's true hero, but a wholly tragic one. Hal Prince wanted the audience to "root" for Anthony and Johanna, to which Sondheim retorted, "if people aren't rooting for Sweeney, then there's no show." The ultimate tragedy is not that Sweeney Todd fails to deliver justice, but that he cannot *stop* delivering it.

———————

There's a twist in the revenge experiment that I've been keeping from you. Player A, when he got cheated, was sometimes levied with a "revenge tax": he had to surrender a bit of his own money before anything would be taken away from Player B. This tax proved no deterrent. In fact, the more eager that Player A had been to seek retribution when it cost him nothing, the more eager he was to do it when it came at a price. (Brain scans measured the eagerness.) So deeply planted was the desire for revenge that a person would gladly suffer if it meant that their enemy suffered more. It's like the Aesop fable about the man who keeps slapping himself in the face to kill the fly that keeps landing there.

Sondheim needed a full month to write "Epiphany," the song in which Sweeney descends from the righteous pursuit of a single malefactor to vowing vengeance upon the whole world. The song's title refers, strictly speaking, not to a bright idea popping into somebody's head, but to a fearsome unveiling of the divine.

Sweeney's hubris leads him to offer himself to a depraved world as the Last Judgment made incarnate. And so his musical motif is a horrific inversion of the "Dies Irae" (Day of Wrath) from the Roman Catholic requiem mass—a hymn of impending, vengeful doom. Sweeney, now transformed into a dark and vengeful god, will spare no one his fateful sword. It must have been disquieting for Sondheim (well, I hope it was) to have lived with this song for a month. If so, it was a purgatory worth enduring.

"The work. The work!" he wrote at the top of his notes for "Epiphany." This song *had* to sound like work—"chugging," Sondheim said—because Sweeney had become a killing machine, never pausing to ponder any man's fate because he was too absorbed in mass carnage:

Not one man, no,
Nor ten men,
Nor a hundred
Can assuage me.

This is the factory logic of the Dickensian workhouse—a hellhole, where people *died* of work—the throbbing assembly lines, and the blazing coal fires that cannot tell night from day. As Sweeney declaims with the blunt staccato force of a hammer swinging down, "the *work waits.*"

Sondheim didn't want the audience to be carried away by "Epiphany." We must, of course, believe that Sweeney converts into the same malignancy that he has vowed to expel. If we don't believe *that*, then the play fails. Even so, we must keep our wits about us; this is not a number to applaud. Sondheim, to forestall that approving response, ended the song not on its final triumphant words—"I'm alive at last / And I'm full of joy!"—but on the two dissonant chords that follow. The orchestra blasts out the first of them while Sweeney is still singing, an outdoing of his own savage exultation. Sweeney's own triumphant chord returns: he is persistent. Then, under the dialogue, the contrary shadow chord is heard once more—but diminished, a bit fainter, its potency ebbing away as the next scene begins.

The mood now shifts from the tragic splendor of Sweeney Todd to the music hall antics of Mrs. Lovett. She frets over how to ditch the dead body in the trunk. It's Signor Pirelli, the rival barber who met a quick end after threatening to blackmail Sweeney. What to do? Times being so hard, and with the price of meat being so high, nothing should go to waste. Here's an appetizing thought: Sweeney's victims would make a tasty mince—but remember, you must grind a corpse *three* times—for popping into Mrs. Lovett's pies.

Sweeney joins this morbid scheme, and the two of them spin out their fantasy of capitalist cannibalism in "A Little Priest," the grisly list song that brings the first act of *Sweeney Todd* to its rousing finish. They conjure an endless line of victims—priest, grocer, tailor, clerk, fop, and, one day soon, judge—to assuage Sweeney's bloodlust. And to earn Mrs. Lovett enough coinage to line the purse she has just filched from a corpse.

This is where Sondheim wanted the applause, and he got a storm of it. Yet "A Little Priest" is nothing other than "Epiphany" wearing the mask of comedy. Sweeney's murderous rampage, far from receding, gains new strength in its intricate plotting. Exactly what, then, are we applauding? Not so much Sweeney's carnage— we've heard about that already—as our own ability to tolerate it.

Sondheim's music has moved us from the fringes of this revenge story to its dark center.

———————

I like to imagine that the learned Judge Turpin owns a volume of essays by Francis Bacon. Not the modern painter, of course, but the sixteenth-century English philosopher and scientist. Perhaps it was Basil Montagu's edition of 1836, the one respectfully dedicated to the Earl of Eldon, that found a place in the judge's private library in Kearney's Lane. I further imagine that he has placed a brass bookmark at page thirteen, where begins Bacon's essay "Of Revenge." The topic fascinates him, especially after he took his own revenge upon Johanna by confining her to Fogg's Asylum, once he discovered that she was about to flee with Anthony.

Judge Turpin doesn't yet know of Sweeney Todd's mania for revenge—though if he did, it would behoove him all the more to ponder Bacon's words. What distinguishes Sweeney's blood quest from mere retaliation is that it refuses to be limited, to be held within bounds, or, indeed, to be brought to its end. To make of your life, as Sweeney has, a study in revenge is to keep your "wounds green," as Bacon wrote—stinging, not soothed; pustulant, not mending; festering but never healed.

There is, admittedly, a brute satisfaction in watching Sweeney as he finally kills the judge—an eye for an eye. But there is nothing at all satisfying about him killing a hundred men, or even ten men. Nor does it much gratify Sweeney himself. Slicing open an innocent man's throat, mopping up the spurted blood, and then disposing of the body—the last bit done so casually, like tossing an empty bottle of hair tonic into the trash—has become his daily habit.

And he does it all while singing in the "Johanna" quartet, one of the loveliest (but not for him) moments in the show. Sweeney takes no pleasure now in the awaited deed—gone is the bubbling joy of "Pretty Women." Executing his routine with a nearly mechanical reflex, he has become the banality of evil.

Banal because he lacks focus. Sweeney's violence sends no message to a single culprit, a named perpetrator, who in receiving his deserved punishment might yet atone at the last hour. Instead of that wild sort of justice, there is only an endless and indiscriminate cycle of harm—"Bless my eyes! / Fresh supplies!" Nothing remains for him but the fixed pursuit of his bloody obsession. Hailed, once, as a "proper artist with a knife," Sweeney now aims no higher than butchery.

———

Yet the greater banality of Sweeney's evil is that it has seeped into, and then stained, the fabric of daily life. So widespread is this evil that it comes to look like the natural appearance of things, obscuring with its filth any trace of original decency.

Filth is everywhere. London is a great pit of shit and vermin. Cockroaches are more plentiful than customers in the city's worst pie shop. Pirelli's miracle elixir is foully made, a swirl of piss and ink. Judge Turpin's unclean heart is shown in his slovenly manner. The price of Mrs. Lovett's climb into the petty bourgeoisie is the bakehouse stench of burning human flesh, a dual repugnance—to morality, to the senses—that she gladly endures. The most abhorrent creature of all is the Beggar Woman, with her dirty face, ratty hair, and soiled clothes no better than rags. "Trash from the gutter," as Mrs. Lovett—who would know—brands her.

When, as a teenager, I first listened to *Sweeney Todd*, I felt that Sondheim made too much of the Beggar Woman. She was critical to the play's climax—that much I understood—but did we need to see and hear quite so much of her? I found the Beggar Woman just as irritating as Sweeney himself did.

It strikes me now that the play was trying to provoke my scorn. That was the hard response it wanted from me. And it was easy for me to look at the Beggar Woman in the same way that almost everybody in the show looked at her—as the loathed outsider. She was someone to be rejected, abandoned, and (like all those mounting corpses) discarded. Like Sweeney, just as he is about to pitch his latest victim into the oven, I was shocked to discover that she was no outsider at all. She was, in fact, Lucy—wife to Sweeney and mother to Johanna—the woman I had been hearing about from the beginning. The pretty woman whose ugly misfortunes had set the entire story in motion. The point was starkly made. There are no real outsiders in our world—but there are plenty of scapegoats, the innocents who are forced into that subjugated role by the powerful few.

The director Hal Prince instructed scene designer Eugene Lee to re-create a glass-and-iron Victorian foundry to dominate the stage of the Uris (now Gershwin) Theatre, then the largest on Broadway. Within that vastness, the characters were confined mostly to tiny platform stages—pie shop, barbershop, Mrs. Lovett's parlor, Judge Turpin's house—that rolled onstage and off. The set dwarfed everyone, putting them all in their proper place, mere cogs in the wheels that grind "beauty into filth and greed." Everyone includes us. We, too, are confined within a social superstructure whose iron frame we cannot bend and whose glass ceiling we cannot smash.

Scaled-down revivals (*Teeney Todd*, the wags dub them) gain in intimacy, but risk obscuring this larger societal point. High status or low, it changes nothing. Rich or poor, it matters not. The same muck is bogging us all down.

When asked what commodity was churned out night after night in the show's factory setting, Prince coolly replied, "they make Sweeney Todds." This notion of industry—forging, melding, assembling—is key to how the play works on us. Sweeney is not someone who by tragic accident alone falls into his evil deeds. No, he is the product—worse, the inevitable product—of a social order corrupt to its core. His descent into serial murder is too outlandish to be sanctioned by even the most sympathetic audience. Still, we understand that Sweeney is provoked into his crimes by a righteous rebellion against the hard structures of injustice. Judge Turpin *is* a profoundly unjust man—to harm another for your own gain is about as morally bankrupt as a person can be. And it is the judge's power and privilege that allow him to get away with inflicting that harm.

Here Sondheim surprises us, and then implicates us, by raising the stakes. What could have been just another gory melodrama has become a reckoning with the forces of oppression. What, the show asks, is *our* response to injustice? Not the trivial wrongdoings that give rise to our petty grievances, but the entrenched suffering that does seem to be the way of the world, its dark and fixed course. This is what *Sweeney Todd* pushes us to confront. Not in a didactic way, and not—for Sondheim loathed all preaching—with ready-made answers. It is enough for theatre to state the question—especially when it's a question we'd rather not hear—and to respect its audience by letting them answer it for themselves. Answer it with the conduct of their lives.

Nor is there a single answer. What anyone can reasonably be expected to do in the face of injustice will depend: on their circumstances, their talents, their flaws, and their obligations to others. For some of us, the issue might be that by underestimating what we can actually do, we end up settling for mere trifles: the virtue-signaling and performative allyship that now taint so much social media. Yet when compared with Sweeney, perhaps that's not so bad. Because Sweeney dangerously *overestimates* himself, believing in his mania that he really can slash and kill his way to righteousness.

Not by chance does Lucy die by Sweeney's own hand. Had he but noticed her, she would have lived—and so, too, would he. Yet noticing what lies around him is precisely what Sweeney cannot do, for he lives wholly in the future. And a dark, warped future it is, in thrall to a twisted fantasy of redeeming past sins through a greater sinfulness. Once again, Sweeney dwells in exile, severed from the common stock. This time, though, the exile comes by his own decree.

Anyone might suppose that Sondheim wrote "By the Sea" to give Mrs. Lovett a star turn in the second act. And indeed, it's a vintage "number," the occasion for a bravura performance. Yet, as he later explained, the song's actual focus was Sweeney's withdrawal from daily life. He has detached himself from whatever—or, in this case, whoever—does not serve his obsession. Sweeney has neither time nor taste for kippered herring, tea and scones, a stroll along the pier, or any of the simple pleasures that make life worth getting up for each morning. Nellie Lovett is hardly a moral exemplar, but her dream of seaside domesticity can remind us that there is a world beyond our own fixations.

Sweeney can instruct us here, but more by what he fails to do.

125

The world is unjust, and we must do our part to combat it. Yet there are aspects of life as we ordinarily live it that still do matter and still do merit our regard. Riches abound in our world, though they may not look like riches at all. An extra tot of gin. A duet warbled at the piano. Pretty daisies brightening up the room. Pretty women combing out their hair. A life shorn of such delights can hardly be called a life.

To treasure the world is not to forsake our struggle against its manifold injustices. We remind ourselves, rather, why the struggle must be borne. For what are protests against climate change but a love of the natural world? What is the fight against health disparities if not a cherishing of the body? And what is the battle for equality of any kind except a delight in humanity's pied beauty? Such labors merit our allegiance not only in themselves, but by virtue of what lies *beyond* them: the world as it will look when at last the struggle is won.

———

Much, and perhaps too much, has been made of how *Sweeney Todd* ends. Once more, the entire company beseeches us to "attend the tale," but now with the chilling reminder that we ourselves are the tale's true protagonist. The actors point accusingly around the theatre, calling out the vengeful Sweeney Todd that lurks inside each of us: "Isn't that Sweeney there beside you?"

This grand meta-theatrical gesture—or, if you prefer, stunt—has never appealed to everyone. The poet and critic James Fenton, in his review of the original West End production, dismissed the ending as "pretentious and fatuous" and branded the entire show "a tissue of bullshit."

I guess I have a higher tolerance for bullshit. No doubt that's because I think the lesson of *Sweeney Todd* is not that we are all prone to seek revenge. (That *would* be fatuous.) I think the lesson is that we mustn't let our desire for revenge, be it justified or not, end up destroying us. It destroyed Sweeney, and his woeful example is a cautionary one. We certainly can, as Sondheim wanted us to, "root" for him. But that hardly means we want to be just like him. We attend his tale, yes, but mostly to learn from it—not to repeat it.

All along, another tale has been told. Perhaps, though, we have not harkened to it so well. It is the tale of Anthony Hope, the naive, kindhearted mariner who rescues the fugitive Sweeney Todd from drowning at sea and then steers him safely home on the good ship *Bountiful*. Anthony is young—as we ourselves were once young, or yet still are—and upon him life only smiles. To him, the whole world, "From the Dardanelles / To the mountains of Peru," brims with rich enchantment. Back home in London, though, he learns (as Sweeney foresaw) to rank cruelty among the world's wonders, and to rank it highly. For he has beheld the awesome sight of Johanna locked in her gilded cage, singing because she cannot fly.

"Is there no justice in this city?" he cries. Disillusion turns out to be not Anthony's undoing, but the very making of him. In the face of the world's magnificent cruelty, he will neither shrink back with indifference nor rush forward in hasty revenge. He will, rather, do the plain good that is plainly his to do. Rescue the lost Mr. Todd and offer him the warmth of friendship. Show what pity he can to the Beggar Woman. Free the innocent Johanna from her captivity. Not even upon Judge Turpin or the loathsome Beadle Bamford does he wish the slightest harm.

Only when Anthony is conscripted into Sweeney's revenge plot, drawn into the older man's dark vision, do things go badly for him. Yet when he aims his pistol at Mr. Fogg, who on the judge's order has locked Johanna up in his asylum, he cannot bring himself to fire his weapon. Johanna, more than ever her father's daughter, finishes the deadly business for him. It is a staggering truth that among the few characters still alive at the end of *Sweeney Todd*, only Anthony is not a killer. He alone renounces violence. He alone forswears revenge. He alone knows that the world is not the great black pit it sometimes seems.

As long as there is an audience to attend his tale—and long may that be so—the vengeful Sweeney Todd will keep rising from his grave. That is a baleful certainty. And in the theatre, at least, he will always claim the last word. Yet there are words for us to speak too; words that we will speak outside the theatre, in the arena of our lives. The one I want beside me there is not the demon barber of Fleet Street, but the lad named Hope.

7

MERRILY WE ROLL ALONG

How to Grow Up

Odd, this new moon. Not waxing and waning, it holds its fullness. Not rising in the east, it appears from the west. Not hanging in the night sky, it races across the firmament. Speeding at 18,000 miles an hour, it takes not a lunar month to encircle the planet but ninety-six short minutes. Though spherical, it is made not of green cheese but polished aluminum alloy. From that metallic orb, about the size of a basketball (if a basketball weighs 184 pounds), protrude four radio antennae. This odd new moon, as the world learned in the early days of October 1957, was named Sputnik—"fellow traveler," in the language of the Russian rocket scientists and engineers who built it.

Sputnik, the first artificial satellite, orbited our planet for ninety days, until early January 1958, when air friction in the earth's atmosphere burned it up. For the first three weeks, until its signal transmitter failed, amateur shortwave radio operators the world over listened to Sputnik's sharp, distinctive beeps. Many others, aided by ordinary binoculars, saw it for themselves when the satellite dropped to within 141 miles of the earth's surface. It wasn't only astronomers who gathered on rooftops at first light to glimpse this stunning herald of the space age.

Among the stargazers is Frank Shepard, a young composer

who shares a crummy apartment on 110th Street in New York City with his playwright pal Charley Kringas. Frank, alone on the rooftop, is poring over his roommate's new script. A bleary-eyed Charley arrives with binoculars. Soon they're joined by a young woman who lives in their building, though they haven't met until now. She is Mary Flynn, an aspiring novelist. Already she's smitten with Frank, just from hearing his piano playing through the walls. Charley catches first sight of Sputnik, but it's Frank who measures the moment: "Nothing's ever going to be the way it was, not ever again. . . . What a time to be starting out."

Or to be ending: because this is the final scene. *Merrily We Roll Along*—like the 1934 George S. Kaufman and Moss Hart play on which it's based, and whose title it shares—tells its story backward. It begins with three old friends in the tatters of midlife disillusion but ends with them all gleaming as brightly as Sputnik itself. Like a satellite returning to the morning sky, this musical returns to its characters' past.

Return. If I had to put *Merrily* into one word, that's the one.

It was likely the librettist George Furth who spotted a parallel between the brave new world of Sputnik and the brave first steps taken by the play's lead characters. But it was Sondheim who made the similarity come alive, in the choral number "Our Time." It's sung three times through in that final scene: twice by Frank and Charley and then by the full company. Through music of pure simplicity, and with lyrics that capture the inflated promises of youth—"Worlds to change and worlds to win"—this song pulls the future into the present. The future that's not ever going to be like the way it was. Small wonder, then, that "Our Time" has become a standard in its own right, the prayer of hopeful youth as its quivers on the brink of change.

Hope was not, however, the response that most Americans had in 1957 to the surprise appearance of a Soviet satellite. In the Cold War era, a foreign scientific breakthrough like Sputnik threatened the security of the United States. Much more than an embarrassing setback in the newly begun "space race," Sputnik was the actual means (so it was feared) by which the Soviet Union might invade its rival superpower. Its passing overhead was met by many Americans with silence—not out of reverence, though, but fear of being spied on. This "new and terrifying danger," as the chairman of the Senate Armed Services Committee warned, could be seen flying across the continental United States an intrusive seven times a day. Sputnik lacked a camera, but it still felt as if the Soviets were tracking everybody's every move. And maybe those beeps were a secret code being transmitted back to Red Square.

Cold War threats aside, Sputnik made America (but not just America) nervous in yet another way. This machine, with its elliptical tracings of the earth's circumference, appeared to surpass its own origins. Made in this world by human hands, it soared beyond the world to chart its own course. Entering a galactic vastness that few could fathom, even as a hypothetical, Sputnik shrank the world that it left behind. It looked small in the distant sky, but those who looked at it felt even smaller.

Except, that is, on 110th Street. Because there, high up on a tenement rooftop, humility is not in residence. Frank, Charley, and Mary gather to watch in awe as the satellite passes overhead, but what they really hold in awe is themselves. Or, rather, all the wondrous things they insist they will do—because now, it's *their* time.

Just one problem. We in the audience know it doesn't turn out that way. For the past two hours, we have watched this trio as they screw up, foul up, and altogether botch everything in their lives. Marriages—friendships—their talent—their morals—you name it—all going, going, gone.

"Our Time" is so alluring not because it is sung with the confidence of youth, but because it is heard with the regret of age. We in the audience, *our* regret. For we know already the certain ruin that awaits these characters. Frank forsakes his calling as a musician to chase fame and wealth as a Hollywood producer. He wins both, but it turns him cynical. Plus he's a serial philanderer. Mary, now a washed-up novelist, finds solace in barbed witticisms and the bottle nearest to hand. Charley, after going berserk on Frank on live television, loses his old friend and writing partner. All the triumphs so confidently foretold in the first scene—for us, though, it's the *final* scene—never do come to pass. Turns out, it never was their time. Or if it was, it was over in a flash.

This moment breaks our hearts. Because what these three young people have yet to go through we may have already gone through. Grieving over a "someday" that never did begin might be nothing new to us. (I'm hearing echoes in my head now of "The Road You Didn't Take," from *Follies*.) What Lindsay Mendez, who played Mary in the 2023 Broadway revival, said about this show will strike for many a familiar, poignant chord: "I don't think theatre is only to make people feel warm and fuzzy, but to make them think and challenge them. And this piece definitely does that."

But it does it so charmingly. *Merrily We Roll Along* boasts one of Sondheim's most tuneful scores. It's a love letter to the "Golden Age" of Broadway musicals, when audiences floated out of the theatre while humming a thirty-two-bar song. And how buoyantly this show ends, with its classic musical comedy promise of "dreams coming true." Long before the final chorus of "Our Time," when the entire company belts "me and you!" a full nine times, they've reached over the footlights and pulled us in. Only the most stiff-necked, uncaring of theatregoers could deny themselves a chance to feel all over again, or maybe for the first time, the joy and optimism that belong especially to youth.

How cannily Sondheim's music returns us to our youth. Not right away—although the nostalgic overture nearly does it—but slowly, gradually, and only after suffering in sympathy with the troubled people onstage. To be released into our *second* youth—that, it seems to me, is what the show does—we first have to earn it. So that when we do roll back into our past, willing to start over, and ready to grow up right, we will do it merrily.

———

I remember when this show flopped on Broadway in 1981. It closed after just sixteen performances, broke the tender hearts of its youthful cast, earned Sondheim some of his most wounding reviews, and nearly had its RCA Records cast album canceled. Before that, during the six weeks of previews, the leading man was replaced, the choreographer was fired, the costumes thrown out, and many in the audience walked out. "I don't want to be in this profession," Sondheim decided after *Merrily*'s abrupt closing; "it's just too hostile, and mean-spirited." Fortunately, he reversed his decision. But he and director Hal Prince, after an astounding decade-long collaboration, called it quits. (They eventually reunited, in 2003, when Prince directed two regional productions of *Bounce*, Sondheim's last fully finished work.)

I also remember taking *Merrily*'s failure personally, as if those snarky New York critics and gossip columnists were stomping on *my* theatrical dreams. Back then I was the same age as Frank, Mary, and Charley as they waited on the rooftop for Sputnik to appear. Like them, I expected the world to make room for me. "Our Time" sounded like the echo of my own greedy desire—it's *my* time—but amplified in ardor and eloquence. It felt like the whole theatrical world was ganging up on Sondheim, and the affront extended to me. Naive and narcissistic, I know. But in my youth, I was young.

A college friend worked on the 1990 revival at Arena Stage, in Washington, DC. Years later, she told me that she wept openly every time the cast sang "Our Time." One night, George Furth spotted my friend crying in the theatre's darkness. He asked her why she found the song so poignant. Furth, though he was a successful librettist, had a notoriously tin ear—"never listened to music, ever," as James Lapine recalled. Still, he was moved by how much my friend was moved. *Merrily* may lack a typical plotline, but it doesn't lack emotional depth.

Like many Sondheim fans, I've been returning to *Merrily We Roll Along*. Not that I ever forgot its score. Who could forget the plaintive "Good Thing Going"? Or the anguished "Not a Day Goes By"? But I had relegated it to the closed category of youth. For me, this musical had become a souvenir of my past. Looked upon fondly, but not too often.

That changed in 2016, when I came across *The Best Worst Thing That Ever Could Have Happened*, Lonny Price's documentary about the doomed first production. (The title is a rueful twist on a lyric from Mary's already rueful song "Now You Know.") Price, who created the role of Charley Kringas, explained how his film was inspired by a question posed from within the show itself: "How did you ever get there from here?" "When you turn fifty," he said, "you start looking at your life, going 'What were the choices?,' which is very reflective of the show." Wise words. They got me thinking that *Merrily We Roll Along* was worth a return visit. Having been away for so long, perhaps I could see it anew. Maybe now I could hear its questions better, and answer them more fully.

In 2023, Broadway audiences flocked to the same show they had once deserted. Maria Friedman's sold-out revival at the New York Theatre Workshop, starring the irresistible troika of Jonathan Groff (Frank), Lindsay Mendez (Mary), and Daniel Radcliffe (Charley), promptly moved uptown to the Hudson Theatre on West Forty-Fourth Street. The production was based on Friedman's acclaimed staging of the musical a decade earlier at the 180-seat Menier Chocolate Factory, a top London fringe theatre with a specialty line in revisionist Sondheim. Forty-two years after its disastrous first outing, *Merrily We Roll Along* returned in glory to Broadway. Tickets that had once found no buyers now sold fast, some of them going for $600 each. By March 2024, the production recouped its initial investment of $12 million and began turning a profit. "No longer lost," critic Jesse Greene declared in the *New York Times*, but "found in the dark." The same darkness that prompts the lyrical question, "How did you ever get there from here?"

Should we be surprised by the return of a show that itself is built around the motif of return? The nature of this motif eluded me at first, but I can plead a legitimate excuse. Being still a teenager when

I first encountered *Merrily We Roll Along*, I had nothing to return to. Nothing lay behind me. Everything loomed before me. At that age—starting out, on the brink, opening doors—I lived solely for the future. I defined myself more by what I might yet do than by the almost nothing I actually had done.

It didn't occur to me back then that Frank, Mary, and Charley, as they got younger and younger with each passing scene, were *recalling* their youth, and not (as I then was) living it. Indeed, they seemed most real to me at their youngest, as if the disasters that befell them were glitches only, a few regrettable incidents in an otherwise joyous tale. The wild cheers that greeted the final scene in the 2023 Broadway revival confirmed much the same. It was lost on me at the time that indulging in a comforting nostalgia for youth is *not* the point of telling the story in reverse. I'm stumbling over my tenses now, but that will happen when you slip between the present and the past.

"Opening Doors" is the song in which Sondheim most noticeably reverts to his own past. It's performed late in the second act, when the year is 1960. Frank and Charley are working on *Take a Left*, a musical whose punning title betrays its earnest politics. They get turned down flat by cigar-chomping producer Joe ("what's wrong with letting them tap their toes a bit?") Josephson. Undaunted by the rebuff, the boys cast and rehearse their own Greenwich Village nightclub revue, *Frankly Frank*.

"Everything in that number is me," Sondheim proudly admitted. The creative frenzy, the spur of camaraderie, and the fight to get a fair hearing from Tin Pan Alley philistines. Joe Josephson is

Sondheim's bitter caricature of the legendary director and producer George Abbott, a man whose definition of a good show tune was one you could hum after hearing it a single time. "The song describes what the struggle was like for me and my generation of Broadway songwriters."

It's not this one song that reveals Sondheim the young composer, it's the entire score. Frank Shepard and Steve Sondheim both started out in the late 1950s. The numbers in *Merrily*, and especially the ones "composed" by Frank, deliberately reprise Sondheim's early style. "I was trying to roll myself back," he said, "to my exuberant early days." The praise long lavished on the score is due largely to Sondheim building it around the traditional thirty-two-bar song that still remains for many fans the purest sound of Broadway music. It's no coincidence that *Merrily We Roll Along* is one of the few Sondheim shows to begin with an old-style overture. First orchestrated by Jonathan Tunick, it pops and fizzes like the one in *Gypsy*, the Jule Styne and Stephen Sondheim musical from 1959 that must have made Frank and Charley sick with envy.

These songs do more than conjure a bygone theatrical era. When a plot moves backward, a musical number's reprise becomes a funny thing. Normally a song in a book musical makes a statement the first time around. The reprise, which is usually shorter, then puts a spin on it, because matters have changed, or the characters have moved on. In *Oklahoma!*, for example, Laurey and Curly sing "People Will Say We're in Love" to hide their true feelings for each other. In the reprise, though, they positively shout their love to the world, not caring who knows it now. Nothing like that happens in *Merrily We Roll Along*. Because instead of charging forward, the characters keep falling back. Which means we start with the reprise, and only later do we get the full song. It's like listening to an echo but not knowing its source.

"Not a Day Goes By," when we first hear it, is a terse and bitter song. It's sung in the first act by Beth, Frank's first wife, on the steps of the courthouse where her divorce from him is about to be made official. She rages at Frank for abandoning her and Frankie, their eight-year-old son. But she rages at herself, too, for obsessing over her deadbeat husband. Beth stares into a future of unremitting anguish, nothing but "thinking and sweating / And cursing and crying." That pounding run of low quarter-note triplets is the sound of pain that must be endured because it cannot be eased.

In the second act, though, the same song is performed as a vow of abiding love. The steady beat that in the reverse reprise felt like misery becomes here the heart's own constancy, its promise of a love that "gets better and stronger / And deeper and nearer." Yet this young love is already divided. Beth and Mary, each unaware of the other, sing to their beloved Frank, and he sings back. For Mary, the song reveals why she, unlike Charley, cannot desert Frank, even though her pining for him brings only grief. The poignancy sharpens with Beth, whose lyrics are now loving and hopeful. She sings without a hint of her later (in the performance, earlier) cynicism.

Can we share her hope? It's hard to, because we know what the characters themselves do not know: their fate. We have beheld what becomes of them. A marriage ends in spiteful divorce. One artist sells out for the sake of the deal. Another squanders her talent. An old friend gets cut dead. Hearing this song for a second time makes me want to edge away from it, knowing as I do that its enchantments will not endure. That makes me a little sad. Just as their nightclub routine "Bobby and Jackie and Jack" also makes me a little sad, in its gentle jibes at the Kennedy clan. In 1960, and "what a swell year it's been," no one guessed how quickly Camelot would vanish into the mist.

These songs do more than tell their own story. What happens in them is more than what happens to the characters. Something is also happening to us, and that's the final resonance of Sondheim's music. What I feel in the score for *Merrily* is my own journey: I'm being escorted back into my past but also being warned not to indulge a false nostalgia for it. After all, when the reprise comes first, what you confront is the effect, not the cause; the consequence, not the incitement; and the rolling aftershocks, not the ground as it first shifted. This, to me, seems the message built into the musical architecture of *Merrily We Roll Along*. If we're going to ruminate over our past, then let's make sure that we're doing it because we want to repair, and not to forsake, our present.

———

Much about the original production looked unfinished: high school gym bleachers passing for a theatrical set, costumes that were little more than khakis and bright T-shirts (whose imprinted character names were illegible beyond orchestra row K), and a cast that was still growing up. Plus the rewrites of the rewrites during the previews that a worried Hal Prince kept extending.

Starting with snide comments—"terrible" and "tacky"—in Liz Smith's *Daily News* gossip column, word spread along Broadway that *Merrily* was trapped in a death spiral. Sondheim long attributed the bad-mouthing to envy that he and Prince were "mavericks" who had the nerve to succeed rather than to starve. Although the cast and artistic team believed the show was improving every night, they were quickly killed off by the chattering "Blob"—just as Charley and Frank, performing "Good Thing Going" at Gussie Carnegie's party, are drowned out by noisy showbiz types with short attention spans. The show essentially closed before it opened. It finished before it started. Like its own characters, *Merrily We Roll Along* lived its life backward.

The backward roll continued, as its creators sought to rebirth the show. The first chance came in 1985, with a production at the La Jolla Playhouse, in San Diego, directed by James Lapine, who was fresh from collaborating with Sondheim on *Sunday in the Park with George*. Sondheim wrote two new songs ("That Frank," "Growing Up") and George Furth reworked his libretto. They tried to soften Frank, to make him more genial—someone whose flaws you could well understand, possibly forgive, and maybe even recognize in yourself.

Lapine wanted youngish, but still experienced, singer-actors to make the characters believable across the plot's twenty-year span. John Rubinstein, the original Pippin, played Frank; Chip Zien, later the Baker in *Into the Woods*, was Charley. Other revivals, further tinkering, and surprising success all followed. Eventually Sondheim and Furth allowed the revised libretto and lyrics to be published, deeming them to be definitive. The London production in 2000 at the Donmar Warehouse, which was the show's long-deferred West End premiere, won the Laurence Olivier Award for Best Musical. In the most ironic return of all, *Merrily We Roll Along* revisited the site of its original shunning—Broadway—only to be welcomed in triumph and with a slick publicity campaign as it settled in for a long run.

No triumph in the story itself, though—only conflict, betrayal, surrender, reproach, and hollow success. The original production obscured the story's darker tones with its juvenile sparkle and flash of primary color. Still, that darkness is there to be found. One reason for *Merrily*'s reversal of theatrical fortune is that we now see it not as a fake regress into youthful innocence but as an honest inquiry into what you should do after you have lost your innocence. How, in other words, do you grow up?

In her New York and London productions, director Maria Friedman framed the show as a long, pensive flashback for Frank in the midst of his own noisy party. Something like the opening of *Company*, another Sondheim work that plays with time. A chorus of spectral voices sings *Merrily*'s title song to an isolated Frank. They press him—Charley and Mary step in, blocking his escape—to justify the unjustifiable truth: "how *did* you get to be here?" As Frank listens to these voices, we get a chance to size him up. We can see him as he's now starting to see himself: a person shaped (or is it torn apart?) by all the errors he has made. A person, that is, formed in our own image and likeness.

Jump forward, or back, to the end. *Merrily* returns us to the primal scene of Frank, Mary, and Charley on the rooftop. It's a buoyant, hopeful morning. Even so, we might detect in their full-throated optimism a trait not nearly so endearing but equally as natural: a willpower born of arrogance. What drives them is not their talent—so far, scant evidence of that—but their need to set themselves apart from the grown-ups. And not just apart, but above: "Tell 'em things they don't know!" These beginners, in their own minds, are the overlooked experts that the rest of the world had better start looking at pretty darn soon. In thundering that it's now *their* time, they are also declaring that somebody else's time has run out. Time for some new names to appear in tomorrow's papers.

They sing dreamily, of course, but the undertone of belligerence is definitely, and necessarily, there. Without it, no dream stands a chance of coming true. I can hardly fault youth for being so like itself—even if that self tends to grin with an easy smugness. Yet there is no other way to be young. To launch yourself into the world, you *do* have to set yourself apart. You *do* have to crash through barriers. You *do* have to act as if nobody older than you knows a damn thing. If you don't, the world will trounce you fast; you'll be finished before you even start.

Eventually, though, we stop being young—and we start growing up. To grow up means to see our place in the world more honestly and with a measure of humility, perhaps even with remorse. If, like Frank, we have climbed straight to the top, we can see from the heights that our success has not been entirely our own doing. What if Mary hadn't urged Frank on? What if Gussie hadn't taken a shine to him? We all have a "what if?" of our own. Maybe our victories are due to a little sneakiness or strong-arming: "Hiya, Buddy, / Wanna write a show?" We all have a buddy ready to do our bidding. The risk of midlife isn't that we will lose our youthful ideals—we will, "It's called flowers wilt, / It's called apples rot"— but that we will replace them with the approval of "the Blob," an entity so formless, and so inherently worthless, that it cannot retain its own shape.

When the chorus rebukes Frank for getting so "far off the track," I hear something more than censure in their words. I hear the call for him to get himself back on track. That these voices might be coming from within Frank's tormented mind only reinforces the point: he knows that he must *change*. To change, though, he must first admit that he long ago became a problem unto himself. If that good thing once going is now irretrievably gone—we know it's gone, thanks to the backward plot—then he's the one who let it go. It did not slip away of its own accord. What is Frank's fitful noodling at the piano—plink, plank, plunk—if not the uneasy sound of a man uneasy with himself?

We must face the truth that the recurring figure in all our tales of grievance is us. If we feel that our life is knotted, then we must concede that our own hands have tightened the knot. If we feel thwarted in our aims, it's likely because we ourselves are doing the thwarting. (This is what the leads in *Follies* won't at first admit, preferring instead to blame their younger selves.) Our motives come in different shapes and sizes—envy, vanity, ambition, greed—but they all behave the same. To confess as much will wound our pride. Yet for none of us can there be any growth at all without the disgrace that leads to it. No rescue for anybody without a prior collapse. To go forward, it seems, we must fall back first.

That's the opening scene: Frank hits bottom. He performs with gusto the role of party host—"Who says, 'lonely at the top'?"—but that doesn't fool us. We know the full anguish behind Frank's cheery facade. He's extracted a curse from none other than Mary Flynn, the woman who can't help loving her unattainable man. He's forbidden the name of Charley Kringas, the oldest of his old friends, from being spoken within his earshot. He's the one whose adultery leads Gussie, his second wife, to walk out on him. But not before she flings corrosive iodine into the eyes of his younger and more fetching mistress, Meg—who will, *of course*, become his third wife. "Now we're finished," Gussie roars, leaving Frank once more on his lonesome.

All this suffering does not end Frank's problem so much as it names his problem. He has been pitched into the fire of a living hell, that's for sure. Yet this calamity is but the premise of his story. What's at stake, now, is whether Frank's agony will be his final ruin, or his path to redemption. He is "conflicted" in himself, as Helen Shaw remarked in her astute *New Yorker* review of Friedman's production. The whole reason for telling his tale, and for telling it backward, is to resolve that inner conflict. Lost in the middle of his life, Frank has been granted the gift of a second youth.

We *do* want Frank to get his life back on track. We *do* want him to grow up. But we know that it's going to take far more than the glib posturing that has always come so easily to him. In the opening scene, the one that begins with a party but ends in purgatory, Frank gets a chance to signal that he's serious about turning his life around. Ru, a young screenwriter, asks Frank, "How do I get to be you?" It's a smiling question, eager and yet more innocent than it knows. Nothing at all like the hectoring chorus in the prologue. At first Frank bats the question away with a bad joke ("the worst vice in the world is 'advice'"). But then he decides to impart a lesson: "Don't just write what you know"—he points to his head—"Write what you know"—he points to his heart. End of lesson. Gussie, not missing a beat, mocks Franks for his pompous banality. His words are trite, she declares, no better than a T-shirt slogan.

It's hard to disagree. How can Frank preach about writing from the heart when he is himself so heartless? As we journey with him backward in time, we find ourselves on the lookout for the heart he once had but misplaced along the way. We hope that by reliving his past, Frank will recover—even better, take with him into the future—the uprightness of character that he long ago disavowed. The question is, how far back in Frank's past must we venture before we find that hidden treasure?

The answer is discouraging—we *never* find it. What the show's action-in-reverse makes clear is not Frank's lost goodness—it wasn't there to begin with—but rather his essential, and ever-worsening, selfishness. Scene by backward scene, we encounter the depth of Frank's failures: two broken marriages, two failed friendships, and the unheard melodies of all the songs that he never composed with Charley. Even in the last (that is, first) scene on the rooftop, and despite its pledge of idealism and amity, the dark roots of the near sociopath that Frank has become are laid bare. It's not so much that Frank fell from grace as that grace was never his proper perch.

———————

The lesson he teaches to Ru may well be a feeble cliché, but the one he indirectly teaches to us is wholly sincere. Frank imparts it, though, as the emblem of a life disastrously lived, a counterwitness to his own facile testimony. His example is offered to us like a cautionary figure in an old morality play: so that we may avoid imitating it. It might be too late for Frank, but it's not too late for us. The fierce egotism of our youth is forgivable, and, in its moment, even justified. The problem starts when we keep fixating on ourselves, for that fixation always comes at the expense of somebody else. To grow up rightly means that at some point we will recognize a mission to pass on whatever we know of the truth. To become the elder, the genuine mentor, that Frank only pretends to be, and not at all convincingly. *Our* destined tomorrow, heralded here, in a play that otherwise spins only backward, is to open doors not for ourselves but for others. The others whose time has now come.

8

SUNDAY IN THE PARK WITH GEORGE

How to Be an Artist

Down in the left corner of Georges Seurat's vast, instantly rec-
ognizable, and weirdly disconcerting painting of a crowded park
on the banks of the Seine—so far down that his lower left leg is
crisply guillotined by the canvas's edge—a man lolls on the grass
and smokes a long clay pipe. His plain cap and sleeveless orange
tunic mark him out as, if not quite a ruffian, then definitely a day
laborer. Much more than the genteel folk who sit nearby, or who
amble through the greenery, he has earned the restful pleasure of
staring out at a bright stretch of water.

Perhaps it was the strength of this man's torso and upper arms
that led James Lapine—when he transformed Seurat's static fig-
ures from *A Sunday Afternoon on the Island of La Grande Jatte* into
the rounded, living characters of *Sunday in the Park with George*—to
suppose him a boatman. A curious fellow, this Parisian rower of the
1880s. He makes his living off the river—up it and down, or just
across, he ferries people and things—yet chooses to spend his one
day of leisure looking upon the place of his own employ.

Even more curious is that in leaping out of the picture, and
onto the stage, he has acquired a black patch worn over his right
eye. (Maybe it was always there but hidden because his painted self
appears in left profile.) We spot it on the Boatman's first entrance,

as he strides downstage and drops into the sidelong slouch that will soon become his forever pose.

Actually, we don't yet know that he's a boatman; that is revealed later. But we do know that he sees with just one eye. Same with me, which doubtless explains why this character intrigues me so. With a single functioning eye, you don't see the world like everyone else. You lose some peripheral vision. Your depth perception is off. Objects and people can look flat, not round. Nor do you travel through the world like most others because you are likelier than most to collide with objects both animate and inert. More than once I have discovered a wall on my left side from the sudden bang of my head against it.

I can well understand, then, why *looking* is such a touchy topic for the Boatman. He doesn't want anyone doing it on his behalf, because even with his one eye he can see the world just fine. No wonder that the Boatman's first lines are a spat with Georges about whether the Seine looks different on a Sunday. (By the way, I will use the French spelling for the Parisian painter in act 1 and the English spelling for his American great-grandson in act 2.) On his day off, the Boatman explains, he doesn't gussy himself up and promenade through the park, as the others do, because unlike them he doesn't want to be looked at. He wants to be left alone to look at the water. So when he spots Georges looking at *him*—and more than looking, sketching away—he turns angry. "Who the hell you think you're drawing?"

His anger is born of pride. The Boatman, scornful of artists who claim a superior talent for "observing" or "perceiving" the world, insists that he is the one who sees it most clearly. *He* is the true artist. Not this bearded man before him, with his sketchpad and charcoal crayons. No, that man sees with two eyes, and one of them is bound to wander into illusion. With just one eye, though, there's no wandering. The Boatman's gaze holds fixed on "what is true." And truth, of course, is the province of artists.

Anyone not creating art in an obvious way might hesitate to call themselves an artist. The *artist*, one might suppose, is an unusually gifted figure, a rare breed, a singular case. And they lead such odd lives. The dancer who all but lives in her studio. The composer who scrimps on heating to save up for a new piano. Or the novelist who nearly gets run over crossing the street because he's lost in thought about how to fix that last sentence. One may admire them, or not—but these creatures are, all of them, unlike us.

Don't believe it. It might appear that *Sunday in the Park with George* is playing an insider's game, addressing itself only to artists in the formal sense. And, indeed, Georges's credo—"Design. Tension. Composition. Balance. Light. Harmony."—has been taken up by theatre artists especially. Two generations of them—and counting—have been inspired by Sondheim and Lapine's work to create works of their own. (As a young director, I would listen to "Putting It Together" before every rehearsal.) Yet if *Sunday* lauds the artist's way only to restrict it to a privileged coterie, then how could the rest of us not feel rebuffed? "Well, screw them," the Boatman would retort on our behalf. Fortunately, though, there's inspiration enough for all.

That's why I've begun with the Boatman, even though he's a minor character. Because he is, in his own crabbed style, speaking the truth. The truth that being an artist is a natural state of being. It's bred deep in our bones, like an instinct, or a reflex, open to us from the start. Every five-year-old is a tiny untutored Picasso.

(Or should I say, a small Seurat?) The only question is whether we nurture, or neglect, what is already there—the artist within.

———————

This is not the dippy claim it may seem. I defy you to find a hint of dippiness in a gruff, eye-patched boatman who scares off polite little girls who just want to say hello to his doggie. Yet he's the one who sees the world in ways that others cannot or will not—which is the gift, and hence the value, of a true artist.

At the top of the second act, the figures in Seurat's canvas, as played by actors, break from their fixed poses as they react to news of his death. He died in March 1891, aged just thirty-one, never having sold a single painting. (In 2022, one of his canvases went at auction for nearly $150 million.) Some of the characters offer mild platitudes, while others barely recall Seurat's hovering presence. It's the Boatman who, with his flat vision, sees the matter in the round: "They all wanted him and hated him at the same time."

Truth be told, Georges *was* a tad peculiar. Looking right at you, but rarely in the way you wanted to be looked at. Or staring at his blank page, or canvas, so immersed in its possibilities that he reneges on his promise to take you to the Folies Bergère, even though you are powdered and rouged and ready to go. Fixed, cold . . . *bizarre*. It's hard to live with a man like that, as Dot—his lover, his model, his muse—tells us in her long first song, delivered while trying, but failing, to stand still in the heavy corseted dress that Georges makes her wear on this sweltering Sunday morning.

Flash-forward a hundred years—and cross, not the Seine, but the Atlantic. His great-grandson George, a trendy multimedia sculptor, hardly cuts a more appealing figure. True, he's genial, but a practiced conniver too. Cocktail party schmoozing. Jockeying for the next commission. Busywork that is not itself the working of art. Worse, he breaks down as completely as his latest piece—a *seventh* "Chromolume"—when its voltage regulator goes haywire during its museum showing. For him, too, the lights have gone out.

How cheerless these artists are. One is a surly lifelong failure, the other a flashy success who has run out of ideas. Not a smidgen of natural charm between them. Neither comes close to Louis the baker, who shows just how lovable he is by marrying Dot, raising as their own the daughter she had with Georges, and then taking them both to a new life in America. We do, in the end, soften toward the painter and the sculptor—but they're not easy to love.

I suppose that's the point. We *do* need to find them a bit distasteful—or sad, or cold, or irksome—because we won't then rush to hoist them onto a proverbial pedestal. We'll keep that plinth of honor vacant for the time being. One day, maybe, they'll deserve it—but not right now. Sondheim makes us wait a long time for their redemption. We wait two hours, and a hundred years.

While we're waiting, the coachman Franz shares a few thoughts. "Work is what you do for others," he explains to his wife, Frieda the cook. "Art is what you do for yourself." His words are meant to demean artistic labor—a hobby merely, not fit or proper work—but actually, they exalt it. Lift it to the highest level of consequence. Artists do not respond, and certainly not with a trained obedience, to snapped fingers or to barked commands, noises only too familiar to a coachman or a household cook. Franz is right: art *is* what you do for yourself—but in the sense that only you can do it. And it's the *only you* part of the task that makes it worthwhile. Dot, after the span of a century, sings it best: "Let it come from you. / Then it will be new."

Many of us are in tears by that point. But it's not due entirely to Dot and Georges realizing at last that they have always belonged together. We are moved, also, by the prospect of what might yet come from within us: all the creative newness that we have yet to summon forth.

———————

How easily it could have gone wrong. An American musical about a neo-Impressionist French painting. Theatre that looks like an art gallery, and vice versa. Two linked stories whose link is hard to find. *Sunday in the Park with George* is not everybody's favorite show. Certainly not the 1984 Tony Award voters, who gave it ten nominations but then heaped nearly all of the awards on Jerry Herman's *La Cage aux Folles*. Still, winning the Pulitzer Prize for Drama—*Sunday* was only the sixth musical to receive it—must have felt to Sondheim and Lapine like the best of all possible consolations.

Yet this musical, for all its grand self-awareness, does not get lost within itself. Quite the reverse, in fact. Its high craft—song motifs, scenery slotting into place, characters who break the picture frame, and a little red book that returns at the end—creates not one particular Sunday, but all Sundays . . . a "*forever*" of Sundays. A forever of looking and noticing and being right where you are.

How can we *not* pay attention to a play that honors so elegantly the lost art of paying attention?

Attending to it, we might glimpse a blurring of the line that by tradition has separated the onlooker from the artist. Blurring was, of course, Seurat's own method. Following, so he believed, the modern science of optics, he filled his canvas with clusters of unmixed paint—thickets of distinct dots—each a single color drawn from the eleven pigments on his palette. Seen up close, his paintings look chaotic and incoherent, a tangle of wild swirls. Yet at a modest distance, the viewer's eye mixes all the colored specks—red, blue, yellow, green, orange, purple—into perceptible shapes, finding in tension a greater harmony. Suddenly, a black straw hat with a pink flower comes into focus. Then a shiny bugle raised to the lips. And look, *look*, there's the bend in the river.

This is pointillism, as Seurat's brush technique came to be known. That the optical mixing didn't happen in precisely the way he supposed hardly negates his achievement: to turn the beholder of art into something nearly like its creator. To insist that what the eye *"arranges"*—receives, yes, but then puts together—is what is beautiful.

What the ear arranges too. By subtle design, Sondheim's music echoes Seurat's pointillist style. In "Color and Light," we see Georges dabbing flecks of paint onto his vast canvas. Each dart of his brush is timed to each jab of the music, while the lyrics—"Red red red red / Red red orange / Red red orange"—name the colors as they overtake the white of the blank canvas. Later, in "Finishing the Hat," when Georges sings of "stepping back to look at a face"—a slight, yet necessary, distance—we are meant to recall how Seurat's own paintings are best seen at a measured remove, so that their swirls of "red red orange" will coalesce into recognizable shapes.

In the stunning act 1 finale "Sunday," when Georges arrests the frenzy of the stage, and then compels it into the serenity of the finished painting, the music *is* that action. While Georges is busy rearranging his images, people included, into the fittest, most balanced place—a parasol here, Louis there, no, *there*—the music is busy with chords played one after another, in a pure adjacency of sound. At times the chords are so thick that seven of the eight notes in a major scale are played at once, like Georges crowding his canvas with every different hue at his disposal.

Sound itself glistens. Just as the painting needs time to resolve itself into an ordered design, so, too, the music needs its own time to nudge those abutting chords into a cadence, a progression toward a final release. And then, "boom"—Sondheim's own word—it happens. Georges ends his conjuring with the word, and at the sound, we have been waiting for: "harmony."

Our ears have listened for the notes to fall into place. Our eyes have merged the colors into a distinctness. Like Georges stepping back to appraise his finished canvas as the act 1 curtain falls, we, too, have stepped back to "look at a face." Which, as Georges has taught us, is the "only way to see."

To step back is what *Sunday* wants us to do. Step back, so that we may see more clearly. Hear more acutely. The show helps us to do that by itself retreating from linear narrative—a clear-cut story—the form long assumed to be the only way for anyone to see, even when the object of our beholding was the pure artifice of musical theatre. *Sweeney Todd* tells its story from start to finish and *Merrily We Roll Along* tells its story from finish to start. But with *Sunday in the Park with George* . . . well, there's not so much a story as a spiral of images.

It's a treasured piece of Sondheim lore that what inspired *Sunday* was not a plot but a picture: namely, a postcard of Seurat's painting. In the early 1980s, Lapine asked Sondheim what sort of musical he wanted to write. He replied, "Theme and variation." Not, then, a story to be told, but a perspective to be taken—an outlook from which to look upon the changing scene. Lapine, by training a photographer and graphic designer, fixed in his mind a climactic image for each act—the tableau of Seurat's original painting, the high-rise buildings on the Island of La Grande Jatte today—and then worked "backward" to write the scenes that would give rise to those final images.

Under Lapine's influence, Sondheim let himself compose with "more formal looseness," as he recalled, "allowing songs to become fragmentary, like musicalized snatches of dialogue." Fidgeting sets the erratic tone for *Sunday*'s opening number, which is also its title song, sung by an itchy, tense, and sweaty Dot as she models in the park for Georges. The music roves, a mimic of her own distractibility. Her rhymes are "near" rhymes, for she's not a precise thinker. And the body's irritations—foot gone to sleep, bustle that slips, pinch of the corset right under the tit—are the song's main focus.

As it starts, so it goes. The rest of the evening turns on predicament more than plot. One artist, in the 1880s, sticks to his chosen path at all costs. Another artist, in the 1980s, strays from his path and greatly to his cost. If we are searching for what unites the two halves of *Sunday in the Park with George*—so unlike in time, place, manner, and mode—we will not find that unity in a story. It is, rather, through *sound*—"theme and variation," parallel songs, echo, reprise, and dissonance converted into harmony—that *Sunday* achieves itself. The entire piece, as Sondheim remarked, is a "continuous love song" between Georges and Dot "that isn't completed until the end of the show."

The irony is that both Georges and George insist upon living within the confines of a traditional plot. Let's call it "The Story of the Successful Artist." In this story, a familiar but formidable one, the artist must win the twin laurels of "finishing the hat" and getting "an exhibition in addition." The artist, that is, must fulfill a vision *and* find commercial success. This is how the story is meant to end. When we refer to the historical Georges Seurat as a failure in his lifetime, a misunderstood genius, we are perpetuating just this kind of story.

For neither character though, does this internalized plot work out. Georges finishes the hat, but who's there to see it? No one—just a dog. He performs a sneering disregard for the art establishment, but Georges does respect Jules, the more esteemed painter, and he does want the public to see his own work. He yearns, though so well he hides the yearning, to be understood. His great-grandson, George, fails in the opposite way. He lands one high-profile commission after another, but brings to them nothing new. He's guessing at things now, drifting in the dark. Just like the darkness that descends after his "Chromolume #7" implodes. Each man is trapped within a narrative that typecasts him in the same role: the chagrined loser. And it's making them sick at heart.

There is counsel in their sad example. It is a perilous, yet also irresistible, temptation to imagine our lives as a story that is meant, and meant from its outset, to reach a certain ending. A fixed destination, be it money, marriage, achievement, or renown. Perilous because such a story can be understood—by ourselves, by others—only in the binary terms of success or failure. Either we're heading in the right upward direction, or we're in decline. There's no escaping the story's judgment because we are its permanent protagonist. The winner, we hope, but maybe all along we've been the also-ran.

It does seem impossible to make sense of life without a narrative. Its metaphors have become our daily speech. We set out on a journey. We chase dreams. We pursue goals. We encounter setbacks. We want closure. And we feel the power of telling our story. Narrative, long ago, became not what we think about, but *how* we think. It is through the prism of narrative that we see our experience and endow it with meaning.

So, here's a question: What would happen if we let the grip of narrative go slack? What might ensue if we resisted, even for a moment, the stranglehold that our inner story has upon us?

Sunday offers an answer. Its own lack of formal cohesion—disjunctive scenes, wandering music, play of images—poses the question. And then its action—what becomes of Georges and Dot—gives the reply. The reply is that what lies beyond the boundary of narrative is neither vacancy nor incoherence, but the swarm and spin of life itself. No longer defined by a story line—for lines have edges, and at edges we must stop—we are free to roam around. At liberty now to traverse the terrain, we might notice a dab here, a fleck there, and all the swirls in between. Instead of dashing away on the freight train of story, we can stay right here—present, mindful, and attentive to what *is*.

But not, like Georges's mother, in a fearful way. Threats, both imagined and real, assail her from all directions. Even from the sky, as Gustave Eiffel's tower climbs beam by iron beam into it. No wonder she longs "for the old view." Nor, like poor Jules, in a judgmental way. Searching for what is not there—"You cannot even see these faces!" he complains about Georges's new painting—he fails to see all the shimmering right in front of him.

Our task is to be present in an open way. To see the world with a loving, and thus an accepting, eye. Only the loving eye finds a "connection" (great-grandson George's favorite word) with all that it meets. In the intimacy of the shared now, it casts nothing aside. Not those shirtless boys bathing in the noonday sun. Not that scary, one-eyed boatman. Not even a long-tailed monkey on a short leash. None of them furthers the story, yet here they are—in this place and of this time. And so they *all* go onto the canvas.

How Georges will stare, and to some his stare feels cold and dark. But as Dot knows best of all, "it's warm inside his eyes." To see the world just as it is—not lamenting what has passed, not pleading for what cannot be—is to find it beautiful. Not pretty, but *beautiful*.

———————

That, it might be objected, is a piece of rhetoric only. Fine words from a struggling artist in need of a client. But consider this: the subject of Georges's painting is ordinary Parisians diverting themselves on an ordinary Sunday in one of their city's not-so-fashionable parks. So prosaic was the setting that Jules mockingly declared his own intention to "paint a factory next!" But, actually, Georges's credo—the beauty of the world is there for all to see, if only they would allow themselves to see it—would be *less* persuasive if his theme were grand or thrilling. A castle besieged. A tempest at sea. A cathedral that soars. But he depicts none of that. He notices, instead, what others might discard or miss entirely. Art historians tell us that Dot's stylish bustle was taken straight from a magazine advertisement of the time. And that little red book, invented for the stage, turns out to be the most valuable object of all.

What is valuable must first be noticed, or else its value fades. Noticing is a difficult skill to master. So readily, then, do we sympathize with Dot in the first scene, as she struggles to be still—"Don't move the mouth!"—while Georges sketches her. She strives to be right *there*, looking out over the water, and not off somewhere else. But somewhere else soon gets the better of her.

How collected, though, she appears at the end. In "Move On," their rhapsodic duet, Dot gently leads George—who has *stopped* noticing—back into the realm of perception. She renews in him a lost ability to see the world and sense its wonder. We feel the full poignancy of Dot giving back in gratitude what Georges gave first to her: "Taught me how to see, / Notice every tree—"

To notice every tree—to *really* notice it, intently, and with a fixed focus—is to make it a part of yourself. And to make yourself a part of it. To blur the line whose only purpose has been to keep you and it on opposite sides.

In "Finishing the Hat," that hymn of every artist who makes a something from a nothing, Georges sings of "entering the world of the hat." Reaching for it, stepping into it, finding his place inside it. One of Sondheim's notes for the song was "Can't you see my heart in the hat?" (Well, yes, I can.) A superb bit of subtext, the line declares Georges's motivating truth. He no longer distinguishes among himself as an artist, his real-life subject, and the art that he makes. Georges—Dot—the painted hat—they are but variations on a single theme. "I am what I do," he insists. Dot, not yet understanding, accuses Georges of escaping into his art—of *not* attending to the world. This he flatly rejects. "I am not hiding behind my canvas—I am living in it."

But not, Georges hopes, living there alone: "*You* will be in this painting." That's his way of telling Dot that art is never an escape from the world. Yet his words are easy to misconstrue. We might presume—as did Dot, as did the Boatman, as did Jules in scorning to sketch in the park—that the artist stands alone, set apart, and, if not always aloof, then certainly at a cautious remove. It's true that Georges must be alone in his studio if he's going to get the red and the orange and the even more red just right. Yet by his side are all those sketches of all those people from all those Sundays in the park. Revising the world because he loves the world, Georges finishes the hat in solitude so that he may entrust to it his whole heart.

The full epiphany occurs in "Sunday," the act 1 finale, when we see—actually see, as its component parts are joined—that Georges's painting exists as an object in the world *and* that the world itself exists within the painting, a simulacrum of order summoned out of chaos. Here reality and artifice dissolve each into the other. Sondheim's lyrics point to this merging, the essential fusion of art and the world. What we perceive in the painting is at one and the same time an illusion of "parasols" and the actual "flecks of light / and dark."

———

There's a babe in arms in the background of Seurat's painting. The stage version names her as Marie, the daughter of Dot and Georges (raised, though, by Dot and Louis). We meet her properly in the second act as George's ninety-eight-year-old grandmother who accompanies him to his museum exhibition.

Marie knows that art can return you to the world. Though she naughtily enjoys acting like a doddering old lady, an embarrassing outsider amid all those trendy art world types, Marie is the most alert, and most alive, person in that crowded room. She quickly corrects the curators when they misidentify the waffle stove in

Georges's painting. Everywhere on his canvas she sees her mother's face: "There she is, there she is, there she is." The music ripples like water underneath, lifting and carrying her on its gently rhythmic tide. Marie is as much a part of that painting as her mother, Dot, the woman who taught her how to notice every tree—and how to nourish the family tree. Now she, too, claims her ancestral song, a song in praise of children and art, those precious twin legacies that like nothing else can sustain the world.

A timely lesson, but George is too distracted ("up on the trapeze") to heed it. His time comes later, when he visits the Island of La Grande Jatte, his first time in France, on the trip that Marie did not live to take with him. But still, "there she is"—in the red grammar book, the family heirloom she bequeathed to George. It belonged first to Dot, who learned from it, and once wrote in it, on this very site. George, in grief, and in the emptiness that he now allows himself to feel, takes up the book, opens it, and starts to read aloud "Lesson #8." The title of that simple grammar lesson becomes the title of the song that he now sings.

George turned to the page at random, but it feels more like the kindness of fate—because it's the same lesson that Dot herself read aloud. We watched her do it. Reciting, and then singing, Dot's words—how emphatic their echoing—George uses the song to work his way back into the past. What "Children and Art" was to Marie, "Lesson #8" is to him. George finds in his past, and finds there almost in spite of himself, the "connection" he has been trying to make—the connection to both his family and his art, for each entails the other. Though murkiness hangs in the Parisian air, and though a brutality of concrete spoils the view, a hardy old tree can still be seen. The tree that is, and always has been, the family tree.

George is reading an old-fashioned grammar lesson, but it's a new lesson in life that he's learning.

It seems inexplicable now that Sondheim didn't write "Lesson #8" until the week before *Sunday* opened at the Booth Theatre on Broadway. Yet once he did write it, the entire show pulled together. Clicked right into place. The cast knew it immediately, because that's when the standing ovations began. Charles Kimbrough, the original Jules, likened George's final solo to a "keystone" in an arch: the one last piece, and not the bulkiest, that holds everything together. And without which everything falls apart. If we are moved to raptures in "Move On," the soaring duet that follows, it is because of what has been achieved in the fifty-eight bars of "Lesson #8."

To see a family tree, and to find your place within it, is, I admit, to tell yourself a story. But it's not a story of success or failure, not a narrative of life on the quick forward march. It is, rather, a tale of affinities and belongings. Lineages and linkages. Wholeness and healing. It is, in other words, a tale of *art*—and how our life may be lived as a true work of art, resplendent in its own abiding coherence and not straining after a prettiness that is forever mutable. This stable center is what enables the artist—which is to say, each of us—to move on, trusting that "Anything you do, / Let it come from you. / Then it will be new." I hear in those words no soft mantra of self-praise. What I hear, rather, is the courage to bind ourselves to the world as we find it, and the resolve to choose how best to live within it. We will surely make mistakes. But it's the "choosing" that matters most.

In her final lyric, Dot emboldens George to "give us more to see." We are unusually alert to those words because they have ceased to rhyme. The full quatrain we were expecting has not been, and will not be, finished. And so this one lyric leaps out from all the rest—not rounding things off but opening them up. What we hear is addressed to us now as much as to George himself. In bidding us to see *more*—to look ahead to what we want, and not to repel it, or judge it, or fear it, or mock it—Dot hails with so much love the artist in each of us. So that where others might see only blankness, we will see "so many possibilities."

9

INTO THE WOODS

How to Choose the Right Path

Into the Woods takes a few well-known fairy tales—Jack and the Beanstalk, Rapunzel and the Witch, Cinderella and Prince Charming, and Little Red Riding Hood —and does strange things to them. In James Lapine's libretto, the tales mix and merge, with characters from different stories crossing paths in the woods. No edition of the Brothers Grimm includes a scene shared by Cinderella's prince and Jack's mother. Yet once the stories get entwined, their disparate plots fused into one, it's not at all clear how things are going to work out.

This musical delivers the expected "happily ever after" ending, but much too soon—just halfway through, at the end of the first act. Which leaves the second act free to do what no storybook fairy tale can ever do: rewrite itself. Unravel all that has been so tightly stitched together. Like *Sunday in the Park with George*, Sondheim and Lapine's previous show, *Into the Woods* is a musical whose two halves appear to contrast more than they compare.

Yet the show's most decisive breaking of fairy-tale rules is the one most likely to escape our notice, for so deftly are the rules broken. Nowhere outside of *Into the Woods* will you find the fairy tale of the Baker and his Wife—the tale around which the plot develops—because it was invented by James Lapine, and then set to music by Stephen Sondheim. It is, to be blunt, a sham fairy tale.

Also, a necessary one. Lapine created the Baker and his Wife not as archetypal figures from a mythical past but as modern-day New Yorkers who awake one morning to find themselves trapped in a medieval fairy-tale world. They blend in surprisingly well—but still, they are misfits in the woods. Sondheim, with his lyricist's gift for specificity, likened them to a bickering "Bronx Jewish couple" whose life revolves around the twin disappointments of having no children and not enough money. They "stand in for the audience," as Lapine explained, because their situation feels so familiar to us. This act of substitution is key to *all* fairy tales, for they must reflect back to us, if only symbolically, an image of ourselves. We must see in the fairy tale a version of the real tale we are living out day after day.

That's why in this chapter I'm going to look mostly at the Baker's Wife. Because it seems to me that her core dilemma—not knowing which path to choose—is one that we all share.

———————

Being childless is the family curse placed upon the couple by the Witch who lives next door, in revenge for the Baker's late father having once stolen beans from her garden. To lift the curse, the Baker and his Wife must find—and then bring to the Witch—"the cow as white as milk," "the cape as red as blood," "the hair as yellow as corn," and "the slipper as pure as gold." Only in the woods will they find what they seek. And so into the woods they go.

Not, though, without a quarrel first. The Baker insists that he will embark on the journey alone because the spell was placed on his house, not his wife's. She is not so easily deterred. Whether it's due to spousal loyalty, injured pride, or just wanting to get the spell lifted, the Baker's Wife decides to follow her husband in secret.

This is no trivial step. For her, venturing onto the path is an overt act of defiance—a blank refusal to accept her husband's order to stay at home. Just as Eve her grandmother did when she bit into the forbidden apple, the Baker's Wife disobeys—and doesn't regret it.

There's more at stake here than she knows. We know it already—it's a fairy tale, so momentous things *will* happen—but she doesn't. Yet in taking that first transgressive step, the Baker's Wife claims for herself the central action of all fairy tales: the hero's quest. The Baker believes that the quest (though he is so obviously ill-suited for it) belongs to him. The universe disagrees—and puts his wife, instead, directly into fate's path. This decision feels to the Baker's Wife like a brazen act of her own will, but really she is being summoned by forces beyond herself.

Or rather, within herself—because every hero's quest is a response to an *inner* call. The call to know the truth of yourself. Not the self as you assume it to be, and not as the world demands it to be, but the self as it longs to be. In a fairy tale's language of symbols, the quest takes the shape of a contest, or a trial, an impossible task that must be accomplished by the tolling of the midnight bell. Empty a lake with a slotted spoon. Fetch a key from the ocean floor. Spin straw into gold. Each challenge, whatever its form, is a metaphor of the self's obligation to fight for itself.

In most fairy tales, including Sondheim and Lapine's musical one, a hero's journey begins with a forbidden act: betrayal, rebellion, deceit, or a reckless gamble. Ignoring her husband's command is the Baker's Wife's first act of defiance, but hardly her last. Before long, she tricks Jack into selling his cow Milky-White for five "magic" beans (they *are* magical, but she doesn't know it yet). When the Baker's Wife lies, it is not because she is a shady character—it is because the high stakes of the moment demand it.

Without a readiness to dissent, to spurn the crowd's judgment, and thereby to risk its spite, there can be no prospect of meaningful change. No hope of finding the right path for yourself. Only the dead-end certainty of a life more endured than fully lived. Far better than her husband does, the Baker's Wife intuits what must be done:

If you know
What you want
Then you go
And you find it
And you get it.

———

Go—find—get. Though she starts her journey with four tangible "gets" in mind—cow, cape, hair, slipper—there's something more waiting for her in the woods. Another treasure for her to find. It is, of course, Prince Charming. Now, as a new fairy tale collides with an old one, the Baker's Wife senses that the journey she thought she was on is not the journey she ought to be on.

She hears about the prince first from Cinderella, straight from her dance with him at the king's festival. Envious of that encounter—"Oh, to be pursued by a Prince. All that pursues me is tomorrow's bread."—the Baker's Wife confesses that she would give anything to be in Cinderella's "shoes." That's no mere figure of speech, because those shoes—glass slippers, really—symbolize her wish to lead a different life, a life in which a handsome prince holds her in his arms as they glide across a ballroom floor in time to music that sounds for all the world like the music of the spheres. No more having to bake tomorrow's bread.

Her gaze now fixed on her new goal, the Baker's Wife draws near it. It takes a little time, though. She hides at first behind an obliging tree, the better to eavesdrop on the prince. Hearing him, but not seeing him. Later they meet—but he is brusque and rushes off. The moment is not yet ripe.

Then, in a pivotal scene, the Baker's Wife crosses paths again with Cinderella, who is now running *away* from the prince. The Baker's Wife can scarcely comprehend this, because she herself wants only to track the man down. The opportunity must be seized. In the play's cleverest bit of stage business, the Baker's Wife and Cinderella swap footwear. Cinderella, no longer encumbered by her glass slippers, can outrun the prince. But there's more to it. In getting hold of those glass slippers, the Baker's Wife *becomes* her own Cinderella. Like an understudy putting on the absent star's costume as the curtain is about to rise, she steps into her longed-for leading role.

Now, at last, she is ready to get her prince. Remember, this is a fairy tale—which means that all its actions and events are symbolic. They are not literal occurrences in the outer world so much as figurative expressions of a character's inner state. When the Baker's Wife claims the prince as her own, she is claiming a neglected part of herself. The part that has nothing to do with staying at home and baking bread. Or looking after her infant child, the result of the Witch's curse being lifted. Figuratively speaking, that's the small self that for so long she has identified with. Yet there's a larger version of herself that has been waiting all this time just to be acknowledged, let alone accepted. The prince symbolizes how she wants to feel, but so far hasn't, about her life: exalted, masterful, and in control. For all of us, and not just for the Baker's Wife, to watch a prince in smooth, princely conduct is to glimpse what life would be like if only we played the hero, and not a supporting role, in our own story.

Merely watching, though, will not suffice. We must *kiss* the prince. For only by kissing the prince—or princess, or whatever lofty symbolic figure compels us—can we make their loftiness our own. "Your choice? How brave," the prince commends the Baker's Wife. He means her choice to search for the boy Jack while a vengeful giant is on the loose. But he also, and more interestingly, hints at a bolder choice: to share this moment with him. In fairy tales, the approval that we must give to ourselves is typically depicted as coming from someone else, a someone like Prince Charming. Such characters are helpful projections of our own internal state, enabling us to see more clearly the truth about ourselves. And so, the prince's approval ("How brave") is the sign to the Baker's Wife that her instinct to overcome whatever constricts or diminishes her—the instinct that led her into the woods in the first place—is a healthy one. She should trust it. She should take the risk now before her.

How could they *not* kiss? This rapturous moment—with its pressing of lips, its darting of tongues, and its sighing of echoed sighs—melds two into one. No longer leading a divided life, the Baker's Wife now moves in harmony with her truest self, *embraced* by herself—though in the guise of a prince's enfolding arms. The union achieved in that kiss is a union with her essential self. The fairy tale of the Baker's Wife has now arrived at its happy ending.

If only. For at precisely this moment, the moment when the Baker's Wife stands on the cusp of a new life, *Into the Woods* renounces its fairy-tale magic and reverts to kitchen-sink realism. It does all that in just a single line.

Sondheim had little patience with actors who lobbied for script changes, because he felt they wanted only to enhance their own role and not to improve the play overall. The one time he altered a lyric because of something an actor told him came after a late-night phone call with Joanna Gleason, the original Baker's Wife. Almost in passing, and certainly not angling for a rewrite, she described her character as being "in the wrong story." Jolted into insight, as he later explained, Sondheim realized just how much the Baker and the Baker's Wife were outsiders in the fairy-tale world they had stumbled into. He turned Gleason's words, which could hardly be improved upon, into the show's biggest laugh line. After the Prince kisses her, the Baker's Wife, stunned, looks straight out at the audience and, deadpanning it, says, "I'm in the wrong story."

Her reaching out is what draws us in. Her address to the audience, her plea issued from the other side of the proscenium arch, puts us immediately on her side. The Baker's Wife is one of us—but, poor thing, she's lost in a land of witches and giants and charming princes. All right, that last part isn't so bad. Still, it's mostly a frightening and alien world. Not a gingerbread house in sight. No wonder the Baker's Wife is looking at us with that expression of befuddled alarm.

Prince Charming, the opposite of her own feckless husband,

has transfixed her from the start. She will do anything to meet him. When, at last, she finds him in a receptive mood, she drops what she's doing (Who cares about Jack? Who remembers the Baker?) to linger by his side, absorbed into his royal radiance. Yet no sooner does she get her kiss than she worries that she was wrong to get it. Maybe her husband was right when he told her to stay put. Maybe Cinderella's shoes aren't the right fit. But then she leans in to return his kiss. It's no coincidence that the Baker's Wife breaks the rules of theatrical illusion at the same time as she breaks the rules of her marriage. This woman has definitely landed in the wrong story—but which one is the wrong one?

To sort it out, Sondheim gives the Baker's Wife her one musical soliloquy, "Moments in the Woods." It's the only time she sings alone. Her task in this question mark of a song is not to do something new, not to drive the story forward, but to reflect on what has just happened. And to figure out what comes next.

The prince speeds off to slay a dragon, leaving her alone and unsure whether she only imagined their dalliance. Then wham, total recall. Snapping out of her waking dream, she scolds herself for having yielded to the prince's wiles. To ease her conscience, she blames the surroundings: "What *is* it about the woods?"

Still, she won't dismiss the kiss. Instead of regretting, or forgetting, this unusual moment, she resolves to learn from it. What she learns is that she has to taste the forbidden fruit to know that she doesn't actually like its taste. She learns that a judicious breaking of her vows can remind her why she vowed them in the first place. And why, indeed, she will keep on vowing them. Not dodge them. Not decry them. Not bargain them down into a nothingness. But, as best she can, honor them.

The insight here is paradoxical: a transgression won't always lead you astray. In fact, it can restore you, and with a new strength, to the life you have already staked out for yourself. A life of duties and standards and promises. Not, mind, a life in which your every desire is fulfilled, for that is sheer fantasy. But rather a life whose horizon runs beyond any solitary, selfish desire. If you can loosen life's grip upon you, then you may well start to feel your life not as a burden weighing you down but a choice setting you free. *Then* you can bind to it more closely, and more gratefully, than ever.

By her song's end, the Baker's Wife understands that she must leave the woods. "Back to life, back to sense." Her lyric's harsh consonants—all those percussive *b*'s and *ck*'s—sit perfectly on the quick new rhythm, an alert and driven sound that begins with the key change. Having begun her soliloquy in dreamy languor, she concludes it with a disciplined vigor, practically barking her own marching orders. Out of the woods, and back to the bakehouse.

In 2022, the magazine *American Theatre* interviewed three actors who played the Baker's Wife on Broadway: Joanna Gleason (1987), Kerry O'Malley (2002), and Sara Bareilles (2022). Their performances are different, but their perspective on "Moments in the Woods" is similar. As they see it, the Baker's Wife repudiates the "princess" cliché—much as Bareilles did in her 2004 feminist pop song "Fairytale"—and recovers her own agency. Absconding with the prince might seem to be the romantic choice, but it would mean sacrificing, as Gleason elaborated, "her Baker, her life, her love." Sacrificing all that is *hers*—what she herself has chosen for herself. For Bareilles, the scene with the prince was a "gift" for her character: it awakened a "new perspective," one that enabled the Baker's Wife to be "present to what is in [her] life." Returning to her husband and infant child is no meek, wifely surrender but an affirmation freely made that, in Sondheim's own words, "it takes two." The Baker's Wife, in the richest, most expansive meaning of the phrase, has woken up.

Tellingly, her character has no personal name. But then, nobody in *Into the Woods* does. The only lead character with a name is Jack—but that's the most generic moniker of all, a bland shorthand for the multitudes. People in fairy tales are not real people; they are abstractions or archetypes of humankind. They exhibit the patterns found not in one individual life but in all lives everywhere. What happens to them are not the concrete events of history—there is no actual Baker's Wife who nurses her baby by the fireside—but the unveiling of a truth through the tale's signs and symbols.

This is precisely how we find *our* way into the story, how we make it pertain to us. In the Baker's Wife's predicament, we catch sight of ours. We, too, are deep in life's dark woodland, maybe lost in its thicket. Yet what she learns we, too, can learn. Through her, and through Sondheim's artistry, we can have our own moment in the woods. So that like the Baker's Wife, we can finally wake up to reality.

———

I have never kissed a prince. Not to my knowledge. But I have most definitely kissed a man who, as I kissed him, became for me a prince. It happened, not once upon a time, but on a December night in Greenwich Village more than thirty years ago. I can still recall the Bleecker Street address of the long-since-shuttered Italian restaurant that John and I had just left. The moment, you see, was unforgettable. Unforgettable not so much for the kiss itself, sweet though it was, as for how it changed me. That is, after all, what a kiss from a fairy-tale prince is meant to do.

We had spent most of that day—watching the ice-skaters at Rockefeller Center, meandering through a Soho gallery, catching a show at the Astor Place Theatre—avoiding what could not much longer be avoided: we had fallen in love.

Yet this was no romantic comedy. In the early 1990s, no effective treatment for HIV was available, gay people were denounced by a sitting US senator as "morally sick wretches," and same-sex marriage was beyond anyone's belief. When love is so categorically forbidden, and maligned as a matter of routine, the closet feels like a safe haven. At least back then it did to me.

It also felt false. The protection offered by the closet came at the intolerable price of living a lie. Of not being who I was. But on that December night, I finally desired my own desires. And I desired one particular man so unboundedly that I kissed him on a crowded street corner. It seemed, to me at least, risky. Yet the risk of not taking the risk was far greater. It would have kept me walled up inside my own life, a prisoner unto myself.

Like a prince in a fairy tale, John revealed to me—because he returned the kiss—all that had been hidden from me. Suddenly I was launched into a new phase of my life; into, indeed, life itself. Into the woods, and then *out*.

Our romance lasted less than a year, but our friendship endures. They do make things happen, those charming princes.

———————

My own fairy tale ended so differently from that of the Baker's Wife and her Prince Charming. While I leapt into a new life, she went back to an old one. Her fairy tale did not carry her across any threshold. But isn't that what fairy tales are supposed to do? The more I thought about the Baker's Wife, the more elusive her story seemed. Something else was happening to her and I hadn't figured it out.

The Swiss psychologist Marie-Louise von Franz, one of Carl Jung's closest collaborators, believed that to interpret a fairy tale you must stalk it like a stag: tread gently, keep alert, and, above all, follow wherever it leads. Hunting metaphors may not be so popular these days, but you take her point. A fairy tale is hard to pin down. It's always a little beyond us, heading in its own direction. Perhaps that's what James Lapine took away from reading some of von Franz's essays when he was writing the libretto for *Into the Woods*.

Her remarks gave me pause. Maybe I had tried too hard to lead the tale of the Baker's Wife when I should have followed it instead. So I started over and let the story take me where *it* wanted to go. This turned out to be a most memorable trip. Because the story of the Baker's Wife, as so artfully condensed in the song "Moments in the Woods," took me into some dark, unexpected places. But then, darkness is exactly what we should expect to find in the woods, where sunlight fights to penetrate the dense canopy of trees.

When I say this song is dark, I mean that it feels tragic to me that the Baker's Wife decides to head back home. Not just regrettable, but utterly catastrophic—the worst possible outcome for her.

Most people familiar with *Into the Woods* will likely agree with Joanna Gleason and Sara Bareilles that the song's ending is redemptive, with an encouraging promise of household reunion. Without question, "Moments in the Woods" bears that interpretation. Indeed, it's the one I have elaborated on in the past few pages.

Yet it's a mark of mature artistry in any creative work when it can sustain multiple, and even contradictory, readings. That stag can and will head off in any direction.

So, hear me out. The tragedy of the Baker's Wife is not that she rejects Prince Charming but that she rejects what he stands for. This larger, ultimate rejection is what dooms her, because the prince symbolizes a forsaken part of her own self. He's an image of the exalted aspect of herself that the Baker's Wife longs to integrate into her life—to be, as it were, reconciled with—but in the end does not. So, in spurning him, she really spurns herself.

After their first kiss, the prince carries the Baker's Wife deeper into the woods, leaving the stage empty. A short scene follows in which the Baker pleads with Cinderella—who now looks more like a peasant than a princess-in-waiting—to seek shelter with him and the others because the avenging giant has rampaged the castle. His act of sober care is doubtless meant to contrast with the prince, who lives only for wanton pleasure. Yet it also shows how the two couples have realigned, with Cinderella and the Baker's Wife trading places—just as they had swapped shoes. Then the lights come back up on the prince and the Baker's Wife, who roll together downstage, locked in a long kiss. The prince breaks their embrace and runs off, declaring his duty to slay the giant.

Prince Charming *must* exit the scene at this point because his work is done. Symbolically, his role was to awaken the Baker's Wife to the larger life that she knew awaited her, but which she had been too terrified to accept. This role he fulfilled exquisitely, sealing the deal with a lush kiss. Departing, the prince speaks his gratitude— "I shall not forget you . . . How alive you've made me feel"—but, really, his words belong to the Baker's Wife. *She* has come alive.

She will not forget herself. *She* has woken up to life, though it took a prince's kiss to do it.

Everything now hangs in the balance. The prince has summoned the Baker's Wife to live the life that is truly hers—and to live it without counting the cost. She is catapulted into a whole new dimension of being, whose symbol is the dark, mysterious woods. The question is whether she will stay a little longer in the transforming woods—or get out fast. Will she live out her new life or revert to the old one?

She mulls it over with music. Sondheim gives the Baker's Wife some tongue-twisting lyrics to convey the emotions twisting inside her. Unsure of herself, she flirts with having it both ways: a husband at home and a lover on the side. But she knows that's impossible—no one can be both in and out of the woods. Savor the moment, by all means, but then, let it go. She does let it go, because, as Sondheim put it, "she likes life as it is." And so her song ends, as every soliloquy should, with a clear resolve: "it's time to leave the woods."

Joanna Gleason, when singing that line, balled up into her fist the red handkerchief that the prince had left behind, and then she threw it away. Not a casual tossing aside, but a forcible expulsion, banishing from her sight the token of the man whom she had just kissed (and likely, more than kissed). How memorable this image of sudden reversal and rebuke. That bloodred handkerchief was a visual perfection, for it flashed out the raw vitality of life.

The story I've just told is the same one as before, except that I've approached it from a different angle—stalked it from another side. Where has it led me? To the unhappy realization that the Baker's Wife opened a long-closed door only to slam it quickly shut. (In this, she is the opposite of Bobby in *Company*, who not only keeps the door open, but walks right through it.) The slamming looks like an act of emotional maturity—the Baker's Wife, returning to her senses, puts all frivolous things behind her. Roll up your sleeves, for there's dough that needs kneading. But really, the door slammed shut is the foreclosing of her own future, the future that the prince has just revealed to her.

How could anyone renounce such a gift? It's a harsh thing to say, but the Baker's Wife heard the call of life—and tuned it out. That's what I find in her story. She squandered her chance. Threw the moment away, just like the prince's red handkerchief. She did not, in the end, attain a greater consciousness. She did not wake up. If that's not a tragedy, then I don't know what would be.

All tragic heroes die—and so what *must* happen now happens quickly. The Baker's Wife falls into the path of the giant's wife and dies instantly, crushed under that colossus. She was retracing her steps, counting them one by one—and counting on them to get her back home. Yet right away, she lost her way. The symbolism here is strong. When the Baker's Wife risked venturing onto the right path, she met a prince who with his kiss promised a new life. But a path is tragically wrong when it leads straight to death.

———

James Lapine is sometimes asked if the Baker's Wife dies because of her fling with the prince. It's an oddly moralizing question, given that other characters in the play do far worse: some steal, another kills. He replies that the Baker's Wife was simply unlucky. Being in the wrong place at the wrong time, she got stomped on by a giant in a stomping mood. Nothing more to read into it.

I'm not so sure about that. Audiences feel cheated by her death (which might explain her ghostly return at the end) and they want to make sense of it. She is, after all, a favorite character and, along with the Baker, a proxy for all of us. To render her death meaningless, a random misfortune only, is to render equally meaningless the story of her life. But then, what would be the point of telling that story—and telling it so well?

Another word for meaning is *lesson*. What lesson can we learn from the Baker's Wife? She herself—in one interpretation, at least—seems not to have learned much at all. Still, we can learn from her failures. This is, of course, exactly what a fairy tale makes possible. It lets us see our problems more clearly by handing them over to someone else. We pretend, for the length of the story, that we are dealing with somebody else's troubles—Jack's or Cinderella's or Rapunzel's—but really we are dealing with our own. Shifting the burden of truth-telling onto these imaginary figures, we entrust them with the responsibility to feel on our behalf—just as Prince Charming did for the Baker's Wife—what we cannot yet fully feel for ourselves. By giving outer expression to an inner turmoil, a fairy tale can show us how to chart a hopeful path through it.

It saddens me that the Baker's Wife embarked upon the right path only to quickly reverse course. I regret her failure (as I see it) to choose wisely when she was gifted with the chance. Yet I also feel compassion toward her—compassion, that most classic of theatrical emotions. My motives here are mixed. I look kindly upon the Baker's Wife because I hope to look upon myself with the same kindness when it's my turn to have a moment in the woods. Should I ever find myself facing what she faced—it happened to me once; it may happen again—I hope I will have drawn the right lesson from her poignant example. I hope that I will summon the courage to choose the right path for me, knowing that right and wrong can be hard to tell apart.

Courage from a prince's lips? O trespass sweetly urged. May we always remember that if a prince kisses us, the best response is to kiss him—or her, or them, for princely pronouns are diverse—right back. And to keep on kissing. They will, sooner or later, get up and leave, for that is what charming princes must do. Yet when they do leave, we won't be left alone to feel any burden of regret. Because by the time their lips withdraw from ours, we will have become the prince in our own lives.

But only, of course, if we wish it.

10

ASSASSINS

How to Let the Darkness In

Perfect theatrical fodder—that was Stephen Sondheim's take on assassins. "They come with built-in motivations and climactic actions." They are the heroes in stories of their own obsessive scripting. The whole world is their stage. Especially in their death scenes, when they can overact appallingly.

Here's an infamous case. In a tobacco barn near Port Royal, Virginia, about eighty miles due south of Ford's Theatre in Washington, DC, where, twelve days earlier, on April 14, 1865, he had shot President Abraham Lincoln, the actor John Wilkes Booth was himself shot dead. "Boston" Corbett, a sergeant in the twenty-man detachment of Union soldiers that had been pursuing Booth, fatally wounded him. Corbett later claimed, though others disputed it—it was hard for anyone to see through the barn's slats—that the fugitive had raised his pistol and was about to fire. Soldiers dragged the now-paralyzed Booth out of the burning barn (it had been set afire to force him out) and carried him to the nearby farmhouse porch. There, a few hours later, he died.

Lieutenant-Colonel Everton Conger, the intelligence officer assigned to the unit, removed from Booth's corpse a red velvet pocket diary. It's now displayed in the museum at Ford's Theatre. In its final entry, dated April 21, 1865, Booth protests at being "hunted like a dog" for "doing what Brutus was honored for."

Marcus Junius Brutus was honored (well, by some) for leading the conspiracy in 44 BC to assassinate Julius Caesar. On the Ides of March, two dozen Roman senators stabbed Caesar to death near the entrance to the Theatre of Pompey, convinced that by slaying this tyrant the old Roman republic would be preserved. Liberators all, they violated a human law to fulfill a higher one—the law of pure morality. This, at least, was how they justified their treachery.

How did Booth justify his? His own words damn him as a Confederate sympathizer, a white supremacist who supported slavery. He reviled Lincoln first for issuing the Emancipation Proclamation and then for endorsing the right of former slaves to vote. (Lincoln did the latter in a speech delivered outside the White House, with his enraged soon-to-be assassin in the crowd.) Never did Booth dedicate himself to America's founding proposition, the one restated by Lincoln at Gettysburg, that "all men are created equal."

Booth was, in his own warped thoughts, a shining redeemer—a new Brutus—the patriot who dared to rescue his country by striking down its hated oppressor. Leaping to the stage floor from the box in Ford's Theatre, after he shot the sitting Lincoln in the back of his head, Booth cried *sic semper tyrannis*—"thus always for tyrants"—the words attributed to Brutus as he sank his blade into Caesar's flesh.

But it was not the Brutus of history who most inspired him. Booth took his cues from Shakespeare's *Julius Caesar*, in which the character Brutus—"the noblest Roman of them all," as Mark Antony eulogizes him—claims the mantle of tragic hero. Booth knew the play intimately, having acted Mark Antony at New York's Winter

Garden Theatre in November 1864, sharing the stage with his brothers Edwin and Junius Jr. Edwin, the most gifted tragedian of his time, took the starring role of Brutus. How envious his younger brother must have been, for the Brutus of Shakespeare is moved by ideals, not greed; seeks the common good, not ruinous faction, and when defeat cannot be itself defeated, he falls valiantly on his sword. A plum role for any actor.

Five months passed before Johnny Booth got his chance to act out that coveted part. And although he played it for one night only, his performance has resounded in America's fraught history ever since. For on that unforgettable and infamous April night, a stage killer became a real one.

––––––––––

How befitting, then, that Abraham Lincoln's assassin returned to the theatre from which he came when, nearly a hundred and thirty years later, Stephen Sondheim put him on the stage and gave him a doleful ballad to sing. When Sondheim and librettist John Weidman made the peculiar decision to write a musical about American political assassins (a concept borrowed, with its author's consent, from an unproduced work by composer-lyricist Charles Gilbert Jr.) it wasn't the politics that intrigued them so much as the *drama* of each assassin. What kind of people were they? What sort of lives did they lead? What led them to violence? Above all, what did they hope to accomplish by killing the president of the United States?

Assassins, which had its premiere in December 1990 at Playwrights Horizons (the off-Broadway theatre where *Sunday in the Park with George* was developed), presented itself not as a darkly realist drama—an American tragedy, enacted over and over—but as sheer carnival extravaganza. Bright lights. Bold colors. Calliope music. Keeping sly watch over all this pageantry is the tooth-picking proprietor of the fairground shooting gallery. His slick patter lures the would-be assassins in: "C'mere and kill a President."

One by one, they walk right up to savor their moment in the limelight. John Wilkes Booth pours out his story, until the Balladeer cuts him off. A barbershop quartet sings in tight harmonic praise of the guns held so gently in their hands. Sam Byck, in a tatty Santa Claus costume, rants his monologues into a 1970s tape recorder. John Hinckley, on his guitar, wafts his love to film star Jodie Foster. United, as it were, in divisive purpose, they eventually join voices in a song of disaffection that no one will ever hear played before a baseball game: the *other* national anthem.

The showstopper, though, belongs to one Charles J. Guiteau—author, idealist, and frustrated seeker of the US consulship in Paris. Facing the crowd that has come to watch him hang for killing President James A. Garfield (whose election, by the way, he supported), Guiteau sings a revivalist hymn he composed in his jail cell that very morning. "I am going to the Lordy," he intones so humbly. "Glory hallelujah!" No American audience can resist a repentant sinner.

Then, in a stunning turnaround of style, Guiteau launches into a cakewalk—"Look on the bright side," he exhorts—strutting and high-stepping his way to glory everlasting, up the gallows steps and down. He's gone from being nearly invisible to the killer you can't get enough of. You're almost sorry (all right, you are) when the hangman tightens the noose around Guiteau's neck and slips the black hood over his head. You know you won't get it—but you *want* that encore.

I've asked myself why Sondheim made the assassins so blatantly theatrical—not reluctant or bashful amateurs, but each one a headliner who can ride a laugh or coax a few tears. John Wilkes Booth styled himself America's own Brutus. The audacious Charlie Guiteau really did compose the hymn "I am going to the Lordy" on the day he left this world. All that, and more, testifies to the gigantic narcissism of such characters, their outrageous belief in themselves as pivotal figures in a national epic. Like tough guys playing the "strongman game" at a carnival—swing the mallet down, ring the highest bell—they delight in displays of raw strength.

But really, they exhibit only their weakness. Guiteau sings of going to the Lord and being remembered for saving his country. Is the man deluded? Nobody in his time, or ours, has ever hailed him as America's savior. "They will understand it later," the dying Booth insists. But no one does understand it—or, rather, we understand it only too well—because the Balladeer, the play's voice of history, starts singing a different tune. Each assassin foretells a gain, yet each inherits only the empty wind. Theirs is a fury of performance that signifies nothing, as Shakespeare's Macbeth—one of Booth's favorite acting parts—would ruefully pronounce.

Consider the cakewalk.

Seduced, as I was, by Charlie Guiteau's nerdy charisma, I had let slip from my mind the origins of his showy dance. (Being a theatre academic, I do think about such things.) Though by the 1880s it had become a staple in minstrel acts—performed by both African American and white actors in blackface, and to mostly white audiences—the cakewalk began decades earlier in the antebellum

South. Its name derives from the cake traditionally awarded to the best performer. Plantation slaves devised it to ridicule white slave owners by exaggerating their genteel airs and carefree manner. (Hence the colloquial meaning of a cakewalk: an easy thing to do.) Its signature moves—the prancing, the bowing, the winking, the high steps, and the proud backward tilts—were all meant as fierce, coded mockery, and not craven flattery.

Wrapped up in the mockery, though, was a longing. A longing for the freedom that all white people enjoyed simply because they were white, but then denied to the people that some of them enslaved. We hear, in the cakewalk's eager music, a grasping beyond its reach. We see, in its flashy and frantic steps, a mimicking of what cannot be owned. It's a song-and-dance of doubleness, of having and of not having. Truly, the cakewalk is the dance of outsiders. It belongs, if but symbolically, to all who feel excluded, to all who have been pushed aside, and to all who suffer under the hypocrisy of ruling elites. Yet the moves of that same dance embody a wish to be on the inside. To occupy, not the peripheries, but the absolute center.

I suppose this is the reason why the characters in *Assassins* are such virtuosos. Less to entertain us—although they do—than to exhibit themselves. Yet their self-revealing has an unexpected depth to it. We see, as it were, past the braggart posturing and into the hurt and the wounding and the pain that makes them do the awfulness that they do. Theatre, in the strangest irony, has turned them real.

———————

So real that they call themselves a *family*. But a family whose members are troubled in different ways. Booth vows to kill the man who killed his country. Guiteau wants not to be overlooked. Leon Czolgosz, the exploited laborer who shoots President William McKinley in 1901 at the Pan-American Exhibition in Buffalo, asks why some people get to keep so much when others have so little. Giuseppe Zangara, the Italian immigrant who fails to assassinate President-elect Franklin Delano Roosevelt in 1933, needs someone to blame for his bad health. The sad loser Sam Byck, who plots in 1974 to highjack a plane and crash it into Richard Nixon's White House, longs to be a winner. A year later, Lynette "Squeaky" Fromme and Sara Jane Moore fail on separate occasions to kill President Gerald Ford. Fromme does it out of her slavish devotion to the imprisoned cult leader Charles Manson, while Moore needs to stand out from the crowd. John Hinckley, proving his love for a movie star, comes close to killing President Ronald Reagan.

I've kept all the generations in the present tense because that's how they appear to us in the play. Still alive (as Fromme, Moore, and Hinckley really are, at the time of this writing) and somehow able to slip over, or slink under, the boundaries of place and time. They're not there and then; they're here and now.

Did you notice who's not on my list? It's Lee Harvey Oswald. The last of the nine to appear, he gets the longest scene—eleven whole minutes. In a creepy family reunion held in the Texas School Book Depository, assassins both past and future—ancestors, that is, and their progeny—cajole a hesitant Oswald into aiming his rifle at *their* preferred target. His appearance in the play may be delayed, but he's never actually gone away. He's always been with us. Odds are that someone you have known, or maybe even you yourself, can state exactly where they were when President John F. Kennedy was shot to death in Dallas, Texas, on the afternoon of November 22, 1963. (My father was lunching at a drugstore counter in West

Chester, Pennsylvania. I, being then fourteen months old, was home in nearby Kennett Square, with my mother and toddler sister.)

This family respects some odd traditions. Early on, we see them moving into the classic regimented routine of the Broadway musical: *a chorus line*. All singing. All dancing. All shooting. By the end of "Everybody's Got the Right," their first number, this shuffling ragtag crew has found its footing. Found its plucky voice—"Everybody / Just hold tight / To your dreams." Found, too, its deadly aim. John Wilkes Booth, triggered by the sound of "Hail to the Chief," gets in a quick first shot and wins his marksman's prize.

A chorus line gives pleasure in being identical to itself. Who can tell the Rockettes of Radio City Music Hall apart? Who needs to? Each spangle twinkles like all the others. Each leg is kicked to the same height, and not an inch higher (or worse, lower). And when dozens of toe taps strike the sprung floor, the resulting thunderclaps clap in unison.

To arrange, then, presidential assassins into a chorus line—the opening gambit of Sondheim's music—is to join them up, to blend and blur them, turning the motley many into a singularity. Though in appearance so varied, they are bred from a single stock: outcasts all, orphans each, the left behind, the unwanted, and the forgotten. Stranded on the outside, they can only look resentfully in. Not for nothing do they call themselves "The ones that can't get in / To the ball park."

How well this all-American metaphor names their grievance. For them, the land of opportunity has run out of room. They never had the chance to hit a home run in the ball game of life. Somebody decided that the "right / To be happy"—the right enjoyed, so they protest, by everybody else—does not extend to them.

It should, they insist. Giuseppe Zangara goes to his death in the electric chair vowing in broken English that "Zangara no foreign tool, / Zangara American!" The music disagrees. The bystanders who "saved Roosevelt" sing to a John Philip Sousa march, classic Fourth of July music, while Zangara gets a tarantella—a folk tune from his native Italy, the song of an obvious foreigner. John Hinckley, though a grown man, indulges in the most wholesome of patriotic childhood fantasies: one day, he will be president. Again, the music disagrees. That calculated wrong note in his opening guitar vamp is the sound of a klutz, not a future commander in chief. As the lights fade all around him, Sam Byck spouts bitterly, "I like to be in America." It's the bitterness of an internal exile, a "decent stand-up guy" who's been made homeless in—and *by*—his own homeland. When a character in one Stephen Sondheim musical quotes lyrics from another Stephen Sondheim musical, you sit up and take note. What you note is that Sam Byck doesn't know the words to "America."

Yet there is not, so they swear, a turncoat in their ranks. They *love* America—the ideal, if not always the fact—but America sure hates them. No job. No health. No justice. No fairness. No love. No prize. America has bolted the door against them. Built its fences high. Bid them wait outside the ballpark. All they want—and is it really too much to ask?—is to sit in the stands, cheer on the home team, and sing proudly of that—*their*—star-spangled banner. Apparently, it is too much.

The assassins won't be deterred. With the gritted gumption that America expects—no, demands—from the same people it has kicked aside, the assassins drive the Balladeer clean off the stage. No longer will they be tricked by his bogus claim that if the "mailman won the lottery," they can too. That's just the kind of hearty, but hollow, promise that keeps the downtrodden down. "We'll never see the day arrive," Byck and Czolgosz sneer in unison. Enough with the "prizes all around" bullshit. There are no winners here.

Yet they have won the stage. There's no intrusive Balladeer to garble their story. Theirs, now, are the only voices to be heard. And so, they sing their victory ode—"*another* national anthem"—to give hope to the disheartened, faith to the doubting, and vigor to the weak. It's the only number in *Assassins* that's not an obvious pastiche. For it's meant to be authentically theirs, and theirs alone.

Not that anybody else would choose to sing this odd anthem. Its brisk, optimistic rhythm fails to subdue a dissonant harmony, that underlying note of primal rage—"I want my prize!" Byck wails in pain—that demands to be heard. This disillusioned crew cannot have what they want—America won't ever allow it—so they do what they can. They move, like troops amassing on a battlefield, down to the foot of the stage, readying themselves for attack. "Spread the word . . . We're alive . . . Someone's gonna listen . . . Listen!"

Listen! To the click of a trigger.

———————

History musicals make historians of us all. "Who gets to pick the story?" they ask, and "Who gets to tell it?" Decisive questions, for the picking and the telling never do happen by chance. It didn't happen that way in *Pacific Overtures*, the first Sondheim-Weidman collaboration, and it doesn't happen that way in *Assassins*. (Or, for that matter, in Lin-Manuel Miranda's *Hamilton*.) Somebody on-stage is using their power—and using it for their own purposes—to decide which voices get lifted up, and which quieted down. Which narratives get repeated, and which remaindered. Which folks get statues made of them, and which get none.

John Wilkes Booth, hiding in that Virginia tobacco barn, knows that no statue will ever be raised in his honor—yet, still, he fancies himself a noble hero. That's *his* story. And though he likens himself to Brutus, he acts more like Hamlet: a dying avenger who begs the man beside him to *tell his story*, and so redeem his wounded name. The Balladeer, though, won't play the obliging Horatio to his Hamlet. He won't tell the story, at least not in the way Booth wants. In fact, he turns on the man—"Why *did* you do it, Johnny?"—damning his legacy of blood and treason. He taunts that Booth "killed a country" out of pettiness alone, riled by "bad reviews." "Leave it to history to tell," Booth loftily allows.

"Damn you, Booth!"—that's history's snap judgment, as pronounced by the Balladeer, of the events of April 14, 1865. It is, like every historical judgment, a choice between opposing narratives, rival interpretations, and views beyond all reconciling. It's not the facts that are disputed—Lincoln is dead, and Booth killed him—it's what they *mean*. Is Lincoln's assassination the end of his tyranny, or the birth of a new age of political violence? Is the American Civil War safely over, or will it never end? To write history, even when you write it to a banjo's tune, is to make *your* version of the truth prevail.

The truth for Lincoln's killer is that pulling the trigger was his most consequential act, his most brilliant performance, and the true pinnacle of his life. "Do not let history rob me of its meaning," Booth implores. Later, when he sweet-talks Lee Harvey Oswald into shooting President Kennedy instead of taking his own life, he preys on that young man's same longing for meaning: "All your life you've

wanted to be something, Lee. You're finally going to get your wish."
The others press the point, with John Hinckley, back from the future,
telling Oswald that he alone can make them "a force of history."

Except that the Balladeer shunts that history aside. Flicks it
away, so lightly, like a stale crumb off a table. He stands for *his*
truth: Abraham Lincoln's murder changes nothing. A life is lost,
and that loss is deeply mourned. But the country survives. Sure,
a "madman" may come along now and then—little we can do
about it—but that's no cause to fret. Nobody can "stop the story"
of America, because the "story's pretty strong."

How smoothly the Balladeer makes this point, as if it were only
common sense, the plainest fact of life, as inarguable as the weather.
He looks the wholesome part, too: a trusted neighbor, chewing the
fat with us over the backyard fence. Gosh darn, it's all so folksy.
Yet beware—he's pushing a dangerously false thesis. The Balladeer
wants us to believe, and believe without question, that the work of
political assassins—even the four "successful" ones—is essentially
pointless. It honors no vow, changes no minds, achieves no end.
All that effort, "and it didn't mean a nickel."

Not so fast. There's a part of American culture—the stub-
born and disingenuous part—that responds to certain acts of
violence with an unworried shrug, attributing each new brutal-
ity to the proverbial "one bad apple" who mustn't be allowed to
spoil the whole bunch. The Balladeer sings of a "madman," but
it's the same breed of duplicitous spin. When bad things happen,
so we are endlessly told, we mustn't dwell on them. They are but
hiccups—blips—minor inconveniences. There's no bigger picture
for anyone to see. No larger story for anyone to tell. Nothing, that
is, for anyone to question, let alone change.

That's hoodwinking on a national scale—and *Assassins* won't let us be hoodwinked.

It was bad timing that the show opened during the Persian Gulf War, a war widely popular with Americans at the time. President George H. W. Bush, in response to Saddam Hussein's invasion of Kuwait, led a forty-two-country coalition ("Operation Desert Storm") in a bombing campaign against the aggressor Iraq. The first bombs fell on January 17, 1991, right in the middle of *Assassins*'s run at Playwrights Horizons.

Sondheim, for a while, attributed the show's mixed-to-harsh reviews—and its lack of an immediate Broadway transfer—to the jingoism of the Persian Gulf War. With the first President Bush enjoying a now-inconceivable 90 percent approval rating, few people dared to gush over a musical about killing his predecessors, including the attempted killing of his immediate predecessor a decade earlier. "I'm still angry about it," Sondheim told a group of students in 1994. In later years, though, he softened: "I'm reluctant to assign blame to such things."

Even so, the subsequent decision to delay, and then cancel, the Roundabout Theatre Company's production of *Assassins* because of the 9/11 terrorist attacks—it was meant to start rehearsals the week after—demonstrates how politically charged this show has always been. (The Roundabout's eventual 2004 production won five Tony Awards.) As Sondheim and Weidman put it at the time, *Assassins* demands that its audiences "think critically about . . . the American experience."

In a theatre, though, critical thinking is never abstract. It's inseparable from the characters on the stage, the ones whose journey we have consented, at least for a few hours, to join. What they face, we face. What they feel, we feel. And when they come to a crossroads, we wonder what we would do—keep going, turn, or turn back—if we found ourselves in their place. In short, we bring empathy into the room. Even when that room is the Texas School Book Depository and even when it's being used by eight presidential assassins, plus the one who's about to join them.

How could we fail to show empathy? So dashing is John Wilkes Booth that he nearly pulls off the feat of converting ugly violence into heroic nobility. He would have, too, if Sondheim hadn't made him shout the N-word in anger at the exact moment—"How we gave up the field / But we still wouldn't yield"—that our pity for him peaks. When anarchist Emma Goldman tells factory worker Leon Czolgosz that his "suffering" has made him "fine," that his coarse life has rendered him "beautiful," we see exactly what she sees: a worthy soul brought to ruin's edge by the greed of others.

Humor, too, reels us in. Charlie Guiteau's cakewalk, Sam Byck's tape-recorded harangues, Sara Jane Moore clutching her big bucket of Kentucky Fried Chicken—even the noir drollery of the "Gun Song" quartet—well, they all disarm us. These gunslingers pry the guns of hard-heartedness from *our* hands, stealing them away with their charm, their poignancy, and their easy laughter.

This was, for some of *Assassins*'s first audiences, too risky a move. They feared that empathy for its characters would stretch to endorsement. Or that the merest fellow feeling—acknowledging their plight, their anguish, and their deviant pursuit of justice—would turn into a tacit acceptance of straight-up murder.

Astonishing to think, but *Time* magazine wondered whether

Sondheim envied the show's killers or was just their most obsessive fan. It was obvious (so wrote drama critic Henry A. Miller III) that he wanted to mythologize them. John Simon, in *New York* magazine, cut to the chase and called for somebody to assassinate *Assassins*. When a national publication titles its review "Glimpses of Looniness"—the award goes again to *Time*—you can be sure that its readership includes people so afraid of their country's past that they won't even *try* to understand it. (The issue is not passé. As I write this, Florida has outlawed in its public high schools the Advanced Placement course on African American studies, banning its teenage citizens from learning their own history, while leaving scores of Confederate memorials untouched.)

Confusion is working its worst. So let's be clear about *Assassins*: to understand with empathy why its characters committed their atrocities; to imagine them feeling that they had no other option; and to allow how in their disordered minds they were bringing a better tomorrow a few strides closer—none of this will wash away our collective moral judgment. None of this challenges the Balladeer's correct verdict that Booth *is* a murdering scoundrel, as are Guiteau, Czolgosz, and Oswald; as Hinckley, Fromme, and all the others might have been. Our empathy does not excuse their guilt. Nor, by some evil alchemy, does it transmute their guilt into a gleaming innocence.

What it does is to hold their guilt up to the light—the limelight, the spotlight, even those flashy carnival lights—so that we may scrutinize it all the better. We must look at guilt, not avert our eyes. We must draw it into the day, not leave it in neglected shadow. For guilt, too, tells a story, as the wrongdoer Booth so rightly states. Difficult to tell, and painful to hear—but not, therefore, absurd.

Not meaningless, as people like the Balladeer will always insist. The story of guilt may be dark, but even darkness tells a truth. It tells us how it hurts and what it wants.

————

It has always perplexed me that this musical drawn from the great American songbook—the homeland stylings of Stephen Foster, John Philip Sousa, Scott Joplin, Woody Guthrie, and even the Carpenters—has been branded by some as unpatriotic. As if to dramatize some of the worst moments in American history were in itself an act of betrayal. How could that be? The distinctively native feel to Sondheim's score—recall, the first music we hear is "Hail to the Chief," played on a merry-go-round—presumes a shared identity, invokes a common culture. We are *all* Americans here.

Yet when the president's tune is played at the fairground to the *wrong beat* (it's a forward march, not a turning waltz), the music adds this reproach: America makes some Americans feel out of step and out of tune. Life in America can get so bad that a wayward few will go to horrific extremes to put things right. It's wrong, but it happens, and it happens for a reason. This is what the darkness sings.

Who will listen? Not everybody cares to know that for some folks the American Dream is no dream at all, but a nightmare shell game, or confidence trick, in which losing is the only outcome, no matter how hard they try. Not everybody wants to be reminded of populism's cardinal rule: for some Americans to succeed, others must fail—and "that's by design." There *must* be a cadre of demonized outsiders—whole populations of so-called shirkers, leeches, losers, perverts, and sundry "not real Americans"—to make all those insiders feel positively angelic. Just ask Sam Byck, the unemployed

Philadelphia tire salesman, who cannot find in the entire City of Brotherly Love one single person to share a beer with him.

Sondheim wrote the choral number "Something Just Broke" for the London opening of *Assassins* in 1992 at the Donmar Warehouse. Sam Mendes, the director, urged him to add a song of America in mourning—a "chain of grief," Sondheim called it—depicting the country as it learned the news, from the 1860s through to the 1960s, that the president had been shot. It's performed late in the show, right after the Oswald scene, to grant the audience a reprieve: an interlude of warmth after so much wanton killing. How well it captures the hurried unity that follows every American tragedy—Pearl Harbor, JFK, Columbine, 9/11, Sandy Hook—and how eloquently it insists that death will not win the last word.

Yet alongside the chorus's plea for release from America's never-ending cycle of political violence, I hear an equally heartfelt plea for them to be excused from the obligation to do something about it. I hear a blunt refusal to learn from those tragedies. They're meaningless, after all, just as the Balladeer taught. And I hear, too, the need to put them quickly behind us: "Till it's only something just passed— / Nothing that will last." These lyrics belong to the "Bystanders." It's a damningly apt name, for getting involved has never been their style. How could it be, when there are bedsheets to wash, shoes to shine, and fields to plow? The beige blankness of their clothes signals their persistent wish to evade all notice, to recede into a passive invisibility.

In their song, "broke" carries a double meaning. It's breaking news, of course, that the president has been killed. But the whole country is breaking too—wrenched past its steady shape and brought to the brink of fissure, and then splinter, and then, finally, fracture.

"Fix it up fast," a child among them cries. So fast that nobody has time to stop and think why so much brokenness lies all around.

Part of me wants to share their grief. Another part of me, though, wants to sneer at them (a bit, anyway) and chide them for ignoring all that is going on. But this I cannot do. Because when the Bystanders sing, I ask myself if *I* have ever been a bystander. Of course, I know the answer already: I have. For so long, it's been easy for me not only to look away from others, but also to look upon myself as one of the fairground winners. One for whom winning is so terribly important that someone else's defeat is the bad news that I don't need to hear. And should that news be forced upon me, then I will fix up that intrusion fast.

That's the chastening truth I hear in this show about myself. Now I know why it sets so many people on edge. Not because it says that deep down we're all assassins—that's facile, and *Assassins* isn't facile—but because it says there are assassins still among us, and we just don't care how that came to be.

I have never had a gun pointed in my face. Though if anything could make time stop, I suspect it would be that. I'd be frozen in fear, halted by panic, and utterly powerless to turn that awful scene to its next page. Yet I also imagine that my mind would be focused as never before, connected entirely to the dangerous reality I was trapped in.

"Connect"—that's what the assassins sing at the end, in their reprise of "Everybody's Got the Right." All reprises benefit from a surprise, and this one's got a doozy. On the last refrain, they move in time—nothing near a dance, but still roughly in sync—down to the edge of the stage, as close to the audience as they've ever been. They fall easily into a final chorus line. At the exact moment in the music when any other chorus line would kick its legs high, the nine of them raise, instead, their pistols—and point them in our face.

A passing second, but it feels like a forever. And it feels like the guns are there not to put a stop to things but to let them commence. To incite, and how shocking a way to do it, the connection they have been wanting from us all evening long. Their methods are sinister, no question. Yet there is something utopian, which is to say, also classically American, in their sunbeam belief that all their dreams can still come true. Even if it means forcing somebody else to stare down the barrel of a revolver. But now that they've got our attention, here's what they ask: "How can I turn your love to me?"

11

PASSION

How to Love

Sometime in the 1860s, Giorgio Bachetti, a handsome young captain in the Italian army, is transferred from Milan, where he has been having an affair with the beautiful, but married, Clara, to a remote mountainous outpost. So remote we never learn its name. There he is pursued by Fosca, the sickly and hysterical cousin of Colonel Ricci, his new brigade commander. How Fosca wins—or, you might say, extorts—Giorgio's love, and nearly destroys him in so doing, is the story of *Passion*, the 1994 musical that Sondheim and James Lapine adapted from Ettore Scola's film *Passione d'Amore* (1981). Scola based his own work on Iginio Ugo Tarchetti's epistolary, and quasi-autobiographical, novel *Fosca*, published posthumously in 1869.

Tarchetti was a leading figure in La Scapigliatura, a fraternity of Italian novelists, poets, and painters whose works rejected the illusions, as they saw it, of cheap romance to embrace instead the messy reality of the heart's obsessions. Their name translates as unkempt (literally, "bad hair"), which tells you how little regard—none, actually—they had for bourgeois niceties. Theirs was an aesthetic of the beyond: beyond decorum, beyond obedience, and, above all, beyond guilt. Where such anarchy prevails, neat plots and contrived happy endings are banished for good. No one in this milieu bothers to comb their hair because no one believes in how things look on the surface.

In *Passion*, Giorgio asks Doctor Tambourri what illness afflicts Signora Fosca, the woman he has not yet seen but whose random screams he has heard every day since his arrival. The doctor replies that she is a "medical phenomenon, a collection of many ills." On the morning they do meet, she looks barely alive: wasting away, clutching the backs of chairs for strength, her taut, pallid face and sunken eyes giving her the gruesome look of a death's-head. Yet Fosca will live on, the doctor hints, because she suffers not from diseased flesh but from a tortured psyche. Her body carries the repellent signs of her trauma—as, in her place, anyone's would—but the trauma itself attacks from within.

The military men who live alongside Fosca are civil to her because she is cousin to their regimental officer, in whose house they are all lodged. Among themselves, though, they speak of her rudely: a lunatic, a witch, and so ugly that she shrieks at the mirrored sight of herself. In so reducing Fosca to her symptoms, and in branding her a figure of deviance, they fail to see the real cause of her odd behavior.

Fosca, of course, knows the deeper truth: "No one has ever taught me how to love," as she confides much later to Giorgio. No one, in fact, has ever thought her worthy of love. It's not so much Fosca's looks that make her unlovable—that's merely the surface—as the degrading way that others have treated her. To her cousin, she's a helpless child. To her parents, a burden. To Count Ludovic, the man from her past, she was a dupe to be swindled. But to no one is she "someone to be loved." That no one includes herself. Fosca's torment is that she believes herself to be unlovable. Her tragedy is that she longs, nonetheless, to be loved.

To feel unlovable is to feel shame in its severest form. To feel the ultimate exclusion, being denied the common joys of life. It's not that we haven't yet found the right person (as well-meaning, but misguided, friends will doubtless say) but that there's no right person for us to find. No one out there will accept the wrongness that is, or so we might believe, intrinsically ours. We are wrong by nature, defective to our core, and marred by all that is integral to our being—such is the lie that we mistake for the truth.

Into my early adulthood, I carried the shame of being gay, the shame of living in a permanently injured body, and the shame of being, so my own family told me, not always a nice person. I hope that I have since then replaced my shame with pride and rejected my self-loathing in favor of a healthy self-regard. But for quite a long time I did feel that I had been pushed beyond love's reach. So ingrained had this feeling become that I stopped questioning it, and just accepted it as a character trait—as much a part of me as my green eyes, my left-handedness, or my slightly twisted right leg.

I was tempted, in writing these words, to insert here a witty, self-deprecating remark. A little jest to lighten the mood. But I decided to keep my nerve and press on, not wanting either of us to be diverted from what *Passion* asks us to confront. If anything, the pain that I endured—a pain that is all too widespread—has made me more alert to the suffering of others. I nod in recognition when Fosca tells Giorgio, "Sickness is as normal to me, as health is to you."

———

Often, those who feel unlovable will protect themselves by rejecting their own desire for love. They shrug it off, and act—for it is *only* an act—as if they have made peace with life as an emotional outcast.

This makes, as I know from my own life, a certain sense. Why value what you can't have? It will only bring you misery.

Such is Fosca's tactic when she gives back to Giorgio the novel by Rousseau that he lent to her. In her first song ("I Read"), she declares to him, as if without lament, that she has measured the "limits of [her] dreams" and does not "cling to things [she] cannot keep." Reconciled, so she affects, to a life estranged from the reality of love, she can only listen for its "echoes" in "other people's lives." Not actual others, though, but the characters in those novels she reads. How preferable fiction feels to her when real people offer only their pity—"passive love . . . dead love," as Fosca coldly puts it.

Yet there's something about Giorgio—she felt it at once, watching him in secret from her window—that gives Fosca new hope. Maybe it's how he sees the beauty of a single flower. That's odd, she reflects, for a military man. But this one prefers gardens to battlefields. And though his comrades talk mostly of their horses, he expounds on literature and lofty ideals. He's so different from them, and, in that difference, so like her: "They hear drums, / You hear music, / As do I."

Fosca, having found an emotional lifeline in Giorgio, grips it tightly and does not let go. No longer forswearing love, she now pursues it. No longer holding back, she now races forward. And instead of apathy, she exhibits only the fiercest resolve. She will, no matter the cost, have him. Suddenly there is *passion*.

Fosca's passion is not, though, what you would call love. She begs Giorgio to understand her and be her friend—but she has no reciprocal intent toward him. She wants only to subdue Giorgio, to bend him to her will, and to coerce him into love. So desperate is Fosca for his love that she will abase herself to gain it. She will kiss Giorgio's hand, throw herself at his feet, slip a letter under his dinner napkin, and fall to pieces in public—"What does it matter if they see me?"—so long as the scene ends with Giorgio carrying her home in his arms.

But if needed, she can play the aggressor too. Fosca implores Giorgio to write to her during his brief visit to Milan, for she must be every day in his thoughts. She stalks him—trails him to the secluded spot where he has gone to read a love letter from Clara—and then collapses at his feet, daring him to ignore the sorry sight of her.

For a time, she withdraws. Not in defeat, though, but in tactical strength: to plot her most audacious move. From her sickbed, Fosca summons Giorgio, who believes she is near death, and entreats him to write a love letter to *her*. She dictates the tender words—"For now I'm seeing love / Like none I've ever known"—that Giorgio grudgingly commits to paper as if they were his own. A love letter is something to be cherished, for it speaks the truth of its writer's open heart. Nothing so honest is happening here. Sondheim, in writing Fosca's song ("I Wish I Could Forget You," the letter's first line), took care to give it "neat rhymes" and "regular rhythms." Why? To show the letter's dictated fakery, and the crafty menace behind it. Count Ludovic was right about Fosca: "You are not quite the victim you appear."

———————

I can hardly blame Fosca for her schemes. Love is a primal human need, as essential to our well-being as food or shelter. A life crowded with love is a fulfilled life, a flourishing life, the kind to which we all aspire. Yet with Fosca—as with anyone who feels unworthy of love—this natural desire gets warped, and ultimately defeats itself.

Fosca doesn't want an honest relationship with Giorgio: no true lover extorts a love letter. What she wants is to be released from the prison of self-hatred. Fosca must prove to herself that she's not the despicable figure the world takes her to be. Yet what is more despicable than coercing another's love?

The first audiences for *Passion* loathed Fosca as much as she loathed herself. So creepy, so vile, and so wholly grotesque that to pity her was an impossibility. Yet instead of cursing this monster, they ridiculed her. Even in the stillness of the train scene, the audience jeered at Fosca, leaving actor Donna Murphy in tears as she left the stage. And earlier, when it seemed that Giorgio would abandon Fosca after she fainted on the ground, a few spectators actually applauded. This was hardly the response that anyone in the show wanted. Be angry with Fosca. Be shocked by her. Be disgusted, even. But take her seriously.

During the previews, Sondheim and Lapine noted whenever the audience scoffed or laughed at Fosca. In each of those scenes, they altered a word, or adjusted a light cue, to soften its tone—and thus keep the audience from spoiling the desired dramatic effect. Their fine-tuning worked. When *Passion* opened at the Plymouth (now Gerald Schoenfeld) Theatre on May 9, 1994, the unwanted laughter was gone.

Still, Fosca remains a challenging character. That audiences have stopped laughing at her doesn't mean they have started loving her. Not, at least, until she dies, when her outbursts can be forgiven, and when her love can live quietly on in the more likable Giorgio. I doubt that our wariness toward Fosca will erode, but for a reason that hardly discredits the score, the libretto, or any particular staging. What we find so troubling about this character—how she depletes the emotions of others, how she extorts love at any cost, and how she demeans herself in one moment only to pounce savagely in the next—may be an unwelcome image of the trouble with us. Sondheim put it pithily: "we are all Fosca."

The *New York Times* critic David Richards was on to something in his review of the original production when he observed that Fosca was so "lonely" that sometimes you had to "look away" from her. If we turn away from Fosca, it's because to look at her—"Look at me. / No, Captain, look at me"—is to look also at ourselves. And if we do look at ourselves, look unsparingly at ourselves, then we may have to admit that some part of us *does* feel unlovable. That some residual shame still attaches itself to us. If we find ourselves, as many theatregoers have, in a hurry to despise Fosca, or in a rush to ridicule her, it might be because we are slow to accept what we find contemptible about us. Not, of course, that we really are contemptible, but that we sometimes do feel that way.

———

This is not, though, how the story ends. If poor judgment were Fosca's only character flaw—all decorum flouted, though with nerve more than style—she would have little hold upon us. We might show our dismay. Or be moved to pity. But we would not, certainly not, get involved. As for the notion that one day we will "see what is beautiful" in her—well, that's as absurd as her own jealous intrigues.

The absurdity ends in the train scene. Giorgio, stricken with illness, and granted forty days' leave, is traveling back to Milan, back to Clara, and back, so he hopes, to good health. In any case, he's headed *away* from Fosca. He sits alone in a train carriage, the blanket wrapped so tightly around him doing little to ease his feverish chills. Just as the whistle blows, and the train pulls away from the track, Fosca appears. The suitcase she carries is an alarming sign: for Giorgio there is no escape from Fosca, other than the death to which she has been hounding him ever since he made the mistake of lending her that novel by Rousseau.

Giorgio is furious, but there is no showdown. No fiery clash erupts between these combatants. He is, of course, too weak to attack. Yet Fosca does not press her advantage. "I'll keep my distance," she offers quietly; "stay out of your path." Her meekness is of a new sort. Instead of a well-rehearsed timidity—Fosca has always been a gifted actor—we see a sincere resolve to accept her fate. And fate has ruled that Fosca must love Giorgio. Love him utterly, without hope of requital, and without care for consequence. For in loving him, she begins to love herself.

Can it be true? A Fosca who gives, but takes nothing in return. A Fosca who keeps to her place. A Fosca who makes no fuss. After everything we've witnessed—recall, she has stalked Giorgio, timing her unwanted entrance down to the last second—it hardly seems credible. "But if Fosca doesn't learn something more from all of this," as Donna Murphy said, "we have a problem."

The problem gets solved in "Loving You," Fosca's remarkable ode to self-possession. She stops fighting with the world and starts to make peace with herself. Never has Fosca looked so settled, acted so poised, or behaved so gently. Hers is no weak surrender to the inevitable. While Fosca does not choose to love Giorgio, she *does* choose to accept that loving him is the purpose of her life. Loving him, even though he does not love her. Fosca, for the first time, accepts this dismaying truth. She has pursued him, but not to create a scene. She will explain herself, but not insist on being understood. She will keep watch over her beloved, but from a distance if need be. In making these choices, Fosca has set herself on the road to her own recovery—already, her symptoms are in retreat—the path back to a wellness that she feared never to reclaim.

Her song is plainly honest. It's too short, just thirty-two bars, to enable plotted deceit. There's no musical "release," because Fosca doesn't change her mind. For her, there is no epiphany in the song. She proceeds, rather, with a sober dignity through its unhurried procession of quarter notes. There's a key change, but it modulates *down*—because, as Sondheim explained, Fosca is not so much rejoicing over her fate as accepting it.

Her obsession motif ("I do not read to think," from her first song) is here reprised, but with new words that give a becalming nobility to her once-unruly passions: "This is why I live. / You are why I live." It echoes one final time in a soft clarinet solo, a lingering solemnity to dispel from our minds any memory of hysteria or chaos. If we trust to the music, we can hear the healing in it.

I believe Fosca when she vows to "live" for Giorgio. I also believe her when she pledges to "die" for him. Which, soon enough, she does. But not before learning from Giorgio the truth that she *is* "someone to be loved." It's reflected back to her in her lover's eyes and returned to her in his most tender kiss—but still, Fosca had to learn it for herself. "In the end," she predicts to Giorgio on the train, "you'll finally see what is beautiful about me." He finally does see it, but only because she has seen it first.

We, too, have to see it for ourselves. If we never catch sight of all that is beautiful in us, then neither will anyone else. If we never claim what is lovable about us, then nobody else ever can. And if we cannot say *this* is why we live, then we will not have a life.

———————

This least ironic of Sondheim's musicals—in *Passion*, the characters do nothing but tell you who they are—opens, nonetheless, with irony: a love duet that unravels the more ardently it is sung. Clara straddles Giorgio in bed, her orgasm so intense that the orchestra must carry its elongated cry. She shudders, and sinks back into her lover's cradling arms. A moment of sweet languor passes. Still naked, still in bed, and their sweaty bodies still entangled, Clara and Giorgio begin to sing as all new lovers do: their love is unique, beyond compare, a "happiness / No one really knows."

Such a scene, in a more traditional musical, would be the last one, for nothing announces *finis* so categorically as the triumph of true love. But here the story has only begun, and begun in a most bothersome way. The love that unites the lovers is, at the peak of its ecstatic voicing, called into doubt. Was it "inevitable," or only a fluke, that they "glanced / At each other in the park"? Do they really feel "more"? Or is their passion "just another love story"? They lie so still, but their anxious thoughts are up and about, disturbing the scene.

Giorgio shifts the mood first, telling Clara that he must leave Milan in five days to join the Fourth Brigade. Chilled by his news, she covers her nakedness, rises from the bed, and pulls back the sheltering curtains. Strong daylight pierces their privacy—it's afternoon already—filling it at once with worldly demands: he must get back to the barracks, she to her husband and son. Clara, it turns out, is another man's wife, beside—and astride—her young lover in stolen hours only, and never beyond the confines of the bedchamber that allows their dalliance and conceals it too. How, when their own lives forbid it, can they sing of happiness?

Though he looks the virile part, Giorgio is not a generous lover. He offers his body to Clara, but he *takes* from her so much more—her pity, her care, and even her marriage vow. Nor will he grant her the safe boundary, which she seeks, of an ordinary love affair: the tacit acceptance that their whispered promises are only make-believe, a little charade to be acted in their little room. Giorgio, at his new posting, tries to sustain their passion in letters—"We'll make love with our words"—forgetting that theirs is a union of bodies, not of souls or even minds.

Clara does her epistolary best, but there's little about letters to keep her satisfied. Still less once Giorgio starts to write about Signora Fosca, the bizarre woman who has somehow intruded into their secret correspondence. It's evident, though not to Giorgio, that Clara is backing away when in one of her letters she encases a gray hair freshly plucked from her head. Her tone is jovial, but her message brings no cheer. When your lover sends you a discouraging token of her age—instead of a racy red ribbon snipped from her garter—it's over between you. So much for the happiness that no one has ever known.

By now the audience has pushed ahead of Giorgio, for we can see that he is fooling himself about love. He doesn't know what love is, and Clara isn't the one to tell him. If anything, she has taught him, and taught him by her own example, how to perform a wild passion on cue. How to tame its recklessness, temper its risk, and squash its exuberance into a "practical arrangement . . . scheduled in advance." That's a valuable lesson in a bourgeois society like theirs, where no limits are set on what is covertly permissible so long as no one gets humiliated out in the open.

————————

Yet being humiliated is the necessary sacrifice of ego without which love cannot be secured. This much is Giorgio's lesson to learn, and the slow painful learning of it forms his story. If Fosca needs to value herself more highly, then Giorgio needs to keep his self-esteem in check. More than a whiff of naive narcissism clings to this young man. Not just in the ennobling purity (so he fancies it) of his love for Clara, but also, and more cruelly, in the insipid counsel he imparts to Fosca—"look to life for whatever pleasures it can offer"—as if her troubles arose from a mere failure to be amused. She rebukes his callousness: "I thought you'd understand."

So begins Giorgio's tutorial in how to love. It proceeds oddly, but then the tutor is herself an oddity. Finding the perfect moment to sit her pupil down, she instructs Giorgio to copy out the words that he must learn—and never was this idiom more fitting—by heart. This is the love letter from him to her, its fraudulent sentences dictated by Fosca herself.

Fosca's conniving need for love is fully indulged here. But that's only half the story. The other half, and it is equally revealing, is that Giorgio—almost against his will—learns how a true lover feels and what a true lover says. He learns it by watching Fosca perform that role, using her own speech as her script. Giorgio comes to know what love is by copying, and then reciting, someone else's words on the subject. He learns, as we all first learn, by imitating.

To imitate is to take up within yourself the thoughts or feelings of someone else. The point is not to inhabit another's character but to expand your own. This is precisely what happens to Giorgio. Later, he refuses to tell the colonel, who misconstrues the love letter as evidence of Giorgio's dishonor, that Fosca coerced him into writing it. He is content to be known as its author. More, he reprises the letter with a profound sincerity—"Your love will live in me"—when a ghostly vision of Fosca appears to him in the last scene. Words that once felt to him like a curse he now pledges as his heart's own truth.

Jere Shea, the original Giorgio, felt that his character's turning point, when he first absorbs a part of Fosca into himself, was the scene in the bedroom with the love letter. After Giorgio writes, and then signs, the false missive, Fosca demands from him a kiss, which Shea likened to a "virus" or a "vampire kiss." The similes are apt. Fosca, in her own way, infects Giorgio, planting deep inside his mind some essence of herself strong enough to overpower his defenses. Though its symptoms are harsh—poor Giorgio, so weak, so feverish, so dreadfully reduced in body and spirit—his illness is not fatal. Indeed, it proves fertile, giving life to a man who was, without knowing it, already half dead. Fosca infects Giorgio, as Sondheim realized when he first saw Ettore Scola's film, not with poison—but with love.

His slow recovery begins in the train scene. At first Giorgio is determined that Fosca must give him up. Yet as he listens to her quiet profession of love (whispers reach a depth that screams never can), he grasps the fuller truth that love, to *be* love, must be unyielding and absolute. This gift will not let itself be rescinded. Nor is the offering of it meant to elicit a favorable exchange. Love seeks nothing but its own expression.

When Giorgio, ill though he is, puts his blanket around Fosca, and then returns with her to the colonel's house, instead of journeying to Milan as planned, he is not merely trading Clara for Fosca. These women are no longer rivals because rivals must be fairly matched. Yet now, the choice between them could hardly be starker—or easier to make. Clara, in her letter, asks Giorgio to "wait" for her love. Wait for what? If you are prepared to defer your love until a more opportune moment, then you are not actually in love. You are in business—which is not wrong, but it's not love either. Giorgio's response to Clara is bitter and biting: "Is this what you call love?"—the same question he used once to harangue Fosca, angered by her obsessive pursuit of him.

Yet anger is now the opposite of what he feels toward her, this woman who has taught him that "Love within reason—that isn't love." In his short, but revelatory, final solo ("No One Has Ever Loved Me"), Giorgio defines love largely by what it is not: "not pretty or safe or easy." This must be the least mawkish love song ever written, and therein lie both its candor and its force. Sondheim grants us neither clever wordplay nor internal rhymes to divert our ears. Nothing in this song permits us even for a moment to step outside it. There is for us no evading what has happened to Giorgio: his gradual, grateful surrendering of every last illusion about love. The moral? When you find yourself assailed by love, battered by its hardness—for softness, as we know by now, is alien to the truest love—do not fight it. Or fear it. Or wish it away. Just accept it. And in accepting it, be ever mindful that the person loving you has no choice.

Giorgio vows in the final scene that Fosca's love will live in him. The story is ending now, but a future is being promised. It's a serious promise—and a serious future—because this lyric is shared first with

Fosca and then taken up by the entire company, sung eleven times as the play's last words. The music is Fosca's obsession motif, those six notes that have haunted us all evening long, but which now are sung with the hushed tenderness of a lover's last vow. Take heart, departing one, for "your love will live in me."

This is no platitude. Giorgio promises not that he will keep alive the memory of Fosca's love for him—though he will, of course—but that the *love itself* will endure, "as permanent as death, / Implacable as stone." Endure, but how? The permanency of Fosca's love will show itself mostly in its effects: what it changes, what it brings about, the difference it makes. Love, having infected Giorgio, now enlarges his perception of the world. Just as he helps Fosca to know that she is "someone to be loved," she helps him to know that he is someone who *can* love. Giorgio thought, wrongly, that he understood what love was; but now, seeing "in a different light," he finally does.

Fosca restores Giorgio to life at the cost of losing hers. Yet in losing it, she finds it. Fosca dies *into* her life, fully and lovingly, not away from it, a cowering victim of fear and shame. She leads Giorgio to her bed, which is also for her a grave, knowing that "to die loved is to have lived."

———

Sondheim was curt in his response if you told him that Fosca behaved so outrageously that she could never be your role model. Who, he would retort, said she should be? *Passion* does not "laud" her stalking, smothering love for Giorgio, he would explain, nor does it urge the audience to "emulate" her. No one is asking us to pattern our life after Fosca's. What an absurd request that would be.

But the play does invite us to heed her life—attend *her* tale, and Giorgio's too. Because there's something in those lives that might emerge, or has already, in our lives. Perhaps it's the need to surmount a learned shame, the toxic falsehood that our very identity has forced us beyond love's embrace. Or maybe it's that we've drunk the elixir of love too deeply, savoring its fabled sweetness but forgetting that its effects are but a hypnotic charade. Not by chance does the first regimental officer we meet launch straight into an aria from Donizetti's *L'elisir d'amore*. In whatever way *Passion* infects us, it's going to reveal, through the responses it provokes, a reality that we have yet to confront fully. We may, of course, resist the disclosure—that, too, is a response—confident that the truth is hardly what we need.

Sondheim will not let us hide from the truth. And in *Passion*, where could we possibly hide? Not in dramatic ironies. There are none after the first scene. Not in applauded musical "numbers." None of those either. And, most assuredly, not in the charm of its lead characters. These usual safe harbors of musical theatre are strictly off-limits to us. Sondheim, with a defiance that would make the novelist Tarchetti proud, dares us to grapple with this story; a story so outrageous, doing such violence to all propriety, that no tidy bargain can be made with it. Either we plunge headlong into this story, or we stand well clear.

But if we *are* in the story—if, like Giorgio, we get drawn in—there is much for us to ponder. Are we willing to lose our dignity to at last find ourselves? Will we hazard ruin if it restores us to wholeness? Can we drop our attachments long enough to figure out if they are worth being attached to? That's what it will take for us to come out the other side of our torments and to know that we are someone to be loved.

EXIT MUSIC

Here We Are

It feels only right to give the last word to Sondheim's last work.

More than a decade after he and playwright David Ives decided to write a musical inspired by two Luis Buñuel films, *Here We Are* had its premiere in September 2023 at the five-hundred-seat Griffin Theatre in The Shed, an arts center in the hyperdeveloped Hudson Yards district of mid-Manhattan. Directed by Joe Mantello, and with a dream cast including Tracie Bennett, Bobby Cannavale, Rachel Bay Jones, Denis O'Hare, and David Hyde Pierce. *Here We Are* extended its run through late January 2024.

Rich in song and humor, the first act ("The Road") is based on Buñuel's *The Discreet Charm of the Bourgeoisie* (1972). As in that surrealist film, some affluent friends—here, a hedge fund tycoon, a talent agent, a plastic surgeon, and an interior decorator—take to the road to do what seems easy but turns out to be hard: find somewhere to eat. Each venue they visit fails to offer the merest morsel of a meal. Not even the promisingly named Café Everything can whip up a basic weekend brunch. The distraught waiter, played to perfection by O'Hare, brings only his apologies to their table. They try a trendy French bistro next. Tracie Bennett, channeling the spirits of both Édith Piaf and Jean-Paul Sartre, plays a server who'd rather wail torch song philosophy than wait on tables.

Salvation arrives at the last moment, when one of the friends—a suave, swarthy ambassador—takes everybody back to his embassy for a grand feast.

In the second act ("The Room"), which recalls Buñuel's *The Exterminating Angel* (1962), the dining room is transformed into a panic room, a veritable doomsday bunker, as the overprivileged few seek refuge from the anarchists amassing outside the door. There's a twist, but I won't spoil things for you. As their confinement drags on, the rich become the poor: water taps run dry, food runs out, and toilets won't flush. Matters turn so dire that a Ming vase is repurposed as a piss pot.

The grand piano in the middle of the room suddenly stops playing. Strike its keys all you like, but it won't make music. The silence is oddly resonant: a warning of the impending apocalypse, perhaps; or maybe it's a metaphor for how the upper crust have been brought low, denied all their customary amenities. Such readings do reinforce the show's critique of hoarded wealth and unshared power. Yet a far more poignant symbolism is all too obvious: we have heard the last of Sondheim's music. (*Here We Are* opened nearly two years after his death.) The piano is silent because nothing more from him—nothing more that is *new*—will ever be played upon it. This may not be what either the director or the librettist intended, but it's certainly how it feels to the audience.

I will always be grateful that I saw the first production of *Here We Are*. Being there was unlike any other evening that I've had in more than forty years of theatregoing. It felt, not like another night out, but more like an occasion: a farewell to Sondheim himself. It was impossible for the audience not to mark that moment, and, indeed, that's why many of us were there. As I watched the production from my seat in the fifth row, what stayed uppermost in my mind was not its satire of a moneyed coterie, not its stellar performances and smart direction, and not even the bounce of Sondheim's music and the snap of his lyrics. What preoccupied me was the silence of that piano—a silence echoed, as it were, in the near-total lack of songs in the second act. In Sondheim's last musical, the music stops in more ways than one.

David Ives and Joe Mantello, the show's surviving creators, regard *Here We Are* as a completed theatrical work. Its musical imbalance, as they told Frank Rich in a lengthy interview for *New York* magazine, was not because Sondheim had failed to finish all the songs. It was, rather, because the second act didn't need more songs. It would be strange, Mantello elaborated, if characters "trapped in a room" behaved in a standard "musical-theater way." So, in the spring of 2021—a low point in the show's long genesis—he told Sondheim, who had completed the score for the first act, not to write any more music. And he didn't.

Sondheim's own remarks on a decade of working, sporadically, on *Here We Are* add some intriguing nuance to the story. For him, the songwriting was agony. Worse than Sondheim's habitual procrastination were the new challenges of his physical frailty and decreased stamina. The intransigence of Buñuel's material (how do you write songs for rich people stuck inside a mansion?) only aggravated the problem. "I'm having a lot of trouble," Sondheim hinted to journalist D. T. Max in March 2019, the month he turned eighty-nine. "Too depressing to talk about . . . a combination of Buñuel and age."

It's open to debate whether *Here We Are* needs (or doesn't need) more songs in the second act. Sondheim fans will probably never stop wrangling over that question. What seems clearer, though, is that Sondheim didn't want to provide any more music, even if he sometimes acted otherwise. He "wants to seem to be writing a musical," Ives explained to Mantello in an email from May 2020, "but doesn't want to actually write a musical." It's not hard to imagine that Sondheim decided for himself that it was time to stop, and so, he stopped. Mantello justified it later in dramatic terms—the second act doesn't require songs—but still, the stopping came first.

Visual artists call it *non finito*, the "not finished." Think of those Michelangelo figures who are both emerging from and falling back into the huge marble blocks from which they were sculpted. Or Leonardo da Vinci's sketches that come to a halt, as if the artist put down his red chalk and resolved not to pick it up again. *His* decision, and not that of circumstance or fate. Jasper Johns, in his 1971 lithograph of a concentric circular target, makes the point explicitly. The thin brittle paintbrush and the three dried cakes of watercolor paint set underneath the image testify to what will *not* happen—no color will be added, ever, to the black and white. *Here We Are* is a perfect theatrical *non finito*: not finished, and that's by design.

When an artist leaves a work *unfinished*—incomplete, partial, still in progress—we regard it as a misfortune. We mourn the absence of what ought to be there but never will be. We feel differently, though, when an artist chooses not to finish what has been started. The artist steps back from their creation, pronounces it good—good, just as it is—and calls it a day. That's an affirmative stance, not a regrettable shortcoming. Whether it's a Michelangelo statue, a Leonardo sketch, or the last Stephen Sondheim musical, such works of art move us to reflect on how something can be *final* and yet also *not finished*.

But then, doesn't that describe life itself? Life, as we live it, feels unalterably final: no chance for anybody to repeat a single moment of it. Our existence is not, after all, a rehearsal. And yet our life can likewise feel to us not finished—the roads we won't ever take, the heights we won't ever climb, the words we won't ever speak, and the dreams we won't ever dare. Not even if we overtook Methuselah in age could we hope to finish the story of our life, let alone to go back and rewrite it, because there would always be yet another part of our story waiting to be completed.

Our task, then, is not so much to fix our life as to *have* a life. Being present to our own life means not getting distracted by the illusion that we could solve all of life's riddles if only we worked a bit harder. Tempting, but a fool's errand. How much wiser to bear witness to all that is unresolvable in our days, all that is vexing and perplexing about others, and all that is flawed in ourselves, admitting (even if sometimes we pretend not to) that things will likely remain that way. Life is less about solving the puzzle—remember, Sondheim *dismantled* his Japanese puzzle boxes—than putting up with the puzzlement. Being alive means accepting that the wild, wondrous mystery of ourselves won't ever be fully revealed: not to the world, not to old friends, and not even to us.

Yet here we are.

ACKNOWLEDGMENTS

It was the "old friends" who got me through it. I could not have written this book without the care, support, and encouragement of Dorothy and Roger Baxter, James Davies, Paul Ewing, James Finegold, Jean Gilson, Daniel Grimley, Michael Hazlett, Erika Lin, Joseph Lordi, Eric Martin, Mike Mathews, Mark McGrath, Lee Anne and Dan Pierce, Liz Robelen, Sally Smith, Tiffany Stern, and Jack Wieland. I thank especially those friends who offered me the gift of their time—and their wisdom—by reading and critiquing the first draft: Lou Bayard, Cynthia Burns Coogan, Jonathan Dyson, Daniel Pollack-Pelzner, and Joe Roach. I will always be grateful to Joe for his many kindnesses, his collegial example, and his unerring expert guidance.

David Forrer at Inkwell Management has been enthusiastic about this book from the time it existed as a mere two sentences in an email. I am fortunate indeed to have him as my literary agent and I thank him for his wholehearted belief in me. My good fortune has continued at Atria Books, where Peter Borland has been the best of editors—strong in championing the book with his colleagues but gentle in helping the author to improve it. I thank Sean deLone, Peter's associate, and an Atria Books editor in his own right, for keeping things on track. I am grateful to Dayna Johnson and Gena Lanzi for their commitment to promoting and publicizing this book. Thanks are also due to Tom Pitoniak for his eagle-eyed copyediting. Giovanna Pugliese at the New York Public Library made it surprisingly easy to obtain nearly all of the book's photographs. For that one elusive image, I thank Mike Markiewicz at ArenaPAL in London.

At Queen's University Belfast I have the privilege of teaching and writing about musical theatre, and Sondheim especially. I thank the university for supporting this book and I thank my students for inspiring me.

Finally, I acknowledge with respect, gratitude, and affection this book's dedicatee, Paul McCarren, SJ. How right Sondheim was to call teaching a "sacred profession." Paul has been my teacher for more than forty years now, first in his acting classes at Georgetown University and then as a trusted friend. In teaching me all about the theatre, he has, of course, taught me all about life.

NOTES

Overture

xiv *unmade bed* Bradley Whitford, video interview, *Variety*, February 3, 2022.

xiv *first-rate work* Steven Levenson, *tick, tick . . . Boom!*, screenplay (2021), 97.

xv *give us more to see* Stephen Sondheim and James Lapine, *Sunday in the Park with George* (New York: Applause Books, 1991), 171.

xvi *our own lives* Isaac Butler, "Stephen Sondheim Solved the Puzzle to Being Alive," *Slate*, November 27, 2021.

xviii *know things now* Stephen Sondheim and James Lapine, *Into the Woods* (New York: Theatre Communications Group, 1989), 35.

xix *his own lyrics* See Sondheim's comments on *West Side Story* in D. T. Max, *Finale: Late Conversations with Stephen Sondheim* (New York: Harper, 2021), 75.

Introduction: The Song Is You

1 *sacred profession* Sondheim calls teaching a "sacred profession" in his taped interview for the Roundabout Theatre's 2010 production of *Sondheim on Sondheim*, a musical revue conceived and directed by James Lapine.

1 *spreading it around* Arthur Laurents and Stephen Sondheim, *Gypsy: A Musical* (New York: Theatre Communications Group, 1994), 104.

2 *pause for a mo'* James Goldman and Stephen Sondheim, *Follies* (1971; New York: Theatre Communications Group, 2001), 70.

2 *exasperating musical comedy* Walter Kerr, *Herald Tribune*, March 19, 1964.

3 *entertainment* Howard Taubman, *New York Times*, April 6, 1964.

NOTES

3 *my name on a flop* Sondheim, quoted in Craig Zadan, *Sondheim & Co.* (New York: Macmillan, 1974), 95.

4 *one of the most irritating* See Stephen Sondheim, *Finishing the Hat: Collected Lyrics (1954–81)* (New York: Knopf, 2010), 111.

4 *being made asses of* Angela Lansbury, quoted in Zadan, *Sondheim & Co.*, 95.

6 *Group 1, Group A* Arthur Laurents and Stephen Sondheim, *Anyone Can Whistle: A Musical Fable* (New York: Random House, 1965), 52, 53.

6 *Who is what?* Laurents and Sondheim, *Anyone Can Whistle*, 78.

6 *You are all mad* Laurents and Sondheim, *Anyone Can Whistle*, 80.

6 *circus music* Laurents and Sondheim, *Anyone Can Whistle*, 80.

7 *Happy and successful* Laurents and Sondheim, *Anyone Can Whistle*, 24.

8 *You must now go home* Jean Genet, *The Balcony*, trans. Bernard Frechtman (London: Faber & Faber, 1966), 96. For the comparison between Genet and Sondheim, I am indebted to David Savran and Daniel Gundlach, "*Anyone Can Whistle* as Experimental Theatre," in *The Oxford Handbook of Sondheim Studies*, ed. Robert Gordon (Oxford: Oxford University Press, 2014), 82–84.

8 *smart-ass* Sondheim, *Finishing the Hat*, 125.

Gypsy: How to Be Who You Are

11 *best, last* Sondheim, *Finishing the Hat*, 57.

12 *you'll never get away from me* Laurents and Sondheim, *Gypsy*, 30.

12 *born too soon* Laurents and Sondheim, *Gypsy*, 104.

14 *playing bingo and paying rent* Laurents and Sondheim, *Gypsy*, 12.

14 *get up and get out* Laurents and Sondheim, *Gypsy*, 12.

15 *all the things that I gotta be yet* Laurents and Sondheim, *Gypsy*, 12.

15 *tough . . . for a singer* See Sondheim, *Finishing the Hat*, 59.

15 *I'll be damned* Laurents and Sondheim, *Gypsy*, 10.

17 *sense of selfhood* On the effect of a parent's unlived life on a child, see Robert A. Johnson and Jerry M. Ruhl, *Living Your Unlived Life* (New York: Tarcher Press, 2007).

17 *As long as we have this act* Laurents and Sondheim, *Gypsy*, 24.

19 *right there* Laurents and Sondheim, *Gypsy*, 27.

19 *I wonder how old I am* Laurents and Sondheim, *Gypsy*, 27.

20 *It's a terrible act* Laurents and Sondheim, *Gypsy*, 47.

20 *six turtles, as private as private can be* Laurents and Sondheim, *Gypsy*, 48.

23 *Momma . . . I'm pretty* Laurents and Sondheim, *Gypsy*, 94.

23 *And if you're real good* Laurents and Sondheim, *Gypsy*, 95.

24 *To be a stripper* Laurents and Sondheim, *Gypsy*, 82.

24 *I didn't have to sing or dance* Gypsy Rose Lee, *Gypsy: A Memoir* (1957; Berkeley, CA: Frog, 1999), 231.

24 *I am Gypsy Rose Lee* Laurents and Sondheim, *Gypsy*, 100.

24 *MAY YOUR BARE ASS* Eleanor Roosevelt, telegram, Gypsy Rose Lee papers, Series I, Box 6, Folder 8, Billy Rose Theatre Collection, The New York Public Library for the Performing Arts, New York City.

25 *for the first time* Laurents and Sondheim, *Gypsy*, 101.

26 *I guess I did do it for me* Laurents and Sondheim, *Gypsy*, 107.

Company: How to Get Close

31 *paucity of connection* Olivia Laing, *The Lonely City: Adventures in the Art of Being Alone* (London: Canongate, 2016), 3–4.

31 *city of strangers* Stephen Sondheim and George Furth, *Company: A Musical Comedy* (1970; New York: Theatre Communications Group, 1996), 54.

31 *off of the train* Sondheim and Furth, *Company*, 54.

31 *shall we let it go?* Sondheim and Furth, *Company*, 54.

31 *rusty fountains* Sondheim and Furth, *Company*, 54.

34 *what might have been* Sondheim and Furth, *Company*, 32.

35 *Instead of ending* On "Sorry-Grateful," see Stephen Banfield, *Sondheim's Broadway Musicals* (Ann Arbor: University of Michigan Press, 1993), 158–59.

35 *You're always sorry, / You're always grateful* Sondheim and Furth, *Company*, 32.

36 *I have no block . . . I don't feel you're really ready* Sondheim and Furth, *Company*, 40.

36 *ready* Sondheim and Furth, *Company*, 71.

37 *You promise whatever you like* Sondheim and Furth, *Company*, 71.

37 *wings down, stay a minute* Sondheim and Furth, *Company*, 96, 97.

38 *Thank you for including me* Sondheim and Furth, *Company*, 5.

38 *titillates a person* Sondheim and Furth, *Company*, 42.

38 *Susan sort of Sarah* Sondheim and Furth, *Company*, 49.

38 *someone* Sondheim and Furth, *Company*, 49.

38 *nobody ever performs in concert* See Sondheim's comment on "Someone is Waiting" in Mark Eden Horowitz, *Sondheim on Music: Minor Details and Major Decisions* (Lanham, MD: Rowman & Littlefield, 2019), 120.

39 *Angel, I've got something to tell you* Sondheim and Furth, *Company*, 8.

39 *Chinese techniques, exotic mystiques* Sondheim and Furth, *Company*, 48.

40 *we loooooooooooove you* Sondheim and Furth, *Company*, 19.

40 *Whatever you're calling about* Sondheim and Furth, *Company*, 4.

41 *good and crazy* Sondheim and Furth, *Company*, 13.

41 *sharing a tear* Sondheim and Furth, *Company*, 80.

42 *Don't stop now* Sondheim and Furth, *Company*, 115.

42 *Stay exactly as you are* Sondheim and Furth, *Company*, 76.

42 *Poor baby* Sondheim and Furth, *Company*, 94.

43 *When're we gonna make it?* Sondheim and Furth, *Company*, 110.

43 *But who will I take care of?* Sondheim and Furth, *Company*, 111.

43 *big favor* Sondheim and Furth, *Company*, 111.

44 *What do you get?* Sondheim and Furth, *Company*, 111.

44 *Somebody crowd me with love* Sondheim and Furth, *Company*, 116.

44 *Somebody let me come through* Sondheim and Furth, *Company*, 116.

45 *To help us survive* Sondheim and Furth, *Company*, 116.

46 *cop-out* Sondheim, quoted in Zadan, *Sondheim & Co.*, 124.

46 *Michael Bennett recalled* See Bennett's comments on Dean Jones as Bobby in Zadan, *Sondheim & Co.*, 129.

Follies: How to Survive Your Past

51 *Broadway baby* Goldman and Sondheim, *Follies*, 25.

52 *old 78 records* Frank Rich, "The Last Musical," *Crimson Review*, February 26, 1971.

52 *happen to me* Goldman, quoted in Zadan, *Sondheim & Co.*, 148.

52 *one foot in present* Sondheim, "*Follies* in Concert," *Great Performances* (1986), directed by Michael Houldey and produced by Ellen M. Krass and Thomas Z. Shepard for the Public Broadcasting Service and WNET. *Follies* was performed with a star-studded cast and the New York Philharmonic at Lincoln Center in September 1985 to make a legacy recording of the full score.

53 *lie about ourselves* Goldman and Sondheim, *Follies*, 4.

53 *Liebchen, it's for you* Goldman and Sondheim, *Follies*, 14.

54 Di-*rect from Phoenix* Goldman and Sondheim, *Follies*, 12.

56 *foolishness and madness* See Hal Prince, *Sense of Occasion* (New York: Applause Books, 2017), 160. Ted Chapin, the future head of the Rodgers & Hammerstein Organization, was a "gofer" on the original production. His notes from the time are the basis of *Everything Was Possible: The Birth of the Musical Follies* (2005), a remarkable insider's account of the show from read-through to opening night.

57 *honest talks* Goldman and Sondheim, *Follies*, 38.

57 *don't look at me* Goldman and Sondheim, *Follies*, 12.

57 *like a shut-in* Goldman and Sondheim, *Follies*, 33.

57 *in Buddy's eyes* Goldman and Sondheim, *Follies*, 33.

57 *worth living* Goldman and Sondheim, *Follies*, 32.

57 *self-hypnosis* Sondheim, quoted in Horowitz, *Sondheim on Music*, 207.

58 *woodwind accompaniment* See Stephen Sondheim, "Theatre Lyrics," in *Playwrights, Lyricists, Composers on Theatre*, ed. O. L. Guernsey Jr. (New York: Dodd, Mead, 1974), 71.

58 *It's the intervals* Barbara Cook, "*Follies* in Concert," *Great Performances* (1986).

58 *On your guard* Goldman and Sondheim, *Follies*, 6.

58 *I don't remember* Goldman and Sondheim, *Follies*, 28.

58 *consists of either/or* Goldman and Sondheim, *Follies*, 28.

58 *Does it?* Goldman and Sondheim, *Follies*, 28, 29.

58 *stabbing dissonance* Stephen Sondheim, "Theatre Lyrics," 71.

58 *boys downstairs* Goldman and Sondheim, *Follies*, 18.

61 *Lord, lord, lord!* Goldman and Sondheim, *Follies*, 35.

61 *very poignant* Phyllis Newman, "*Follies* in Concert," *Great Performances* (1986).

62 *I could kill you* Goldman and Sondheim, *Follies*, 58, 60.

63 *everybody lives to love* Goldman and Sondheim, *Follies*, 61.

63 *into the Follies* Goldman and Sondheim, *Follies*, 70.

63 *betwixt and between* Goldman and Sondheim, *Follies*, 70.

63 *very perturbed* Goldman and Sondheim, *Follies*, 70.

64 *bright* Goldman and Sondheim, *Follies*, 77.

64 *Not going left* Goldman and Sondheim, *Follies*, 77.

64 *spend sleepless nights* Goldman and Sondheim, *Follies*, 77.

65 *two unhappy dames* Goldman and Sondheim, *Follies*, 78.

65 *proud of me* Goldman and Sondheim, *Follies*, 31.

65 *feel just fine* Goldman and Sondheim, *Follies*, 80.

66 *Mister Whiz* Goldman and Sondheim, *Follies*, 80.

66 *Me, I like to love* Goldman and Sondheim, *Follies*, 82.

66 *forgotten the lyrics* See Sondheim, *Finishing the Hat*, 241.

66 *I DON'T LOVE ME!* Goldman and Sondheim, *Follies*, 84.

66 *Can't you see it?* Goldman and Sondheim, *Follies*, 85.

67 *martyred looks* Goldman and Sondheim, *Follies*, 56.

67 *cryptic sighs* Goldman and Sondheim, *Follies*, 56.

67 *Bet your ass* Goldman and Sondheim, *Follies*, 56.

67 *reason is undone* Goldman and Sondheim, *Follies*, 5.

A Little Night Music: How to Handle Your Regrets

72 *la, lie* Stephen Sondheim and Hugh Wheeler, *A Little Night Music*, in *Four by Sondheim* (New York: Applause Books, 2000), 161–319; citation at 176.

72 *whipped cream with knives* See Sondheim, *Finishing the Hat*, 253.

74 *try to forgive me* Sondheim and Wheeler, *A Little Night Music*, 304.

74 *years of muddle* Sondheim and Wheeler, *A Little Night Music*, 302.

75 *tip him off* Glynis Johns, quoted in Paul Salsini, *Sondheim & Me: Revealing a Musical Genius* (La Crescenta, CA: Bancroft Press, 2022), 101. Johns recounted the story of how "Send in the Clowns" was written in her interview with Salsini, 102.

75 *I want to right it all* Sondheim, manuscript notes, cited in Mark Eden Horowitz, "Biography of a Song: Send in the Clowns," *Sondheim Review* 11, no. 3 (Spring 2005): 15–20; citations at 15, 16.

76 *a little pissed off* Len Cariou, quoted in Salsini, *Sondheim & Me*, 102.

76 *isn't it rich?* Sondheim and Wheeler, *A Little Night Music*, 303.

77 *middle-aged regret* See Tunick, Introduction, *A Little Night Music*, 170.

77 *easy to remember* Sondheim, quoted in Meryle Secrest, *Sondheim: A Life* (London: Bloomsbury, 1998), 251.

77 *enormous regret and irony* Sondheim, interview with Sheridan Morley, "London Stage 95," London Weekend Television, November 5, 1995.

78 *I'm the other* Judi Dench, interview with Sheridan Morley, "London Stage 95," London Weekend Television, November 5, 1995.

78 *in mid-air* Sondheim and Wheeler, *A Little Night Music*, 303.

78 *don't ask where is it* Sondheim and Wheeler, *A Little Night Music*, 197.

79 *recorded and then broadcast* Videos of both "Send in the Clowns" master classes can be seen on YouTube.

80 *no one is there* Sondheim and Wheeler, *A Little Night Music*, 303.

80 *dignity* Sondheim and Wheeler, *A Little Night Music*, 203.

84 *just passing through* Sondheim and Wheeler, *A Little Night Music*, 299.

85 *many a bed* Sondheim and Wheeler, *A Little Night Music*, 307.

85 *meanwhile* Sondheim and Wheeler, *A Little Night Music*, 306.

85 *mouths to be fed* Sondheim and Wheeler, *A Little Night Music*, 307.

85 *everything that passes by* Quoted in Secrest, *Stephen Sondheim: A Life*, 252.

85 *everything / Passing by* Sondheim and Wheeler, *A Little Night Music*, 307.

86 *tiny Titian* Sondheim and Wheeler, *A Little Night Music*, 221.

86 *love of my life* Sondheim and Wheeler, *A Little Night Music*, 313.

86 *indiscriminate* Sondheim and Wheeler, *A Little Night Music*, 220, 221.

87 *who know too much* Sondheim and Wheeler, *A Little Night Music*, 180.

87 *discretion of the heart* Sondheim and Wheeler, *A Little Night Music*, 221.

87 *danse macabre* On the link between the nineteenth-century waltz and mortality, see Banfield, *Sondheim's Broadway Musicals*, 246–47.

NOTES

Pacific Overtures: How to Be a Part of the Whole

93 *Perry's own words* Matthew Calbraith Perry, *Narrative of the Expedition of an American Squadron to the China Seas and Japan* (New York: Appleton, 1856), 300. "But it is expected that the government of your imperial majesty will . . . acced[e] at once to the very reasonable and pacific overtures contained in the President's letter."

94 *four black dragons* Stephen Sondheim and John Weidman, *Pacific Overtures* (New York: Theatre Communications Group, 1991), 15.

94 *the Americans were never here* Sondheim and Weidman, *Pacific Overtures*, 40.

95 *will have come and gone* Sondheim and Weidman, *Pacific Overtures*, 40.

96 *oblique* Weidman, interview with Frank Rich, "Anatomy of a Song," a *Camera Three* CBS documentary, first broadcast March 28, 1976. The documentary can be seen on YouTube.

96 *everythingness* Sondheim, interview with Frank Rich, "Anatomy of a Song."

96 *no authentic Japanese account* Sondheim and Weidman, *Pacific Overtures*, 55.

97 *was there* Sondheim and Weidman, *Pacific Overtures*, 56.

97 *I was younger then* Sondheim and Weidman, *Pacific Overtures*, 57.

98 *droning* Sondheim and Weidman, *Pacific Overtures*, 62.

98 *Tell us what you hear* Sondheim and Weidman, *Pacific Overtures*, 56, 62.

98 *Whatever happened* Sondheim and Weidman, *Pacific Overtures*, 64.

99 *ready to be performed* Frank Rich, "Anatomy of a Song."

99 *The song's about history* Sondheim, interview with Frank Rich, "Anatomy of a Song."

100 *relentlessness* Sondheim, *Finishing the Hat*, 304. See also Sondheim's remarks on "Someone in a Tree" in Horowitz, *Sondheim on Music*, 158.

100 *more Indonesian in tone* See W. Anthony Sheppard, *Extreme Exoticism: Japan in the American Musical Imagination* (Oxford and New York: Oxford University Press, 2019), 377.

100 *stretching out of time* Sondheim, interview with Frank Rich, "Anatomy of a Song."

NOTES

102 *Let the pupil show the master* Sondheim and Weidman, *Pacific Overtures*, 105.

103 *Ryosenji Treasure Museum* See Lionel Lambourne, *Japonisme: Cultural Crossings Between Japan and the West* (London: Phaidon Press, 2005).

104 *feel like homework* See Zadan, *Sondheim & Co.*, 227.

105 *it's the details that count* Sondheim, interview with Frank Rich, "Anatomy of a Song."

105 *stroke not the painting* Sondheim, interview with Frank Rich, "Anatomy of a Song."

105 *fragment of the day* Sondheim and Weidman, *Pacific Overtures*, 59.

105 *pebble, not the stream* Sondheim and Weidman, *Pacific Overtures*, 64.

106 *part that's underneath* Sondheim and Weidman, *Pacific Overtures*, 59, 61.

Sweeney Todd: How (Not) to Deal with Injustice

111 *equal amounts of money* See Dominique J.-F. de Quervain et al., "The Neural Basis of Altruistic Punishment," *Science* 35 (August 2004): 1254–58.

113 *musical thriller* "A musical thriller" is the play's subtitle. Stephen Sondheim and Hugh Wheeler, *Sweeney Todd, the Demon Barber of Fleet Street* (London: Nick Hern Books, 1991).

114 *hour has come* Sondheim and Wheeler, *Sweeney Todd*, 18.

114 *throats / Of hypocrites* Sondheim and Wheeler, *Sweeney Todd*, 59.

114 *tonsorial parlor* Sondheim and Wheeler, *Sweeney Todd*, 45.

114 *dreamed all your days* Sondheim and Wheeler, *Sweeney Todd*, 20.

115 *precious / Rubies* Sondheim and Wheeler, *Sweeney Todd*, 21.

115 *seven count is irregular* See Sondheim's comments in Horowitz, *Sondheim on Music*, 132.

116 *Patience, enjoy it* Sondheim and Wheeler, *Sweeney Todd*, 74.

118 *if people aren't rooting* Sondheim, quoted in Horowitz, *Sondheim on Music*, 147.

119 *The work, chugging* Cited in Horowitz, *Sondheim on Music*, 139.

119 *can assuage me* Sondheim and Wheeler, *Sweeney Todd*, 80.

119 *the work waits* Sondheim and Wheeler, *Sweeney Todd*, 80.

119 *not a number to applaud* See Sondheim, *Finishing the Hat*, 355.

120 *And I'm full of joy* Sondheim and Wheeler, *Sweeney Todd*, 80–81.

120 *contrary shadow chord* On the shadow chords in "Epiphany," see Steve Swayne, *How Sondheim Found His Sound* (Ann Arbor: University of Michigan Press, 2007), 38.

121 *wounds green* Francis Bacon, *The Essays of Counsels, Civil and Moral . . .* , ed. Basil Montagu (London: W. Pickering, 1836), 14.

122 *fresh supplies* Sondheim and Wheeler, *Sweeney Todd*, 105–06.

122 *proper artist with a knife* Sondheim and Wheeler, *Sweeney Todd*, 15.

122 *trash from the gutter* Sondheim and Wheeler, *Sweeney Todd*, 51.

123 *into filth and greed* Sondheim and Wheeler, *Sweeney Todd*, 10.

124 *they make Sweeney Todds* Hal Prince, quoted in Martin Gottfried, *Sondheim* (New York: Harry N. Abrams, 2000), 127.

125 *obligations to others* On how individuals might respond to structural injustice, see Kieran Setiya, *Life Is Hard: How Philosophy Can Help Us Find Our Way* (New York: Riverhead Books, 2022), 114–18.

125 *does not serve his obsession* See Stephen Sondheim, "Larger Than Life: Reflections on Melodrama and *Sweeney Todd*," in *Melodrama*, ed. Daniel Gerould (New York: New York Literary Forum, 1980), 14.

126 *attend the tale* Sondheim and Wheeler, *Sweeney Todd*, 156.

126 *there beside you* Sondheim and Wheeler, *Sweeney Todd*, 155.

126 *tissue of bullshit* James Fenton, "The Barberous Crimes of Sondheim and Prince," *Sunday Times* (London), July 6, 1980.

127 *mountains of Peru* Sondheim and Wheeler, *Sweeney Todd*, 7.

127 *no justice in this city?* Sondheim and Wheeler, *Sweeney Todd*, 113.

Merrily We Roll Along: How to Grow Up

132 *time to be starting out* George Furth and Stephen Sondheim, *Merrily We Roll Along* (New York: Theatre Communications Group, 1998), 160.

132 *worlds to win* Furth and Sondheim, *Merrily We Roll Along*, 155.

133 *terrifying danger* Senator Richard Russell, quoted in Daniel Sage, *How Outer Space Made America* (New York: Routledge, 2016), 35.

134 *someday* Furth and Sondheim, *Merrily We Roll Along*, 156.

134 *definitely does that* Lindsay Mendez, interview with Diep Tran, "Hey, Old Friend: Lindsay Mendez Returns to Broadway with *Merrily We Roll Along*," *Playbill*, September 5, 2023.

135 *dreams coming true* Furth and Sondheim, *Merrily We Roll Along*, 161.

135 *me and you* Furth and Sondheim, *Merrily We Roll Along*, 161.

135 *too hostile, and mean-spirited* Sondheim, quoted in James Lapine, *Putting It Together: How Stephen Sondheim and I Created* Sunday in the Park with George (New York: Farrar, Straus & Giroux, 2021), 16–17.

136 *never listened to music* Lapine, *Putting It Together*, 45.

137 *get there from here* Furth and Sondheim, *Merrily We Roll Along*, 3.

137 *reflective of the show* Lonny Price, *Theatre Talk*, interviewed by Susan Haskins and Jesse Green, January 18, 2017.

137 *turning a profit* Brent Lang, "*Merrily We Roll Along* Broadway Revival Recoups Investment . . . ," *Variety*, March 20, 2024.

137 *found in the dark* Jesse Green, "'Merrily We Roll Along': Finally Found in the Dark," *New York Times*, October 10, 2023.

137 *get there from here* Furth and Sondheim, *Merrily We Roll Along*, 3.

138 *tap their toes* Furth and Sondheim, *Merrily We Roll Along*, 145.

138 *Everything in that number* Sondheim, quoted in Horowitz, *Sondheim on Music*, 42.

139 *my generation of Broadway songwriters* Sondheim, *Finishing the Hat*, 419.

139 *exuberant early days* Sondheim, *Finishing the Hat*, 381.

140 *And cursing and crying* Furth and Sondheim, *Merrily We Roll Along*, 76.

140 *And deeper and nearer* Furth and Sondheim, *Merrily We Roll Along*, 133.

141 *swell year it's been* Furth and Sondheim, *Merrily We Roll Along*, 120.

141 *terrible, tacky* Liz Smith, "Not So Merrily They Roll Out of the Theatre," *Daily News* (New York), October 18, 1981.

141 *mavericks* Sondheim, quoted in Stephen Schiff, "Deconstructing Sondheim," *New Yorker*, March 8, 1993, 76–87. See also Lapine, *Putting It Together*, 16.

142 *Blob* Furth and Sondheim, *Merrily We Roll Along*, 100.

142 *Other revivals* See Sondheim, *Finishing the Hat*, 381–85.

143 *how did you get to be here* Furth and Sondheim, *Merrily We Roll Along*, 4.

143 *things they don't know* Furth and Sondheim, *Merrily We Roll Along*, 156.

144 *Wanna write a show?* Furth and Sondheim, *Merrily We Roll Along*, 44–45.

144 *It's called apples rot* Furth and Sondheim, *Merrily We Roll Along*, 81.

144 *far off the track* Furth and Sondheim, *Merrily We Roll Along*, 3.

145 *lonely at the top* Furth and Sondheim, *Merrily We Roll Along*, 10.

146 *Now we're finished* Furth and Sondheim, *Merrily We Roll Along*, 28.

146 *conflicted* Helen Shaw, review of *Merrily We Roll Along*, *New Yorker*, December 26, 2022.

146 *Write what you know* Furth and Sondheim, *Merrily We Roll Along*, 25.

Sunday in the Park with George: How to Be an Artist

152 *think you're drawing?* Sondheim and Lapine, *Sunday*, 57.

152 *observing, perceiving* Sondheim and Lapine, *Sunday*, 44.

153 *what is true* Sondheim and Lapine, *Sunday*, 57.

153 *Harmony* Sondheim and Lapine, *Sunday*, 172.

153 *screw them* Sondheim and Lapine, *Sunday*, 44.

154 *wanted him and hated him* Sondheim and Lapine, *Sunday*, 133.

155 *do for others* Sondheim and Lapine, *Sunday*, 55.

155 *do for yourself* Sondheim and Lapine, *Sunday*, 55.

155 *Then it will be new* Sondheim and Lapine, *Sunday*, 171.

156 *forever* Sondheim and Lapine, *Sunday*, 88.

157 *arranges* Sondheim and Lapine, *Sunday*, 78.

157 *Red red red red* Sondheim and Lapine, *Sunday*, 37.

157 *look at a face, red red orange* Sondheim and Lapine, *Sunday*, 66, 37.

158 *chords are so thick* On the "pointillism" of Sondheim's score, see Mark Eden Horowitz, "Biography of a Song: Finishing the Hat," in *Sondheim Review* (Fall 2005): 24–29.

158 *boom* Sondheim, quoted in Horowitz, *Sondheim on Music*, 113.

158 *harmony* Sondheim and Lapine, *Sunday*, 87.

158 *look at a face* Sondheim and Lapine, *Sunday*, 66.

158 *only way to see* Sondheim and Lapine, *Sunday*, 66.

158 *Theme and variation* Stephen Sondheim, *Look, I Made a Hat: Collected Lyrics (1981–2011)* (New York: Alfred A. Knopf, 2011), 4.

159 *backward* Lapine, *Putting It Together*, 70.

159 *formal looseness* Sondheim, *Look, I Made a Hat*, 11.

159 *song's main focus* See Sondheim, *Look, I Made a Hat*, 11.

159 *continuous love song* Sondheim, quoted in Zadan, *Sondheim & Co.*, 90.

160 *finishing the hat, exhibition in addition* Sondheim and Lapine, *Sunday*, 65, 149.

161 *old view* Sondheim and Lapine, *Sunday*, 79.

161 *see these faces* Sondheim and Lapine, *Sunday*, 71.

162 *connection* Sondheim and Lapine, *Sunday*, 148.

162 *warm inside his eyes* Sondheim and Lapine, *Sunday*, 38.

162 *paint a factory next* Sondheim and Lapine, *Sunday*, 29.

163 *Don't move the mouth* Sondheim and Lapine, *Sunday*, 25.

163 *notice every tree* Sondheim and Lapine, *Sunday*, 169.

163 *world of the hat* Sondheim and Lapine, *Sunday*, 66.

163 *my heart in the hat* Sondheim, quoted in Horowitz, "Biography of a Song: Finishing the Hat," 24–29; citation at 26.

163 *I am what I do* Sondheim and Lapine, *Sunday*, 75.

163 *living in it* Sondheim and Lapine, *Sunday*, 74.

163 *in this painting* Sondheim and Lapine, *Sunday*, 74.

164 *flecks of light* Sondheim and Lapine, *Sunday*, 88. For an extended analysis of "Sunday," see Robert L. McLaughlin, *Stephen Sondheim and the Reinvention of the American Musical* (Jackson: University Press of Mississippi, 2016), 121–22.

165 *There she is* Sondheim and Lapine, *Sunday*, 161.

165 *on the trapeze* Sondheim and Lapine, *Sunday*, 144.

165 *there she is* Sondheim and Lapine, *Sunday*, 161.

166 *keystone in an arch* Charles Kimbrough, quoted in Joanne Gordon, *Art Isn't Easy: The Theatre of Stephen Sondheim* (New York: Da Capo Press, 1992), 291.

166 *Then it will be new* Sondheim and Lapine, *Sunday*, 171.

166 *choosing* Sondheim and Lapine, *Sunday*, 169.

166 *give us more to see* Sondheim and Lapine, *Sunday*, 171.

167 *opening them up* See Sondheim, *Look, I Made a Hat*, 55.

167 *so many possibilities* Sondheim and Lapine, *Sunday*, 174.

Into the Woods: How to Choose the Right Path

172 *Bronx Jewish couple* Sondheim, interview with Craig Carnelia, "In Conversation with Stephen Sondheim," *Sondheim Review* 15, no. 1 (Fall 2008): 15–20; citation at 15.

172 *stand in for the audience* Lapine, interviewed by Mark Eden Horowitz, "Guidance for the Journey," *Sondheim Review* (Winter 2014): 16–19; citation at 18.

172 *slipper as pure as gold* Sondheim and Lapine, *Into the Woods*, 16.

174 *And you get it* Sondheim and Lapine, *Into the Woods*, 29.

174 *tomorrow's bread* Sondheim and Lapine, *Into the Woods*, 39.

176 *How brave* Sondheim and Lapine, *Into the Woods*, 108.

177 *Jolted into insight* See Sondheim, *Look, I Made a Hat*, 92.

177 *I'm in the wrong story* Sondheim and Lapine, *Into the Woods*, 109.

178 *What is it about the woods?* Sondheim and Lapine, *Into the Woods*, 111.

179 *Back to life, back to sense* Sondheim and Lapine, *Into the Woods*, 112.

179 *her Baker, her life, her love* Joanna Gleason, quoted in Carey Purcell, "The Baker's Wife: More Than Just a Moment in 'Into the Woods,'" *American Theatre*, July 18, 2022.

179 *new perspective* Sara Bareilles, quoted in Purcell, "The Baker's Wife."

180 *it takes two* Sondheim and Lapine, *Into the Woods*, 54.

181 *morally sick wretches* The homophobe was Jesse Helms, who represented North Carolina in the US Senate from 1973 to 2003.

183 *made me feel* Sondheim and Lapine, *Into the Woods*, 11.

184 *she likes life as it is* Sondheim, *Look, I Made a Hat*, 69.

184 *time to leave the woods* Sondheim and Lapine, *Into the Woods*, 113.

185 *Baker's Wife was simply unlucky* See Lapine's comments in Purcell, "The Baker's Wife."

Assassins: How to Let the Darkness In

191 *Perfect theatrical fodder* Sondheim, *Look, I Made a Hat*, 112.

192 *Brutus was honored* See *Right or Wrong, God Judge Me: The Writings of John Wilkes Booth*, ed. John H. Rhodehamel and Louise Taper (Urbana and Chicago: University of Illinois Press, 1997), 117.

194 *C'mere and kill a President* Stephen Sondheim and John Weidman, *Assassins* (New York: Theatre Communications Group, 1991), 5.

194 *going to the Lordy* Sondheim and Weidman, *Assassins*, 65.

194 *Glory hallelujah* Sondheim and Weidman, *Assassins*, 65.

194 *Look on the bright side* Sondheim and Weidman, *Assassins*, 66.

195 *understand it later* Sondheim and Weidman, *Assassins*, 21.

196 *longing for the freedom* On the history of the cakewalk, see Soyica Diggs Colbert, *The African American Theatrical Body: Reception, Performance, and the Stage* (Cambridge: Cambridge University Press, 2011), 105–7.

196 *family* Sondheim and Weidman, *Assassins*, 101.

198 *hold tight / To your dreams* Sondheim and Weidman, *Assassins*, 13.

198 *right / To be happy* Sondheim and Weidman, *Assassins*, 7.

199 *the ballpark* Sondheim and Weidman, *Assassins*, 85.

199 *Zangara American* Sondheim and Weidman, *Assassins*, 34.

199 *saved Roosevelt* Sondheim and Weidman, *Assassins*, 30.

199 *calculated wrong note* See Sondheim's comments on "Unworthy of Your Love" in Horowitz, *Sondheim on Music*, 62.

199 *I like to be in America* Sondheim and Weidman, *Assassins*, 56.

199 *stand-up guy* Sondheim and Weidman, *Assassins*, 56.

199 *mailman won the lottery* Sondheim and Weidman, *Assassins*, 82.

200 *We'll never see the day arrive* Sondheim and Weidman, *Assassins*, 83.

200 *prizes all around* Sondheim and Weidman, *Assassins*, 82.

200 *another national anthem* Sondheim and Weidman, *Assassins*, 84.

200 *I want my prize* Sondheim and Weidman, *Assassins*, 80.

200 *Spread the word* Sondheim and Weidman, *Assassins*, 83, 84.

201 *Why did you do it, Johnny?* Sondheim and Weidman, *Assassins*, 16.

201 *bad reviews* Sondheim and Weidman, *Assassins*, 16.

201 *Leave it to history to tell* Sondheim and Weidman, *Assassins*, 21.

201 *Damn you, Booth* Sondheim and Weidman, *Assassins*, 23.

201 *rob me of its meaning* Sondheim and Weidman, *Assassins*, 19.

202 *get your wish* Sondheim and Weidman, *Assassins*, 96.

202 *force of history* Sondheim and Weidman, *Assassins*, 100.

202 *madman* Sondheim and Weidman, *Assassins*, 15.

202 *story's pretty strong* Sondheim and Weidman, *Assassins*, 15.

202 *didn't mean a nickel* Sondheim and Weidman, *Assassins*, 81.

203 *I'm still angry about it* Sondheim, quoted in Salsini, *Sondheim & Me*, 39.

203 *I'm reluctant to assign blame* Sondheim, quoted in Salsini, *Sondheim & Me*, 39.

203 *think critically about* Sondheim and Weidman, quoted in "*Assassins* Postpones Broadway Debut," *Playbill*, September 13, 2001.

204 *still wouldn't yield* Sondheim and Weidman, *Assassins*, 21.

204 *suffering, fine, beautiful* Sondheim and Weidman, *Assassins*, 38.

205 *wanted to mythologize them* See William A. Henry III, "Glimpses of Looniness: *Assassins*," *Time*, February 4, 1991.

205 *cut to the chase* See John Simon, *New York*, February 4, 1991.

206 *that's by design* Sondheim and Weidman, *Assassins*, 53.

207 *chain of grief* Sondheim, *Look, I Made a Hat*, 142.

207 *Nothing that will last* Sondheim, *Look, I Made a Hat*, 142.

208 *Fix it up fast* Sondheim, *Look, I Made a Hat*, 142.

208 *Connect* Sondheim and Weidman, *Assassins*, 106.

209 *turn your love to me* Sondheim and Weidman, *Assassins*, 59.

Passion: How to Love

214 *on the surface* On "La Scapigliatura," see Ann Caesar, "Construction of Character in Tarchetti's *Fosca*," *Modern Language Review* 82, no. 1 (January 1987): 76–87.

214 *collection of many ills* Stephen Sondheim and James Lapine, *Passion: A Musical* (New York: Theatre Communications Group, 1994), 17.

214 *taught me how to love* Sondheim and Lapine, *Passion*, 100.

214 *someone to be loved* Sondheim and Lapine, *Passion*, 130.

215 *Sickness is as normal to me* Sondheim and Lapine, *Passion*, 21.

216 *limits of [her] dreams, things [she] cannot keep* Sondheim and Lapine, *Passion*, 22, 23.

216 *echoes* Sondheim and Lapine, *Passion*, 22.

216 *passive love* Sondheim and Lapine, *Passion*, 30.

216 *They hear drums* Sondheim and Lapine, *Passion*, 35.

217 *What does it matter* Sondheim and Lapine, *Passion*, 44.

217 *For now I'm seeing love* Sondheim and Lapine, *Passion*, 61.

217 *neat rhymes* Sondheim, *Look, I Made a Hat*, 162.

217 *the victim you appear* Sondheim and Lapine, *Passion*, 83.

218 *spectators actually applauded* See Donna Murphy, quoted in Salsini, *Sondheim & Me*, 31.

218 *unwanted laughter* See Sondheim, *Look, I Made a Hat*, 150.

219 *we are all Fosca* Sondheim, *Look, I Made a Hat*, 177.

219 *lonely, look away* David Richards, "Sondheim Explores the Heart's Terrain," *New York Times*, May 10, 1994.

219 *Look at me* Sondheim and Lapine, *Passion*, 23.

219 *see what is beautiful* Sondheim and Lapine, *Passion*, 111.

220 *keep my distance* Sondheim and Lapine, *Passion*, 100.

220 *we have a problem* Donna Murphy, quoted in Salsini, *Sondheim & Me*, 32.

221 *modulates down* See Sondheim, *Look, I Made a Hat*, 172.

221 *This is why I live* Sondheim and Lapine, *Passion*, 101.

221 *live, die* Sondheim and Lapine, *Passion*, 101.

221 *someone to be loved* Sondheim and Lapine, *Passion*, 130.

221 *what is beautiful about me* Sondheim and Lapine, *Passion*, 101.

222 *No one really knows* Sondheim and Lapine, *Passion*, 5.

222 *glanced / At each other* Sondheim and Lapine, *Passion*, 2.

222 *more* Sondheim and Lapine, *Passion*, 5.

222 *another love story* Sondheim and Lapine, *Passion*, 4.

223 *make love with our words* Sondheim and Lapine, *Passion*, 7.

223 *practical arrangement* Sondheim and Lapine, *Passion*, 116.

224 *pleasures it can offer* Sondheim and Lapine, *Passion*, 30.

224 *I thought you'd understand* Sondheim and Lapine, *Passion*, 35.

225 *Your love will live in me* Sondheim and Lapine, *Passion*, 131.

225 *virus, vampire kiss* Jere Shea, quoted in Salsini, *Sondheim & Me*, 32.

225 *Fosca . . . infects Giorgio* See Stephen Sondheim, "Sondheim on *Passion*," *Dramatists Guild Quarterly* 31, no. 3 (Autumn 1995): 9.

226 *wait* Sondheim and Lapine, *Passion*, 114.

226 *Is this what you call love?* Sondheim and Lapine, *Passion*, 115.

226 *Love within reason* Sondheim and Lapine, *Passion*, 122.

226 *not pretty* Sondheim and Lapine, *Passion*, 122.

227 *your love will live in me* Sondheim and Lapine, *Passion*, 131.

227 *permanent as death* Sondheim and Lapine, *Passion*, 61.

227 *someone to be loved* Sondheim and Lapine, *Passion*, 130.

227 *different light* Sondheim and Lapine, *Passion*, 61.

227 *to die loved* Sondheim and Lapine, *Passion*, 123.

227 *laud, emulate* Sondheim, quoted in Sandor Goodhart, "'The Mother's Part': Love, Letters, and Reading in Sondheim's *Passion*," in *Reading Stephen Sondheim: A Collection of Critical Essays*, ed. Sandor Goodhart (New York and London: Routledge, 2000), 221–58; citation at 257.

Exit Music: Here We Are

233 *completed theatrical work* See Frank Rich, "The Final Sondheim: The Complete, From-Beginning-to-End Story of How Stephen Sondheim, David Ives, and Joe Mantello Created the Musical *Here We Are*," *New York*, August 28, 2023. An extract from their conversation was reprinted in the program for the show's original production at The Shed.

233 *Too depressing* Sondheim, quoted in D. T. Max, *Finale*, 210. See also 86, 108, 139–40, 147, and 152 in the same book for Sondheim's other comments on the work-in-progress later produced under the title *Here We Are*.

234 *seem to be writing* David Ives, email to Joe Mantello, May 2020, cited in Rich, "The Final Sondheim."

BIBLIOGRAPHY

Works by Stephen Sondheim

Furth, George, and Stephen Sondheim. *Merrily We Roll Along*. New York: Theatre Communications Group, 1998.

Goldman, James, and Stephen Sondheim. *Follies*. 1971; New York: Theatre Communications Group, 2001.

Laurents, Arthur, and Stephen Sondheim. *Anyone Can Whistle: A Musical Fable*. New York: Random House, 1965.

——. *Gypsy: A Musical*. New York: Theatre Communications Group, 1994.

Sondheim, Stephen. *Finishing the Hat: Collected Lyrics (1954–81)*. New York: Alfred A. Knopf, 2010.

——. "Larger Than Life: Reflections on Melodrama and *Sweeney Todd*." In *Melodrama*, ed. Daniel Gerould. New York: New York Literary Forum, 1980.

——. *Look, I Made a Hat: Collected Lyrics (1981–2011)*. New York: Alfred A. Knopf, 2011.

——. "Sondheim on *Passion*." *Dramatists Guild Quarterly* 31, no. 3 (Autumn 1995): 3–9.

——. "Theatre Lyrics." In *Playwrights, Lyricists, Composers on Theatre*, ed. O. L. Guernsey Jr. New York: Dodd, Mead, 1974.

Sondheim, Stephen, and George Furth. *Company: A Musical Comedy*. New York: Theatre Communications Group, 1996.

Sondheim, Stephen, and James Lapine. *Into the Woods*. New York: Music Theatre International, 1996.

——. *Passion: A Musical*. New York: Theatre Communications Group, 1994.

———. *Sunday in the Park with George*. New York: Applause Books, 1991.

Sondheim, Stephen, and John Weidman. *Assassins*. New York: Theatre Communications Group, 1991.

———. *Pacific Overtures*. New York: Theatre Communications Group, 1991.

Sondheim, Stephen, and Hugh Wheeler. *A Little Night Music: Four by Sondheim*. New York: Applause Books, 2000.

———. *Sweeney Todd, the Demon Barber of Fleet Street*. London: Nick Hern Books, 1991.

Selected Works about Stephen Sondheim

Banfield, Stephen. *Sondheim's Broadway Musicals*. Ann Arbor: University of Michigan Press, 1993.

Chapin, Ted. *Everything Was Possible: The Birth of the Musical* Follies. 2005. New York: Applause Books, 2022.

Everett, William A., and Paul R. Laird, eds. *The Cambridge Companion to the Musical*. Cambridge: Cambridge University Press, 2002.

Ford, Paul. *Lord Knows, At Least I Was There: Working with Stephen Sondheim*. New York: Moreclacke, 2022.

Francis, Ben. *Careful the Spell You Cast: How Stephen Sondheim Extended the Range of the American Musical*. London: Methuen Drama, 2023.

Goodhart, Sandor, ed. *Reading Stephen Sondheim: A Collection of Critical Essays*. New York and London: Routledge, 2000.

Gordon, Joanne. *Art Isn't Easy: The Theatre of Stephen Sondheim*. 1990. New York: Da Capo Press, 1992.

———, ed. *Stephen Sondheim: A Casebook*. New York and London: Garland, 1997.

Gordon, Robert, ed. *The Oxford Handbook of Sondheim Studies*. Oxford: Oxford University Press, 2014.

Gottfried, Martin. *Sondheim*. New York: Harry N. Abrams, 2000.

Grinenko, Aleksei. "'Is That Just Disgusting?' Mapping the Social Geographies of Filth and Madness in 'Sweeney Todd.'" *Theatre Journal* 68, no. 2 (June 2016): 231–48.

Lapine, James. *Putting It Together: How Stephen Sondheim and I Created*

Sunday in the Park with George. New York: Farrar, Straus & Giroux, 2021.

Lofton, Kathryn. "Pausing on a Sunday: Sondheim and the Composition of the Secular in the American Musical." *Modern Drama* 65, no. 3 (September 2022): 355–80.

Horowitz, Mark Eden. "Biography of a Song: A Bowler Hat." *Sondheim Review* (Spring 2006): 20–27.

———. "Biography of a Song: A Little Priest." *Sondheim Review* (Summer 2006): 20–29.

———. "Biography of a Song: Finishing the Hat." *Sondheim Review* (Fall 2005): 24–29.

———. "Biography of a Song: Losing My Mind." *Sondheim Review* (Summer 2005): 29–33.

———. "Biography of a Song: Not a Day Goes By." *Sondheim Review* (Winter 2005): 22–29.

———. "Biography of a Song: Send in the Clowns." *Sondheim Review* (Spring 2005): 15–20.

———. "Biography of a Song: You Could Drive a Person Crazy." *Sondheim Review* (Winter 2006): 25–33.

———. "Guidance for the Journey." *Sondheim Review* (Winter 2014): 16–19.

———. *Sondheim on Music: Minor Details and Major Decisions.* Lanham, MD: Rowman & Littlefield, 2019.

Lahr, John. "Sondheim's Little Deaths: The Ironic Mode and Its Discontents." *Harper's*, April 1979, 71–78.

Max, D. T. *Finale: Late Conversations with Stephen Sondheim.* New York: Harper, 2022.

McLaughlin, Robert L. *Stephen Sondheim and the Reinvention of the American Musical.* Jackson: University Press of Mississippi, 2016.

Mollin, Alfred. "Mayhem and Morality in *Sweeney Todd*." *American Music* 9, no. 4 (Winter 1991): 405–17.

Mordden, Ethan. *On Sondheim: An Opinionated Guide.* Oxford: Oxford University Press, 2016.

Pender, Rick. *The Stephen Sondheim Encyclopedia.* Lanham, MD: Rowman & Littlefield, 2021.

Salsini, Paul. *Sondheim & Me: Revealing a Musical Genius*. La Crescenta, CA: Bancroft Press, 2022.

Secrest, Meryle. *Sondheim: A Life*. London: Bloomsbury, 1998.

Sheppard, W. Anthony, ed. *Sondheim in Our Time and His*. Oxford: Oxford University Press, 2022.

Silverman, Stephen M. *Sondheim: His Life, His Shows, His Legacy*. New York: Black Dog & Leventhal, 2023.

Swayne, Steve. *How Sondheim Found His Sound*. Ann Arbor: University of Michigan Press, 2007.

Symonds, Dominic. "Putting It Together and Finishing the Hat? Deconstructing the Art of Making Art." *Contemporary Theatre Review* 19, no. 1 (2009): 101–12.

Zadan, Craig. *Sondheim & Co*. New York: Macmillan, 1974.

Selected Works about Musical Theatre

Blank, Larry. *I Was Playing Their Song*. Amazon Digital Services, 2023.

Colbert, Soyica Diggs. *The African American Theatrical Body: Reception, Performance, and the Stage*. Cambridge: Cambridge University Press, 2011.

Cook, Barbara, and Tom Santopietro. *Then and Now: A Memoir*. New York: Harper, 2016.

Harbert, Elissa. "*Hamilton* and History Musicals." *American Music* 36, no. 4 (Winter 2018): 412–28.

Hirsch, Foster. *Harold Prince and the American Musical*. Cambridge: Cambridge University Press, 1989.

Jacobs, Alexandra. *Still Here: The Madcap, Nervy, Singular Life of Elaine Stritch*. New York: Farrar, Straus & Giroux, 2019.

Jones, John Bush. *Our Musicals, Ourselves: A Social History of the American Musical Theatre*. Hanover, NH: University Press of New England, 2003.

Kirle, Bruce. *Unfinished Business: Broadway Musicals as Works-in-Process*. Carbondale: Southern Illinois University Press, 2005.

Knapp, Raymond. *The American Musical and the Formation of National Identity*. Princeton, NJ: Princeton University Press, 2004.

———. *The American Musical and the Performance of Personal Identity*. Princeton, NJ: Princeton University Press, 2006.

———. "*Assassins, Oklahoma!* and the 'Shifting Fringe of Dark around the Camp-Fire.'" *Cambridge Opera Journal* 16, no. 1 (March 2004): 77–101.

Lee, Gypsy Rose. *Gypsy: A Memoir*. 1957. Berkeley, CA: Frog, 1999.

Loud, David. *Facing the Music: A Broadway Memoir*. New York: Regan Arts, 2022.

Mandelbaum, Ken. *Not Since Carrie: Forty Years of Broadway Musical Flops*. New York: St. Martin's Press, 1992.

Miller, D. A. *Place for Us: Essay on the Broadway Musical*. Cambridge, MA: Harvard University Press, 1998.

Prince, Hal. *Sense of Occasion*. New York: Applause Books, 2017.

Rodgers, Mary, and Jesse Green. *Shy: The Alarmingly Outspoken Memoirs of Mary Rodgers*. New York: Farrar, Straus & Giroux, 2022.

Rogers, Bradley. *The Song Is You: Musical Theatre and the Politics of Bursting into Song and Dance*. Iowa City: University of Iowa Press, 2020.

Sheppard, W. Anthony. *Extreme Exoticism: Japan in the American Musical Imagination*. Oxford and New York: Oxford University Press, 2019.

Weiner, Laurie. *Oscar Hammerstein and the Invention of the Musical*. New Haven, CT: Yale University Press, 2023.

Wolf, Stacy. *Beyond Broadway: The Pleasure and Promise of Musical Theatre Across America*. New York: Oxford University Press, 2019.

———. *Changed for Good: A Feminist History of the Broadway Musical*. New York: Oxford University Press, 2011.

———. *A Problem Like Maria: Gender and Sexuality in the American Musical*. Ann Arbor: University of Michigan Press, 2002.

ILLUSTRATION CREDITS

1. Stephen Sondheim in rehearsal for the original Broadway production of *Merrily We Roll Along* (1981). Photo by Martha Swope ©The New York Public Library for the Performing Arts.
2. Angela Lansbury as Cora Hoover Hooper in the original Broadway production of *Anyone Can Whistle* (1964). Photo by Friedman-Abeles ©The New York Public Library for the Performing Arts.
3. Sandra Church as Louise in the original Broadway production of *Gypsy* (1959). Photo by Friedman-Abeles ©The New York Public Library for the Performing Arts.
4. George Coe as David, Larry Kert as Bobby, and Teri Ralston as Jenny in the original Broadway production of *Company* (1970). Photo by Friedman-Abeles ©The New York Public Library for the Performing Arts.
5. Ethel Shutta as Hattie in the original Broadway production of *Follies* (1971). Photo by Martha Swope ©The New York Public Library for the Performing Arts.
6. Glynis Johns as Desirée Armfeldt in the original Broadway production of *A Little Night Music* (1973). Photo by Martha Swope ©The New York Public Library for the Performing Arts.
7. James Dybas as the Old Man and Gedde Watanabe as the Boy in the original Broadway production of *Pacific Overtures* (1976). Photo by Martha Swope ©The New York Public Library for the Performing Arts.
8. Len Cariou as Sweeney Todd and Edmund Lyndeck as Judge Turpin in the original Broadway production of *Sweeney Todd* (1979). Photo by Martha Swope ©The New York Public Library for the Performing Arts.
9. Ann Morrison as Mary, Lonny Price as Charley, and Jim Walton as Frank in the original Broadway production of *Merrily We Roll Along* (1981). Photo by Martha Swope ©The New York Public Library for the Performing Arts.
10. Mandy Patinkin as George and Bernadette Peters as Dot in the original

Broadway production of *Sunday in the Park with George* (1984). Photo by Martha Swope ©The New York Public Library for the Performing Arts.

11. Joanna Gleason as the Baker's Wife in the original Broadway production of *Into the Woods* (1987). Photo by Martha Swope ©The New York Public Library for the Performing Arts.

12. Victor Garber as John Wilkes Booth and Terrence Mann as Leon Czolgosz in the original off-Broadway production of *Assassins* at Playwrights Horizons (1990). Photo by Martha Swope ©The New York Public Library for the Performing Arts.

13. Elena Roger as Fosca and David Thaxton as Giorgio in the Donmar Warehouse, London, 2010 production of *Passion*. Photo by Johan Persson. © Johan Persson / ArenaPAL; www.arenapal.com.

INDEX

INDEX

V

vulnerability
  Company on, 43–44
  Follies on, 61

W

"Wait," 116
Waiting for Godot (Beckett), 3
Watanabe, Gedde, 106
Weidman, John, xx
  Assassins and, 103, 193, 203
  Pacific Overtures and, 92, 96, 99, 102, 105, 200
West Side Story (Sondheim), xix–xx, 2
Wheeler, Hugh
  A Little Night Music and, 74, 75
  Sweeney Todd and, 113

Whitford, Bradley, xiv
whole, being part of (*Pacific Overtures* on), 105–7
"Who's That Woman?," 53, 60–62
Winter Garden Theatre, 66
Woolf, Virginia, xv

Y

"You've Got to Be Carefully Taught," 102

Z

Zangara, Giuseppe, 197, 199
Zien, Chip, 142
Zürich Opera, 111, 113